BLUE DIXIE

BLUE DIXIE

Awakening the South's
Democratic Majority

★ ★ ★

BOB MOSER

TIMES BOOKS

HENRY HOLT AND COMPANY   ★   NEW YORK

Times Books
Henry Holt and Company, LLC
Publishers since 1866
175 Fifth Avenue
New York, New York 10010
www.henryholt.com

Henry Holt® is a registered trademark of
Henry Holt and Company, LLC.

Some material in this book previously appeared, in slightly different form, in
The Nation, Rolling Stone, The Intelligence Report, and *Independent Weekly.*

Library of Congress Cataloging-in-Publication Data
Moser, Bob.
   Blue Dixie : awakening the South's democratic majority / Bob Moser.—1st ed.
     p.   cm.—(Times books)
   Includes bibliographical references and index.
   ISBN-13: 978-0-8050-8771-0
   ISBN-10: 0-8050-8771-0
   1. Democratic Party (U.S.)   2. Southern States—Politics and
government—21st century.   3. Political culture—Southern States.   I. Title.
JK2316.M67 2008
324.2736'0975—dc22   2008018135

Henry Holt books are available for special promotions
and premiums. For details contact: Director, Special Markets.

First Edition 2008
Designed by Victoria Hartman
Printed in the United States of America

3   5   7   9   10   8   6   4   2

In memory of Sidney T. Moser Jr.

This is the great danger America faces—that we shall cease to be one nation and become instead a collection of interest groups: city against suburb, region against region, individual against individual. . . . If that happens, who then will speak for America? Who then will speak for the common good?

—Congresswoman Barbara Jordan of Texas, keynote, 1976 Democratic National Convention

CONTENTS

★

Introduction

MESS OF TROUBLE

THE LAST THING my daddy wanted to do on a fine crisp fall Saturday in 1972, he made quite clear, was drive forty-five minutes in traffic just to hear "a bunch of Republicans yammering their rich man's nonsense." But I begged and whined until he caved. By the time Air Force One glinted down the runway of the Greensboro, North Carolina, airport for the big rally, this lifelong Democrat—a working-class veteran of the Great Depression and World War II who would sooner cast a posthumous vote for Mussolini than pull the lever for a candidate of the Grand Old Party—was straining under my bulk on his shoulders as I chanted along with the lusty throng of pent-up crackers: "Nixon now! Nixon now!"

No wonder I was carried away by the excitement: we were witnessing one of the most brazen acts of political thievery in American history. Since Reconstruction, the Democrats had held the South with a grip so tight that there was not a single Republican governor and just one U.S. senator in the old Confederate States when I

was born. The Democratic Party had long personified a political philosophy that had knit together white Dixie voters almost as strongly
as their segregated "way of life": the shape-shifting beast called
"populism." The region's Republicans had long been so anemic that
in 1949 historian V. O. Key wrote that the Dixie GOP "scarcely
deserves the name of a party," more closely resembling an "esoteric
cult on the order of a lodge." My maternal grandfather, who was
known to wield his cane with a bloodthirsty gusto against outspoken Republicans, called it the "lily-livered cocktail party." That was a
nearly universal opinion in the South. After Hooverism and Roosevelt's
New Deal response, blacks had become almost as vehement as
whites in their dismissal of the "party of Lincoln." Republicans were
meddlesome, superior, big-business Wall Streeters endlessly devising
fresh schemes for screwing "regular" folks over. For all their faults,
Democrats were us.

Now Republicans were doing the unthinkable: convincing regular folks—of the white variety, at least—that they were on their side.
Up on a makeshift platform erected on the runway, two key architects of the GOP's Southern strategy, President Richard Nixon
and North Carolina's Jesse Helms, were railing against long-hairs,
liberal elites, and other "criminal forces" holding down the "silent
majority" of Caucasian working stiffs. Mixing pietistic appeals for
school prayer and nostalgia for "traditional American values," they
mouthed a neopopulist pitch borrowed from Alabama governor
George Wallace's scarily successful white-backlash campaign of
1968 and honed by Nixon for a more mainstream audience. The
president broke from his prepared text to acknowledge the hundreds
of antiwar protesters who'd been exchanging epithets all afternoon
with his fans. Directing the "three television networks over here,
ABC, CBS, NBC, who will have this on the program tonight," to
"turn their cameras" to the demonstrators, Nixon sneered, "Let
them see the kind of people that are supporting our opponents over

here"—clearly, just the sorts of people he meant by those dark references to criminal forces. Then he directed the camera to refocus, "in the name of equal time," on "the thousands over here and let's hear and see the kind of people that are supporting us."

The newly converted Republicans let out a sustained guttural roar. But not my father, whose grumpiness about wasting a perfectly good afternoon on Nixon had degenerated into a grim sullenness. Glancing around at a sea of white guys sporting crew cuts, work shirts with stitched-in name tags, and rebel-flag mesh caps, he had muttered, "Good grief. Looks like a bunch of Democrats." The massive fissure in the old Southern Democratic coalition was in stark view on both sides of the barricades erected by the state troopers on that sunny day, with the textile, tobacco, and furniture workers symbolically and literally separated from their progressive allies, a wall going up between them. No matter if they agreed on just about every working-people's economic issue. No matter if they mostly agreed on the senselessness of Vietnam. No matter if they were almost all, on both sides, church-going Christians. The upheavals of the '60s and the Republicans' wedge politics had them cursing each other with gusto.

It was a neat trick by the GOP, stepping into the void created when the Democrats became the party of social, not economic, liberalism and postwar prosperity lifted millions of Southerners into the great suburban middle class. Republicans were adapting the old "us versus them" populism—a sword long wielded *against* them—to "flip" white Southerners and create their own new electoral stronghold. They weren't just stealing Democrats, they were stealing populism. But Republican populism shunted aside that pesky business of bashing the wealthy and lifting up the "little guy" in favor of God-fearing, gun-waving, leave-us-alone rhetoric and coded appeals to white cultural unity. The enemy was no longer the greedy corporate "Big Mules" scorned by legendary populist governor Jim Folsom of

Alabama but a broad coalition of "pointy-headed intellectuals" concocted by Folsom's protégé, Wallace.

Far more than Nixon, who privately cursed conservative Southerners' "right-wing bitching" while publicly chasing their votes, Jesse Helms embodied the new Republican breed. The son of a small-town police chief in a sleepy Piedmont mill town, the owl-faced Helms had become the voice of white backlash in 1960s North Carolina with race-baiting, Bible-thumping, and "librul"-whacking newspaper columns and nightly TV commentaries. "What is needed is a revolt against revolution," he prophesied in 1964. A longtime lobbyist for the state's burgeoning banking industry, the bespectacled, buttoned-down Helms hardly fit the profile of an old-time populist. But in the emergent Republican movement, authenticity was a matter of attitude and presentation. Helms was a master. In his 1972 campaign to become the state's first Republican senator in the twentieth century, the former Democrat found himself up against a moderately progressive Greek American congressman named Nick Galifianakis. Helms, the newfangled culture warrior, knew just what to do: on billboards, TV ads, and brochures, he boiled down his Republican "populism" to a campaign slogan that spoke volumes: "He's One of Us."

The code worked like a charm—or, better yet, like a spell. Just three days after my disgusted daddy and I watched Nixon and Helms clasp paws in a "V" for victory at that raucous airport rally, Helms got his breakthrough win on the coattails of the president's stunning Southern sweep. Not only was Nixon the first Republican ever to ride a "solid South" to victory, he positively napalmed the old "Southern Democracy," capturing a showy 70 percent of the region's votes. Giddy with triumph, one of Nixon's top strategists, the archsegregationist and Strom Thurmond aide Harry Dent, boasted that "the South will never go back." Folks in Dixie, Dent said, "now realize they have been Republicans philosophically for a long time."

★

So commenced the single most destructive myth of contem
American politics: the notion that the century-long Dem
"solid South" had morphed, practically overnight, into an
solid and enduring Republican South. "The story of the Rep
Party's march to political dominance over the last five de
New York Post columnist Ryan Sager wrote in the *Atlantic* i
"has been, at its core, a story about the political realignmen
South, first at the presidential level in 1968 and 1972 and the
congressional level in 1994. That realignment is by now com
the GOP could hardly dominate the region more thoroughly

Actually, the GOP *could* dominate the region more compl
much more completely. In 1944, the Republican nominee fo
dent, Thomas E. Dewey, received less than 5 percent of
Carolinians' votes (making John Kerry's 41 percent in 20
worst showing in the South, sound quite a bit less anemic
was a solid South. The real story of Southern politics si
1960s is not the rise to domination of Republicanism but th
gence of genuine two-party competition for the first time
region's history. Democrats in Dixie have been read their la
with numbing regularity since 1964, and there is no questi
the region has become devilish terrain for Democrats i
for "Washington" offices (president, Senate, Congress). I
widespread notion that the South is one-party territory
some powerful evidence to the contrary. For one thing
Southerners identify as Democrats than Republicans. For a
more Democrats win state and local elections in the Sou
Republicans. The parity between the parties was neatly sym
by the total numbers of state legislators in the former Conf
states after the 2004 elections: 891 Republicans, 891 Dem
The South is many things, not all of them flattering. But i
politically "solid."

Just as the strength of the GOP's Southern edge has been routinely exaggerated, the story of how the South became the Republicans' largest presidential base has been distorted over time. The decline of Dixie Democrats is generally chalked up to the party's support for civil rights and other enlightened social policies and to the evil genius of the GOP's Southern strategists, who preyed on a simmering cultural backlash in the South. But what really befell Southern Democrats is a far murkier tale. It's a story that speaks less to the principled nobility of non-Southern liberals than to an uneasy melding of arrogance and willful ignorance. The Democrats' prejudices against the South led the party to a political betrayal dwarfed only by the consequences of Northern Republicans' capitulation in 1877, when they struck a deal to withdraw federal troops from the region to end botched Reconstruction efforts. The inglorious end of a failed Reconstruction left the vast majority of black Americans, just a decade out of slavery, to fend for themselves among white Southerners who had been disenfranchised and economically laid to waste after the war. On the Democrats' modern watch, those left behind are also disproportionately African Americans—more than half of whom reside in the South and vote overwhelmingly for a party that has, for all practical purposes, stopped courting their votes in presidential elections because of where they live. White rural and working-class Southerners and progressives—the twenty million folks in Dixie who call themselves "liberal"—have also been sidelined and disenfranchised by the party.

These abandonments have opened a larger void: 115 million Americans fed a steady political diet of fearmongering, culture warring, tax cutting, and flag-waving, with Washington Republicans broadcasting their message in a virtual echo chamber. By the 2032 elections, the U.S. Census Bureau projects that the South will control almost 40 percent of the electoral vote for president—more than the declining Northeast and Midwest *combined*. Many parts of the South will also have become "majority minority" by then. Thanks to

a thirty-year migration of millions of Yankees, a historic remigration of blacks from the industrial North, the nation's fastest-growing Hispanic population, and a generational shift away from religious right politics, Democrats can no longer afford to accept the myth of the red-state South. They leave the region uncontested at the peril of the party's future. And the country's.

1

THE SOLID SOUTHERN STRATEGY

★

"There is a party for Caesar, a party for Pompey,
but no party for Rome."

—TOM WATSON,
Georgia populist and Democratic senator

THE TALE OF how Republicans "won" the South, and why
Democrats gave it up, has been ironed out into a quintessentially
American fable of good and evil and reduced to its satisfying essence
for retelling every four years, when Democratic strategists and
media pundits begin their ritual debate about whether, and how,
Democrats should try to reclaim a slice of Dixie with a Southern
strategy of their own.

The legend goes like this: The Democratic Party became the unity
party of white Southerners—a political extension of the Confederate States of America—after the Civil War. (True enough.) From
Appomattox through the civil rights movement, the national Democratic Party was really two parties, with an enlightened Northern
wing and a Southern wing wallowing in the muck of benighted tra-
ditionalism. (The exaggerations begin.) The "good Democrats" of
the North swallowed hard and accommodated their Dixie cousins
for the very practical reason that without their "solid South" vote in
nearly every presidential contest, they would not have *been* contests.

(Right.) Even Franklin D. Roosevelt put up with the racist demagogues of the Southern leadership, the Bilbos and Vardamans and
Talmadges, because of political expediency. (Right again.) And even
though white Southerners didn't have a liberal bone in their bodies,
they kept making an X in the boxes next to Democratic presidential
candidates' names. (Well . . .)

But "with a stroke of the pen," as the saying always goes, the
first Southern president since Andrew Johnson, Texan Lyndon B.
Johnson, intrepidly signed the Voting Rights Act of 1965 and
brought a sudden and irrevocable end to the Democrats' solid South.
Why, even LBJ himself said so; in a quote that has become an inex-
tricable part of the fable, the president worried out loud to one of his
aides, the future journalist Bill Moyers, that he had "delivered the
South to the Republican Party for a long time to come."

By doing the right thing, we are told, the Democratic Party sacri-
ficed Dixie and purified its sullied soul at last. And as soon as
Johnson's pen did its work, the legend continues, Republicans were
ready to pounce. With the brilliant Southern strategy brewed to
wicked perfection by Richard Nixon and his henchmen, the die was
cast. After a quick post-Watergate blip, with Jimmy Carter's election
in 1976, the popular presidency of Ronald Reagan and the ascen-
dence of religious right politics cemented the Republicans' new solid
South. While the region continued to grow in prosperity—thanks, of
course, to its supposedly militant antiunionism and the resulting
abundance of cheap labor that big business loves—the South
remained what it had always been: backward, xenophobic, racist,
and ignorantly susceptible to the rankest emotional appeals to Jesus,
miscegenation, and militarism. The only difference was that the parties had switched places, with the Democrats laid as low as the sad
old Southern Republicans once were. If anybody needed fresh proof
of that, it came along in the 2000 election, when even a Tennessee
Democrat, Al Gore, could not break through the brick wall of
Caucasian conservatism to win a single state in Dixie. "The South is

no longer the swing region," proclaimed political science professor and pundit Thomas Schaller, author of a "non-Southern" manifesto published in 2006 called *Whistling Past Dixie: How Democrats Can Win Without the South.* "It has swung."

That's the story, and a sweet one it is for both Republicans and—in a perverse way—blue state Democrats. For Republicans, this neat little fiction confirms their superior command of political strategy—the canny ruthlessness with which they appropriated white backlash against '60s liberalism, then rode the angry tide of evangelical politics in the '80s. It also offers them the charming promise of starting every presidential election with one-third (and climbing) of the country's electoral votes already sewn up. Meanwhile, Democrats outside the South—those who actually believe this Disneyesque version of political history—can recount the legend and view themselves, and their party, as martyrs for racial justice. The party's sad record in national politics, post-LBJ, has indeed been a cross to bear. But such is the price of righteousness.

But nobody told Southerners they weren't supposed to be Democrats anymore. During the 2006 midterm elections, Gallup pollsters discovered that more folks still said they were Democrats than Republicans in all but three Southern states—Texas, South Carolina, and Mississippi. In half of the South, it wasn't even close: Democrats led by more than 10 percentage points in six Southern states. It's not just the partisan leanings of Southerners that confound the solid South myths. Southerners are more conservative only if you winnow down American politics to cultural or "moral" issues alone. They still tack the furthest right on gay marriage and abortion and still lead the nation in church going. They also back withdrawal from Iraq and strongly favor progressive populist economic policies—more spending on social welfare, stronger environmental and business regulations, universal health care—that are anathema to the GOP and, in many cases, markedly to the left of the national Democratic leadership.

But you'd never know that by listening to the conventional wisdom. The South has, in the popular mind, always been "solid"—solidly white, solidly conservative, solidly fundamentalist, and of course, solidly racist. But never solidly populist—and that is where the Democrats made their mistake.

★

It's true that Democrats were bound to take a hit in the South after LBJ signed the Civil Rights and Voting Rights acts of 1964 and 1965, which ended all forms of legal segregation and doomed the various schemes—literacy tests, violent intimidation—that had long suppressed black registration and turnout. But as Johnson knew, the cracks in the "solid" Southern Democracy had been widening since 1948, when Harry S. Truman's modest civil rights plank sent Deep South Democrats stalking out of the national convention in protest. After the Dixiecrats' attempt to block Truman's reelection failed miserably, most returned—mad and determined, rather than chastened—to their ancestral party. The strains showed throughout the 1950s, especially after the Supreme Court's *Brown v. Board of Education* decision outlawing "separate but equal" schools. But it wasn't until 1964 that the awkward Democratic coalition of such long standing—working-class whites, ruling-class whites, working-class blacks, middle-class Jews, liberals, moderates, evangelical Baptists, and neo-Confederate reactionaries, to name a few—started to unravel in the South.

The day before the 1964 election, Republican insurgent Barry Goldwater chose to make his final campaign stop in Columbia, South Carolina. Matched against a popular president leading the ticket of America's dominant party, Goldwater had made the fatal mistake of being honest in his acceptance speech at the GOP convention, proclaiming his view that "extremism in the defense of liberty is no vice" and instantly snuffing out the remote hopes he had entertained of occupying the White House. But Goldwater did not give up on what became the mission—the sole possible rationale, really— for his foundering campaign: building a new Republican base by breathing reactionary life into its moribund Southern wing. He stumped hard in Dixie, often accompanied by Strom Thurmond, the South Carolina senator who had topped the "Dixiecrat" (States Rights Party) ticket in 1948 and was now leading the segregationist exodus into the GOP. While Goldwater avoided overt race-baiting, his anti–civil rights voting record and Thurmond's enthusiastic backing were more than enough to signal to Southerners—both whites, who voted in unprecedented numbers for a Republican, and blacks, who voted in unprecedented numbers for a Democrat—just where the new GOP stood on the "race issue." More directly, with his "states' rights" rhetoric, Goldwater fully embraced the fierce distrust of the federal government that Southern traditionalists had felt in their collective gut since long before the Civil War. "Forced integration," Goldwater liked to tell his fans in Dixie, "is just as wrong as forced segregation." Richard Nixon would later pick up that refrain, sometimes verbatim.

The day after Goldwater's Columbia rally, the national results were disastrous; Johnson racked up what was, at the time, the largest percentage of the popular vote in U.S. history. But Goldwater had broken through in what Southern journalist John Egerton calls "the five-chambered, race-obsessed heart of Dixie." These were the same old cotton states—Alabama, Mississippi, Louisiana, Georgia, and South Carolina—that had revolted in 1948. But even in President Dwight D. Eisenhower's cakewalk reelection of 1956, four of the five had still stuck with Democrat Adlai Stevenson (along with only three other states in the country). Goldwater had staked a claim in the South's—and the nation's—most "solid" Democratic territory. At the same time, Republicans had lost the majority of Southern states, including the economically booming, fast-growing cities and suburbs that had been friendly to Ike in the '50s.

Republican progress was hardly as relentless or deadly as Sherman's

March. Richard Nixon's 1968 election was nearly derailed by the Deep South, which voted in big numbers for George Wallace's third-party effort and nearly swung the election to Democrat Hubert Humphrey. But that year, and more emphatically in 1972, Nixon made important inroads with the region's fastest-growing demographic: suburbanites, who would later form the base of Ronald Reagan's Republican realignment in the South. "In too many accounts of southern political realignment during the post-war era, the Deep South is the tail that wags the dog," wrote Matthew Lassiter in his brilliant revisionist history, *The Silent Majority: Suburban Politics in the Sunbelt South.* But in fact, "the suburban strategies developed in the Sunbelt South, not a Southern Strategy inspired by the Deep South and orchestrated from the White House, provided the blueprint for the transformation of regional politics and the parallel reconfiguration of national politics." As Lassiter pointed out, every full-blown incarnation of a race-based Southern strategy—the Dixiecrat rebellion of 1948, the Goldwater wipeout of 1964, the Wallace campaign of 1968, and the GOP's experiment with raw racial appeals in the 1970 midterm elections— backfired spectacularly, failing "to carry the high-growth states of the Upper and Outer South and instead achiev[ing] pyrrhic victories in the Deep South."

Nixon's 1972 Southern strategy, like Reagan's in the 1980s, certainly appropriated coded racial appeals—the "one of us" shtick, the opposition to "forced busing," and incessant invocations of "law and order." But the core of the GOP's rise in the South "revolved around the incisive recognition that an insurance agent in Charlotte or a middle manager in Atlanta welcomed the same combination of conservative economic policies and moderate racial rhetoric that resonated for an aerospace engineer in Southern California, a homemaker in Omaha, or an accountant in New Jersey." These were the folks Nixon cozied up to in his signature four-minute political ad in 1968, declaring, "Let us listen now to . . . the voice of the great majority of Americans, the forgotten Americans, the non-shouters, the non-demonstrators." Lassiter concluded, "Republicans turned out to be neither the defenders of civil rights nor the demagogues of white supremacy, but instead the regional and national party of middle-class entitlement, corporate power, and suburban protectionism." This was a national phenomenon, of course, not strictly a Southern one. But its impact on Southern politics was outsized because the non–Deep South's population, wealth, and suburbs were all booming faster than any other region's from the 1940s through the 1990s. Only one party calibrated its pitch and its organizing methods—focusing on the megachurches that were becoming the community centers of Southern suburbs—to the region's evolving culture and new economic realities.

★

The homogeneity of political views in Dixie has been taken as a given ever since the decades leading up to the Civil War. That's when the South began to be painted—by both Northern abolitionists and Southern plantation interests—as an impenetrable fortress for the defense of slavery. But many white Southerners opposed slavery; in fact, prior to 1830, the abolitionist movement was mainly a Southern phenomenon.

"The great popular heart is not now and never has been in this war," said North Carolina congressman and governor Zebulon Vance, a unionist. His fellow Tar Heels defeated a statewide referendum on secession in February 1861. Two months later, after the firing on Fort Sumter, state legislators had to choose a side—and North Carolina became, despite widespread opposition, the last state to join the Confederacy. "It was a revolution," said Vance, "of the politicians and not the people." Such historical complication was quickly erased, of course, by the bloody sectional resentments brought on by the incomparably brutal war and its wretched aftermath. When Northern

Republicans botched Reconstruction and the South remade itself as an apartheid region two decades later, the North-South divide was starkly drawn for generations. Democrats, who had led the campaign to terrorize and disenfranchise Southern blacks in the 1890s, became the party of the vast majority of white Southerners for most of the next century. This was true one-party domination. The former Confederate states had only a solitary Republican in the Senate before 1964, when Strom Thurmond switched allegiances and turned his powerful South Carolina machine into a GOP juggernaut.

The typical, and typically reductive, view of Southern politics has thus been that it has always revolved obsessively around race. "The South is a big, complicated region," journalist Nicholas Lemann acknowledged in 2006 in the *New Republic,* "but the simplest available explanation of its politics is that they are primarily racial." But even the overwhelming solid support for "the Southern Democracy" through the early 1960s obscured a lively mix of allegiances and ideologies fought out within the party. Elections were always decided in Democratic primaries, but those contests were often bitter slugfests between traditionalist conservatives and either populist reformers or "good government" moderates.

In what is still, by default, the most insightful book on the subject, 1949's *Southern Politics in State and Nation,* historian V. O. Key found that "even on the question of race the unity of the region has been grossly exaggerated in the national mind. Nor do the conventional stereotypes of Southern politics convey any conception of the diversity of political attitude, organization and tradition among the southern states." Chronicling the political history of each state, rather than lumping them together, Key demolished the myth of the solid South by describing their divergent voting habits. The differences were stark even in neighboring states like South Carolina, a former plantation stronghold where a rabid anti-government, cultural conservatism historically held sway, and North Carolina, where the conservative Democratic wing often lost to a "respectable" progressive faction.

Furthermore, the solid South stereotype leaves no room for the generations of peace, racial, and labor activists who have waged pitched—and not always losing—battles in Dixie with little support from the national progressive movement. There's no room for some of the most epochal figures in Southern political history—no room for Georgia's Tom Watson, who in the early phase of his career led a rural populist movement that united blacks and whites. No room for the legendary quasi-socialist Louisiana populists Huey and Earl Long, whose economic reforms benefited both races alike. (Regarding the imperial wizard of the Ku Klux Klan, Huey once declared, "Quote me as saying that that imperial bastard will never set foot in Louisiana, and that when I call him a sonofabitch, I am not using profanity but am referring to the circumstances of his birth.") Little room, too, for Alabama's midcentury governor, Big Jim Folsom, the economic populist who stirred up his state with a Christmas address in 1949, declaring, "As long as the Negroes are held down by deprivation and lack of opportunity, all the other people will be held down alongside them. Let's start talking fellowship and brotherly love, and doing unto others. And let's do more than talk about it; let's start living it."

The reduction of all Southern political questions to matters of "race" (sometimes with "religion" thrown in for good measure) belies the pervasive influence of economics on how folks vote. Through the disfiguring lens of racial politics, Folsom's protégé, Alabama governor George Wallace, is remembered as the quintessential Dixie politician of the civil rights era: not for the liberal (and biracial) economic policies that got him labeled "practically a communist" and "downright pink" by Alabama conservatives, but for the chest-jutting resistance to integration that marked his first term as governor. From a decade overendowed with black-and-white images of chaos and horror, Wallace is the central figure in two of the most unforgettable: standing rigidly in the "schoolhouse door" of the University of Alabama to officially protest its integration in 1963, and declaiming fustian racist poesy from atop the marble steps of the state capitol at his inauguration. "In the name of the greatest people that have ever trod this earth, I draw the line in the dust and toss the gauntlet before the feet of tyranny, and I say segregation now, segregation tomorrow, segregation forever."

While Wallace was the most infamous in a sorry line of gut-bucket Democratic demagogues who had, as he infamously said, "niggered" their way into office, he was not, as most Democrats and Republicans alike today believe, the archetypal Southern politician of his time. As usual with the South, there *was* no archetype. While few politically minded Americans have forgotten Wallace's drawling gasps of segregationist folderol, you would be hard-pressed to find anybody—anywhere—who recalls a once-famous inaugural address given two years earlier, when North Carolina's new Democratic governor, Terry Sanford, the first Southern governor to call for employment without regard to race or creed, announced, at the height of the white civil rights backlash, "No group of our citizens can be denied the right to participate in the opportunities of first-class citizenship." As the writer Jonathan Yardley later noted, those were "fighting words" in 1961, every bit as bracing and ultimately far more significant than Wallace's antics.

Sanford was not the only Southern Democrat looking forward. In South Carolina, the same year Wallace took office, newly elected governor Ernest Hollings—a populist firecracker who had promised to defend segregation earlier in his political rise—informed an aghast state legislature that integration had arrived, and "must be done with law and order." One week later, the second-largest state university, Clemson, was integrated without violence. "That speech made quite a difference," said South Carolina congressman Jim

Clyburn, who became the first African American majority whip in Congress in 2007.

Yet, Hollings's unpopular gesture has fallen into historical obscurity while Wallace's hateful defiance marches along in the history books as characteristic behavior among the region's white politicians. When the "national mind" thinks "South," it has long flashed back to the grimmest moments of the 1960s—a sepia-toned montage of police dogs and fire hoses and blown-up black girls in Birmingham, of housewives spitting racist epithets in Little Rock, and of a murdered saint on a hotel balcony in Memphis. The politics of Dixie are still presumed, particularly by the most "liberal-minded" of non-Southerners, to be as race-soaked, simplistic, and wrongheaded as the Ricky Bobbys and Jeeter Lesters and Jerry Falwells who supposedly blanket, or rather infest, the kudzu-choked landscape that looms below the Mason-Dixon.

"The term 'southern,'" Key concluded, "conjures up notions that have little resemblance to reality." His observation has never been more true than today. Nearly sixty years later, four long decades after the demise of Jim Crow opened up new economic and political possibilities in the South, the solid South myth still retains the power to distort and derange American politics. The baseless concept of a "solid Republican South" dictates national campaign strategies for both political parties. Democrats consider the South hopelessly lost to them—or winnable only with the most crippling sorts of compromises on core issues. Republicans, on the other hand, like to assume the South is theirs for perpetuity—or at least as long as the old, "solid" Southern Democracy endured.

★

The Republicans' Southern surge has been picked apart and celebrated by scores of political scientists and pundits. But just as much as the GOP won the region with its appeals to suburbanites and cultural traditionalists, the Democratic Party lost it by failing to build on its new black base. The story of how, and why, the Democrats surrendered Dixie is well worth chewing over. Segregationist whites did, unquestionably, begin defecting in large numbers to the formerly hated "cocktail party" in the wake of the civil rights movement. But they were outnumbered by the massive infusion of Southern blacks into the Democratic Party. Between the midterm elections of 1966 and 1970, more than 1.7 million African Americans registered to vote, spiking the regionwide percentage of registered blacks to nearly 60 percent. At the same time, white Southerners' racial attitudes were, in Matthew Lassiter's terms, undergoing one of the "most pronounced shifts in the history of opinion polling." In a May 1970 Gallup Poll, for example, only 16 percent of white parents in the South opposed sending their children to schools with a small number of black students—compared to 61 percent in 1963. In the North, meanwhile, white support for a federal role in school integration dropped from 47 percent in 1966 to 21 percent in 1976.

Liberals had long nourished the hope that integration would spawn a new Democratic coalition of blacks and moderate and progressive whites. Even as Nixon swept Dixie in 1972, there were encouraging signs. While Harry Dent was roostering about the new "Republican South," the eleven former Confederate states had already elected 665 blacks to local and state offices. (Nowadays, more than two-thirds of the nation's black elected officials are Southern.) Even more strikingly, every single Southern state but Alabama (stuck with Wallace) had elected a moderate-to-progressive governor calling for racial reconciliation and "lift-all-boats" economic reforms.

In Florida, young governor Reubin Askew was hailing the emergence of a "humanistic South, which has always been there, just below the surface of racism and despair, struggling for a chance to emerge." In Arkansas, Democratic governor Dale Bumpers was promoting a "future . . . shaped and shared by all Arkansans—old and young, black and white, rich and poor." South Carolina's new-breed

Democratic governor, John C. West, pledged a "color-blind" administration and followed through by immediately appointing a black adviser to a top staff position, a first in that state.

"The era of defiance is behind us," announced Virginia's new governor, Linwood Holton—a moderate Republican, no less. Even Wallace, reelected in 1970, was whistling a new tune—postelection, of course—that was most certainly not "Dixie." Eight years after his "segregation forever" address, Wallace delivered a startlingly different inaugural message: "Our state government is for all, so let us join together, for Alabama belongs to all of us—black and white, young and old, rich and poor alike."

"We in the South have an exciting opportunity," wrote Atlanta's first black mayor, Maynard Jackson, in 1972, "to prove that, ultimately, black and white have only one enemy: not each other, but those economic, social, educational, and political conditions which cause and maintain hunger, neglect, bigotry, and disease." One of the giddiest signs of progress had come in Georgia two years earlier, when voters had replaced Democratic governor Lester Maddox, a clownish Wallace wannabe who had gained statewide fame by chasing blacks away from his fried-chicken restaurant with an axe, with the relatively liberal Jimmy Carter.

Carter had run a classic populist campaign, trying his damnedest to shake every hand in the state. In a precursor to his 1976 grassroots presidential campaign, he tallied some 1,800 speeches to small-town civic groups, schools, and agriculture associations, inveighing against Georgia's entrenched power brokers and big-money interests. Carter made one campaign gesture to the old-line white Democrats, coming out against "forced busing" to integrate schools. But he steered clear of demagoguing on race. And on his inaugural day in 1971, surrounded by monuments to both Confederate soldiers and legendary bigots like Eugene Talmadge ("The Negro belongs to an inferior race"), Carter made his sentiments known in stronger and clearer terms than Terry Sanford or Ernest Hollings had used eight years earlier: "I say to you quite frankly that the time for racial discrimination is over."

When a near-solid South—all but Virginia—propelled Carter to the presidency in 1976, it looked as though the Democratic dream could, just maybe, become a reality. After Carter accepted the nomination, the strains of "We Shall Overcome" echoed around New York's Madison Square Garden as an unlikely smorgasbord of Democratic luminaries crowded the stage, singing and swaying. Up there with Carter were Coretta Scott King, Ted Kennedy, the African American congresswoman Barbara Jordan of Texas, and—*could it be? Yep, singing right along*—a wheelchair-bound George Wallace. Old wounds were binding. Tears were flowing, especially among the Southern delegations. As *Time* magazine had declared earlier in that first post–Jim Crow decade, "the region is abandoning the fateful uniqueness that has retarded its development and estranged its people." A progressive and biracial South, at long last, was announcing its arrival.

But Carter's star-crossed presidency, hampered by stagflation and doomed by Iranian hostage taking, failed to live up to its promise on nearly every count. Carter's economic policies strayed far from the progressive populism he had championed back home. Rather than reinvigorating—or reinventing—the New Deal spirit that had brought together blacks and whites in the South (however partially and tenuously), Carter's term in office signaled the start of the Democratic Party's slide toward a feckless, defensive posture of "moderation."

Meanwhile, a right-wing political revival among evangelical Christians was delivering another chunk of traditional Southern Democrats into the Republican camp. There was more than a touch of irony in this, of course, since Carter had been America's first "born-again" president, a Sunday School teacher throughout his adult life. But the Deep South Baptist lost evangelical votes in droves in 1980 to the Moral Majority's new hero: Hollywood actor, divorcé, former union president, and faithful nonchurchgoer Ronald Reagan.

The Republicans' Southern strategy had left the Democrats an opening: Translate the South's economic populist tradition into a forward-looking, class-based politics with broad appeal to blacks and whites alike. And run, as Southern Democrats have continued to do on the state and local levels, on progressive "good-government" issues—better schools, better roads, better jobs. While Republicans had latched on to the fearmongering, "watch-out-for-Washington" style of traditional Southern populism, the Democrats had a chance to adapt the equally appealing, vote-getting substance of economic populism. Instead, they ran from it.

"The party abandoned its New Deal legacy as a positive force for change and hunkered down behind a defensive shield," lamented journalist John Egerton, author of *The Americanization of Dixie: The Southernization of America.* "The leaders failed to comprehend that Harry Truman and Lyndon Johnson died for their sins, and in so doing freed the Democrats to reclaim their heritage as the fountain-head of egalitarian opportunity."

★

"Today the Democratic Party stands between two great forces," an eminent populist once said. "On one side stands the corporate interests of the nation, its moneyed institutions, its aggregations of wealth and capital, imperious, arrogant, compassionless. . . . On the other side stands the unnumbered throng which gave a name to the Democratic Party and for which it has presumed to speak. Work-worn and dust-begrimed, they make their mute appeal, and too often find their cry for help beat in vain against the outer walls."

That was thirty-three-year-old William Jennings Bryan, shaking the rafters on Capitol Hill in 1893. The Democratic Party then stood at a historical crossroads similar to today's. Republicans had ruled national politics for three decades, with Democrats offering an ever-more-mushy centrist alternative. When they heeded Bryan's call, the Democrats began to transform from a small-government, "states' rights" coalition into the progressive force behind Woodrow Wilson's New Freedom and Franklin D. Roosevelt's New Deal—both of which won unparalleled support in the South.

When Democrats devolved from the Great Society proponents of the 1960s to the free-trading welfare reformers of the '90s, they lost their identity as the "people's party" in the process. A Bryanesque revival is sorely needed. "Bona fide Democrats need to be reaching out to their natural constituency," wrote John Egerton—a constituency that includes "young people, the working class, women, African Americans, immigrants, the elderly, the poor, small business owners and the millions of middle-class citizens who have been whipsawed by the greedy elite." The stakes could hardly be higher. "Now, all that stands between these loyal, hard-working Americans and a permanent condition of underclass subjugation is the Democratic Party."

But just as it was in the 1890s, a new Democratic populism is anathema to party leaders who have counseled middle-of-the-roadism as a way to neutralize both Republican cultural populism and the flow of corporate cash into GOP coffers. Besides, the very mention of populism stirs ancient fears among non-Southern liberals. Up north, populism has always been tainted, understandably enough, by the ugly legacy of the most colorful "people's champions" of the South—from Tom Watson to George Wallace—who became fire-breathing defenders of white supremacy.

As Michael Kazin wrote in *A Godly Hero,* his majestic 2006 biography of William Jennings Bryan, it is nearly impossible in today's climate to imagine "an officeholder who was a flagrant racist being anything else worth mentioning." But in the pre–civil rights South, populism was a double-edged phenomenon. Many of the very figures who led the bloody campaign to disenfranchise black voters in the 1890s—the snarling "Pitchfork" Ben Tillman in South

Carolina; the "Karl Marx for hillbillies" in Arkansas, Senator Jeff Davis—were also catalysts behind landmark progressive legislation: corporate regulation, income taxes, protection for strikers and union organizers, child-labor laws, federal support for education, and voting reforms such as ballot initiatives and party primaries.

With Jim Crow long dead and buried, the preservation of white privilege is no longer the supreme issue of Southern politics. There *is* no supreme issue in the region, no such powerful force binding together white voters. A new Democratic populism doesn't have to preach hate and fear—or cozy up to traditionalist "moral values." As a Young Democrats leader in South Carolina asked not long ago, "The Dixiecrats are dead, right?" Mostly they are—quite literally— and the civil rights backlash that soured so many white Southerners toward the Democratic Party is going to the grave with them. The South's heady half century of rising education levels and unprecedented in-migration, as well as manufacturing-job losses since the early 1990s, have made the region fertile territory for a reborn Democratic populism. Maybe the soundest advice for Democrats comes from Pete MacDowell, a fierce and funny liberal warrior from North Carolina who cofounded the advocacy group Democracy South. "Shit," he said, "just try being Democrats here. Remind Southern people what progressives actually believe. People aren't being told that they're getting poorer because of corrupt, crony capitalism. The anticorporate critique is not being made. People need to understand that the rich aren't paying taxes. They haven't had that gospel preached to them in a hell of a long time."

This gospel would get an enthusiastic hearing in today's South. Almost half of America's self-defined populists—47 percent—live in the region. That's according to the pollsters at Pew, who define populists as people who "favor an active role for government in both the economic and social spheres." Exit polls from the 2006 midterms sketched a political portrait of a region that will grow only more receptive to a progressive Democratic populism over the next few decades. While their elders leaned Republican by a slim margin, 51 percent of young Southerners (under thirty) favored the Democrats. That wasn't the most ominous news for Republicans: a relatively modest 62 percent of white Southerners, that supposedly "solid" core of Republicanism, said they voted for the GOP—while 87 percent of African Americans, 57 percent of Hispanics, and 52 percent of "others" went the other way. Among Southerners making less than fifty thousand dollars a year, 55 percent voted Democratic; among evangelicals, the largest GOP base in the South, support for Democrats rose from 19 percent in 2004 to 27 percent in 2006.

On economic issues, the progressive leanings of Southern populists are overwhelming: In 2006, just 25 percent said they wanted President George W. Bush's tax cuts to become permanent. Ninety-one percent of self-described populists favored raising the minimum wage. Only 42 percent thought free-trade agreements were good for the country—fewer even than those in Pew's poll, nationally, who called themselves "liberals." While many populist Southerners leaned in a conservative direction on taxes in the 1980s and '90s, the vast middle of Southern voters consists of folks whose ideology has tilted back in the opposite direction: they want the government to do more, not less, to make incomes more equitable. And they say they are willing, by a generous margin, to pay more taxes if it will help the poor.

The ranks of these populists are being swelled by millions of Hispanic immigrants. Nine of the nation's fastest-growing Hispanic populations are in Southern states, and over the next three decades, these new voters will become the biggest swing demographic from Alabama to Virginia. The majority of those Southern Hispanics eligible to vote went for Bush in 2004, but they swung back to the Democrats' camp in 2006. Hispanic voters are anything but sure bets to become a large and loyal voting bloc for the Democrats—especially if the party continues to kiss off the South and blow its chance to make early and lasting connections with millions of immigrants learning American politics afresh.

The Democrats also risk losing touch with their most dedicated Southern voters—African Americans—though their voter turnout soared during Senator Barack Obama's 2008 primary campaign. What the Democrats must do in the South—to inspire black voters, reconnect with white voters, and woo Hispanic voters—is reverse their almost forty-year pattern of fighting elections on the Republicans' turf. "Why does the Democratic Party persist in a national political strategy that seems to play into the Republicans' hands?" asked political scholar and writer Adolph Reed Jr. on behalf of millions of rank-and-file Democrats. By failing to strongly assert the primacy of economic fairness in their campaigns, the Democrats have passively allowed the Republicans to transform too many elections, for too many voters, into referendums on cultural flash points like gay marriage. These wedge issues were once distractions; they are now, often, the entire basis upon which Southern campaigns are waged.

"The answer to the question of why white Southern identity is 'unmeltable,'" said Alabama native Sheldon Hackney, the former National Endowment for the Humanities chair, "is that it has been periodically reactivated, awakened from its wary nap by changes that are perceived as threatening by whites who themselves feel alienated, marginal, and at risk." Meanwhile, Democrats are not engaging these same voters with alternative explanations—and far more plausible ones—of why they're feeling so glum about their prospects and their childrens' futures.

The Democrats' post-'60s emphasis on cultural liberalism, as both the liberal white scholar Todd Gitlin and the African American historian Henry Louis Gates Jr. have argued, has kept the left from articulating a broad common purpose for the country. Identity politics, Gates wrote, is "about the priority of difference, and while it is not, by itself, undesirable, it is—by itself—dangerously inadequate."

When Democrats fret about having to compromise their party's soul to win down south, they are fretting only about identity politics. Democrats would certainly not have to move right on social safety-net issues to win Dixie. They would need to move left, in fact, on issues like health care, corporate regulation and taxation, and antipoverty initiatives. On these issues, the very Democrats who fear the dark consequences of "looking south" have already sold down the river many of the principles the party once held dear. Democrats as champions of unfettered free trade? Democrats reluctant to fight against the outsourcing of manufacturing jobs? Democrats doing little to halt an unjust war fought almost exclusively by the sons and daughters of the working poor? A Democratic administration (Clinton/Gore) presiding over a "prosperous" decade of widening income inequality? These are hardly the characteristics of a party of such high-flown nobility that it cannot risk contamination by contact with Southerners.

★

In 2008 and beyond, Democrats have a historic opportunity to snatch back some of their old Southern turf. Thus far, that has less to do with Democrats' seizing the opportunity—though the Democratic National Committee's grassroots fifty-state strategy has enlivened many formerly moribund party organizations in Southern states—and more to do with demographic trends and disarray on the other side. For the first time in two generations, the GOP machine is sputtering. The religious right, such a mighty force in 2004, quickly became fractured and demoralized by the corruption and sex scandals of its political champions. At the same time, evangelicals began to grope their way toward a "purpose-driven" social gospel that looks beyond the moral wedge issues of abortion and gay rights to poverty and the environment. Many of the evangelical right's most prominent politicians—including Ralph Reed in Georgia, Senator Jim Talent in Missouri, Roy Moore in Alabama, Representatives

Anne Northup in Kentucky and Katherine Harris in Florida—lost convincingly in 2006. Moderate "business" Republicans, many of whom are Yankee transplants, have increasingly split with their right-wing compatriots. And it hasn't helped the GOP's standing with independent-minded Southern voters—a fast-growing group— that Republicans have had a hard time governing in Southern states once they take power. "The Republicans have failed the most important test of any political movement," opined the *Economist* in 2007, "wielding power successfully."

Southern Republicans have also been deflated by the national and international power-wielding failures of George W. Bush. In many ways, Bush was the ultimate product of the Republicans' faux populism. Though many tried, no politician ever embodied the "one of us" style more devotedly than ol' 43, with his swagger, his snigger, his "dead or alive" bravado, his brush clearing on the Crawford ranch (home to perhaps five cows)—and with his singular devotion, when not in public, to multiplying the profits of Halliburton and Chevron. Like the greatest of actors, Bush seemed to not just be playing a role but actually inhabiting his character's skin. Unlike Al Gore, Bush walked, talked, and even laughed like a good ole boy. And Southern populists, along with most other middle Americans, cheered him on. But soon after the 2004 elections, they turned on him—hard—over the war and his dismaying attempt to privatize Social Security. When Bush became discredited in the South, so too did his political style and message—the one that had been so indispensable to the Republicans' Southern appeal.

The glue holding white Southerners together in today's Republican Party is nowhere near as strongly adhesive as the old segregationist politics that kept whites in Dixie voting for Democrats for so long. The Southern GOP remains a queasy coalition of mutually suspicious parties—evangelical Christians and chamber of commerce types—who banded together in a shotgun marriage of political convenience. And the wedge issues used to stir up social traditionalists at election time—those quadrennial proddings of white people's phobias—appear to be drying up. Bans on stem-cell research won't work; the grounds for opposition are too cloudy and abstract compared to the happy promise of breakthroughs in curing major diseases. (A 2006 Pew poll found that more evangelicals favored stem-cell research than opposed it.) Immigrant bashing won't work; the business end of the GOP won't let that go too far. There are only so many times you can vote on gay marriage—and in 2006, the first of these ballot issues actually failed (in Arizona) and made no appreciable difference to the Senate race in Virginia, though the Democratic candidate, Jim Webb, opposed the antigay amendment and Republicans worked hard to hold it against him. If the Republicans' strategic wizards are running out of wedges that can awaken white identity en masse, the keys to the weird kingdom of Southern politics will increasingly slip from their greedy grasp.

But will Democrats be ready to take the reins? Making a genuine effort to win the South will require nothing less than the reanimation of the Democratic Party's populist soul. Democrats, or at least their presidential nominees, can only regain Southern territory by articulating a fresh progressive vision for the country, with a focus on the kitchen-table issues that hit home with Middle Americans: health care, schools, subprime mortgages, Social Security, rural jobs and infrastructure, college tuition, suburban sprawl, and the soaring cost of living. The party of centrist triangulation will have to find its populist voice again, taking meaningful aim at such fat targets as skyrocketing corporate profits and the organized thievery practiced by deregulated insurance, investment, communications, and lending companies. To forge a new Southern Democracy, the party's leaders will have to wrench their eyes away from the latest polling data and devise bold proposals on a contemporary set of "moral" issues including global warming and poverty—the surest way to counter the GOP's edge on "values."

Rather than running from their core principles, Democrats' long-term prospects in the South hinge on whether the party can frame and articulate those principles with a brand-new vigor. To win in Dixie, Democrats must learn to be Democrats again. It sounds straightforward. But given the twisted history of Democrats' approaches to the South since 1965, it could be a rough row to hoe.

2

THE LITE BRIGADE

★

"Don't nobody get moved by any milder, modified version of anything. People rather have fire in their face than just warm spit down their back. If people have to choose between the authentic and an imitation, they'll choose the authentic every time."

—REVEREND JESSE JACKSON, 1987

EVER SINCE THE social and partisan upheavals of the 1960s turned the once-reliably Democratic South into what Southern journalist John Egerton called "the eight-hundred-pound, stogie-puffing gorilla in the smoke-filled rooms of national politics," the Republicans have been relentlessly aggressive in delivering a clear message designed to appeal to rural and suburban whites: low taxes, strong military, high morals, and a laissez-faire assumption of color-blindness on race. Sure, the wedges have evolved—from "forced busing" to gay marriage—but you would be hard-pressed to find a Southerner, white or black, poor or rich, who couldn't give you a quick summation of what the Republican Party says it stands for. Ask about the Democrats, and Southerners would proffer a thousand different theories about what the party was all about, with a high incidence of blank, silent stares.

The national Democrats' superstitious belief in the solid South myth has fatally warped the party's approach to winning elections. At various points since 1972, the party has looked south with wariness, suspicion, and hostility—or pandered to its most reactionary elements. The thread holding together the Democrats' various Southern and non-Southern strategies has been an unmistakable ambivalence: we will try to win some Southern states if we must, but only because we must. (Steve Jarding, who teaches politics at Harvard's Kennedy School of Government when he's not running Southern campaigns, has never forgotten the moment when he fully comprehended this attitude. At a DNC meeting in 2000, party chairman Terry McAuliffe was listening to grim reports about Gore's poll numbers in the South and Midwest when, according to Jarding, he erupted: "I don't give a shit about Missouri and Kentucky! All we care about is getting to 270!")

The Democrats' post–civil rights infighting broke out in earnest after George McGovern's landslide defeat in 1972. A group of conservatives, led by Senator Henry "Scoop" Jackson, started the Coalition for a Democratic Majority, a group dedicated to winning back white working-class voters who had left the party over "the social question." Their bible was *The Real Majority,* a study of demographic shifts in the electorate by moderates Ben J. Wattenberg and Richard M. Scammon, who chronicled the wherefores of the backlash that had led whites in the South, West, and Midwest to change political horses.

Wattenberg and Scammon's backlash theory (which was later picked up by the DLC) was sound enough. But as John B. Judis and Ruy Teixeira argued in their 2002 book, *The Emerging Democratic Majority,* "as strategists, they were as blind to reality as the McGovernites they opposed. The constituency they championed was a dwindling part of the electorate, and at least some of the voters they coveted—white Southerners who had left the Democratic Party over race issues—simply weren't ready to come back unless the party was ready to repudiate its commitment to civil rights."

The influx of black voters into the party, combined with the historic migration of non-Southern natives to the region, offered the

Democrats a chance to build a new Southern majority. It would not be easy, by any means: the backlash of the "silent majority," however much its political import might have been exaggerated, was real. People were tired of tinkering, tired of ideas. And, in the South, white people were also resentful of the villainous reputation they had reacquired in the national mind. Not a few white Southerners came to agree with Senator Jim Webb, who hotly claimed in his book, *Born Fighting: How the Scots-Irish Shaped America,* that liberal activists in the 1960s had converted "an issue of social justice designed to eradicate demeaning laws of exclusion into a full-blown war against the entire value system of a region," turning "many of the very people who might have worked for racial justice into their most virulent enemies. To provoke and blame disadvantaged whites for the plight of disadvantaged blacks was either naïve or politically manipulative. And to expect that the disadvantaged whites would happily assist in revamping the entire social and economic order without attention being paid to their own situation was absurd."

To say the least, the backlash spawned by the '60s was a daunting obstacle to a new Democratic majority. It was tough for blue state party leaders to take the post-civil-rights-movement South seriously and engage with the African American and white progressives and moderates who could make up a new Southern Democracy. The party had models. Rather than split between liberalism and conservativism, Southern governors like Terry Sanford and Reubin Askew had won with a message of responsible reform—appealing to voters, black and white, to rise and meet the opportunities that had come with the much-belated casting off of Jim Crow's fetters.

Pat Caddell, the young McGovern pollster who became Jimmy Carter's political brain, was among those who tried to point the way forward. In 1976, following Carter's victory, Caddell wrote his boss a memo about how best to expand their tiny electoral majority into a new Democratic coalition. To forge a "political realignment," he argued, Democrats had to shift their focus from "Old America"—working stiffs in farm states and the Manufacturing Belt—toward "the younger white-collar, college-educated, middle-income suburban group that is rapidly becoming the majority of America." Sunbelt suburbia became, instead, the backbone of the new Republican majority that stampeded to power on Ronald Reagan's coattails in the 1980s.

In the early 1980s, moderate Democrats like Senators Paul Tsongas and Gary Hart began to call for a "neoliberal" shift, away from Great Society–style income redistribution and toward "growth-based" economic policies. Their movement, built on similar premises as that of the old Coalition for a Democratic Majority, made sense on the surface. The economic calamities of the '70s, and the Republicans' effectiveness in blaming them on the Great Society Democrats, had certainly made voters wary of "tax and spend" liberalism. But there was no ideological underpinning for what came to be known as the "New Democrat" approach—no foundational set of beliefs, like those held by the small-government Republicans who began to take over their party in 1964.

By and large, Democrats continued to believe in government, rather than market solutions to economic injustice. Instead of crafting fresh ways to articulate and sell that vision to voters, Democratic leaders balled themselves up in what Democratic strategist Donna Brazile called "their fetal crouch," and became almost indistinguishable from the Republicans on issues like free trade and business regulation. The party's political strategies, while they changed from election to election, became fundamentally defensive—and the Democrats' connection with Southern voters increasingly superficial and flimsy.

When dissident Democrats finally crafted their own sort of Southern strategy to counter the Republicans in the mid-1980s, it was one big fetal crouch. The strategy came courtesy of the centrist

Democratic Leadership Council, cofounded by Governor Bill Clinton of Arkansas. The DLC called for cutting taxes, "reinventing government," and holding hands affectionately with big business, and Clinton's election in 1992 made it the de facto strategy of the Democratic Party. Twenty years after the Voting Rights Act, the party of civil rights was becoming the party of Republicans Lite.

"They spend 95 percent of the time trying to sway white moderates and even conservatives," Willie Legette, a professor at South Carolina State University, told me in 2003. "The message is, 'We're no longer the party concerned with reducing racial and class inequities.' They're so bent on not being identified as the party of liberalism that they give us no reason to vote."

Democrats' nods to economic populism began to revolve almost entirely around labor unions—never much of a force in the "right to work" South—because they had to hold on to the Northeastern and Rust Belt states. That left Republicans a clean run at the Sunbelt South and West, which were sprawling and booming and soon found themselves in the thickets of brand-new economic and governmental challenges—with only the Republicans offering fresh-sounding solutions. By flooding these states with cash, organizing them from the bottom up, and lavishing praise on them come campaign time, the Republicans won themselves a new base that would continue growing for generations to come, while the other side's population percentage kept shrinking.

"That's the irony," said Donna Ladd, the feisty editor of the liberal weekly *Jackson* (Mississippi) *Free Press*. "The Republican Party understands us, and our potential, better than the Democratic Party does. The Democratic Party is just so afraid of their shadow. They have spent so much of their time just running off potential Democrats." While the Republicans continued to build their machine, the Democrats were dreaming a new dream: not of a transformational party in the South but of figuring out a way to fight back using the Republicans' own weapons.

★

If, as William Jennings Bryan once contended, the "Democratic Party cannot serve God and Mammon; it cannot serve plutocracy and at the same time defend the rights of the masses," then the Democratic Leadership Council was a damned endeavor from the start. Rather than provide a new counterweight to the Republicans' breakneck advancement of the entitlements of wealth, the DLC's goal was to convince Democrats to sing a curious song: "We're with the people, and with Wall Street, too."

Founded in 1985, on the heels of the Reagan landslide that swept the Southern GOP to unprecedented power, the DLC's mission was to staunch the Democrats' bleeding in Dixie by recapturing the party's old image as "one of us"—one of us white folks, that is. Financed primarily by Washington business lobbyists, the DLC called on the party to downplay its support for abortion rights, gun control, and economic redistribution while racheting up its rhetoric on crime, national defense, and "personal responsibility," a phrase that became a mantra for neoliberals like DLC cofounder Bill Clinton. By arguing for more cops on the streets, backing tougher mandatory sentences for drug offenses (which would further devastate blacks), supporting capital punishment (as Clinton did), and aiming government reforms at middle-class families, the Democrats could overcome their identity as "liberal fundamentalists." A Democratic government's role would be "to steer, not to row." Rather than contest the premises of the GOP "culture war" used to distract voters from their economic interests, the Democrats joined in.

This was the antithesis of the approach that "Goldwater Republicans" used to forge a new conservative majority. When they lost in 1964, as former senator Bill Bradley has noted, "they didn't try to become Democrats. They tried to figure out how to make their own ideas more appealing to the voters." But the challenge for Democrats, in the DLC view, was not so much to forge a new vision for a progressive America—it was to change the party's image in pursuit of 270. The aim was to strategically "pick off" moderate white voters, rather than build a new political force capable of fighting the Republicans' pro-corporate economics and hollow cultural pandering. The DLC cooked up a bizarre, defensive recipe for winning back white Middle Americans with a pro-corporate, small-government agenda—an effort, in other words, *to win back populists with ideas that were antithetical to populism.* But with progressive Democrats stymied for ideas and pinning their Southern hopes too much on registering more black voters, the DLC's strategic brew of ideological contradictions at least had the virtue of novelty. Nothing else was working.

As DLC acolytes increasingly came to dominate the national party, the idea that a new, genuinely progressive Southern Democracy might be built by mobilizing blacks and moderate and progressive-minded whites—by organization and persuasion, rather than microtargeting and pandering—was effectively snuffed out. "The point was to look as much like Republicans as possible," said South Carolina activist Legette.

The DLC's first power play was convincing the party to hold a "Super Tuesday" of early primaries in 1988. The idea was that by giving Southern voters a bigger say in the Democratic nominating process, the party would be more likely to pick a moderate candidate, like DLC leader Al Gore. In turn, a middle-of-the-road Southern candidate would be the Democrats' ticket to the White House in a general election. But when Super Tuesday rolled around, the big winner was the ultimate anti-DLC candidate, Jesse Jackson; the big loser was Gore. So intent was the DLC on winning back white Southerners that it had seemingly forgotten about the combined power of black voters and white progressives to sway Democratic primaries in Dixie. When the eventual nominee, Massachusetts governor Michael Dukakis, lost every Southern state that November, the DLC asserted itself again, insisting that the party had lost by picking a candidate too "liberal" for the South. As Adolph Reed Jr. wrote, the DLC's "response to every election cycle, win or lose, is a commitment to the proposition that the party should move farther to the right." And for a while, that response defined the Democrats' "me too" approach to competing in the South.

It took Bill Clinton's once-in-a-generation charisma, not to mention his creative admixtures of empty populist rhetoric with DLC moderation, to make New Democratic politics a winning proposition nationally in the 1990s. But while Clinton—with an assist from third-party candidate Ross Perot, who siphoned off mostly Republican votes in 1992 and 1996—won half the South in both campaigns, Democrats continued their slow but steady Southern decline on the state and local levels during Clinton's presidency. "Bill Clinton blew an opportunity in the nineties to counter the Republicans' grassroots machine," said Jay Parmley, former state Democratic chair in Oklahoma. "The DNC was a wholly owned subsidiary of the Clinton administration; they put their people in place, they paid their consultants, they paid their pollsters. And that is as it should be. But they didn't lift a finger to get the state parties organized and motivated."

By 2000, the GOP had so thoroughly out-organized and out-messaged the Democrats in the South that when Al Gore ran again for the presidency, he abandoned his home state of Tennessee. After all those years of image-driven repositioning—all those years of defensively responding to a reactionary, myth-driven view of Southern voters—Democrats hardly knew themselves anymore. Especially the Southern Democrats.

★

"Liberal?!" cried Rose Marie Lowry-Townsend, rearing back in her seat and tossing up her hands. "Don't be accusing me of *that*. Lord—you could get me in a lot of trouble!"

She was laughing, but she meant it. A middle-school principal from eastern North Carolina who lost a primary runoff for Congress in

1996, the Native American had shown up for the first day of the 2000 Democratic National Convention in Los Angeles impeccably done up in a gleaming white dress, looking ready to take the podium at any moment if called upon. She laughed heartily, shaking her shoulders, when I told her I was hunting for liberals in the North Carolina delegation. The state had historically been the South's most progressive. But after eight years of Bill Clinton and his pro-corporate, anti–New Deal, Republican-Lite DLC having assumed near-complete control of the national party, were there any liberals still active enough to be delegates? If so, what did they think about their party's rightward drift—and about nominating another DLC stalwart, Vice President Gore, for president? These were questions worth asking; after all, polls showed that nearly 20 percent of Southerners still called themselves "liberal," making them, after three decades of Democratic neglect, maybe the most invisible and stifled base in contemporary politics.

"Well, good luck finding them," Lowry-Townsend said. "I'll tell you what *I* am. I'm a yellow-dog Democrat. An attack-dog Democrat. And I'm ready to attack this fall." So was she gung-ho about Gore and his chosen running mate, DLC chairman Joe Lieberman? Lowry-Townsend narrowed her eyes at me. "Look—do *you* want to see George W. Bush in the White House? Huh-uh. End of discussion."

Lowry-Townsend was an old-fashioned Southern Democrat—one of the remaining faithful more likely to vote for the proverbial yellow dog than for a Republican. Yet the Democratic Party had morphed into an entity that really seemed to put the test to whether she was voting for the Democrat or the dog. And so it went as I approached delegate after delegate: young, old, black, white, Hispanic, uptown, rural. Nobody would own up to the "L"-word. Until I came to John Wilson, a ruddy-cheeked, middle-aged fellow leaning forward in his seat, listening attentively to the opening-day speakers. Wary by now of my choice of terms, I asked him: "Are you, by any chance, progressive?"

"You *could* say liberal!" Wilson replied, his face opening into a generous grin. His liberalism had first sprouted forty years before, he explained, when as a seventh-grader, "I led the Kennedy campaign in my class, which was quite a thing to do because my teacher was a Republican." Back then, the odd Republican teacher aside, an open, avowed liberal was a perfectly respectable thing to be in North Carolina—and in the Democratic Party. John F. Kennedy's narrow victory was made possible in 1960, in no small part, by the early and enthusiastic support of North Carolina's Democratic candidate for governor, Terry Sanford. With most of the region wallowing in the big stink over integration, Sanford's endorsement made it more comfortable for other Southern Democratic leaders to support Kennedy, who carried most of the region in spite of fears that his Catholicism and civil rights sympathies would make it impossible.

At Wilson's first Democratic convention, in 1984, the North Carolina delegation was still full of sturdy lefties, satisfied with Walter Mondale but whooping it up for Jesse Jackson. But after the three Republican landslides of the '80s, even the liberals had been ready to hush up and try something new—and Clinton and the DLC arrived, right on time. "I think that when we had to go through Reagan, it became a chilling effect on liberals," Wilson said. "It's like, 'My God, we could have something *worse.*' So it's all gone underground," he said of liberalism, "waiting for the right time to emerge."

During Clinton's "Putting People First" tenure, millions of poor Americans had lost their safety net while the rich got richer. No-strings trade agreements had opened the way for hundreds of thousands of good manufacturing jobs to move overseas—leaving workers to minimum-wage service jobs with no benefits. The South's textile mills and furniture plants had been among the hardest hit. Still, Clinton had made good on one of his DLC-inspired campaign pledges. "Today we've gone from the largest deficits in history to the largest surpluses in history," he boasted at the 2000 convention.

"And, if we stay on course, we can make America debt-free for the first time since Andy Jackson was president in 1835." As Jackson himself might have pointed out, the Republican Lite tactic had put the spotlight on fiscal health for America, not *Americans*.

"Coming out on the plane I was like, 'Am I going to the right convention?'" another proud Southern liberal, Stella Adams, told me. "When I looked at the platform, I didn't see housing. I didn't see the issues that I really care about. It's pretty to the right of me." Passing by Adams in the hallway of the Staples Center, you'd never have expected her to say such things. Adams, president of the North Carolina Fair Housing Center, had come decked out in a tall, baggy hat covered with red, white, and blue sequins—and an improbably matching dress. From the get-up, you'd never guess, either, that this woman had made headlines back home for staging a hunger strike protesting predatory lending practices. At least not until you talked politics with her.

"Corporations run everything now," Adams said. "We have to find a way to bring power back to the people. If we don't we'll end up right where we were. We're setting ourselves up to repeat the Depression of the 1930s."

Adams's own political history suggested one reason why African Americans and liberal Southerners were not in full-scale revolt against the party that had begun to take them for granted. "The day I turned eighteen, the first thing my mother did was take me to register to vote. Voting is such a privilege in my family. My aunt had to take a literacy test in order to vote. She was a very intelligent woman, but when it was her turn to take the test, she was asked to interpret Article 3 of the Constitution. And she failed. Those are the kinds of obstacles we will face again. We've had the vote and had it taken away from us before. We've had equal opportunity and had it ripped out from under us with Jim Crow laws. And this time we'll have it ripped out from under us if we let people reinterpret civil rights laws to our disadvantage." As she spoke, another Southern liberal, Jesse Jackson, mounted the podium to make his appeal. Like Adams, he warned that there was too much to fear from the Republicans to desert the Democrats. There may be little to vote *for,* he as much as admitted, but there was still something to vote *against.*

Such was the condition to which even the most stalwart of Southern Democrats had been reduced by 2000—defensive, uninspired, and desperate for something to believe in beyond the evils of Republicanism. Lo and behold, on the final night of a dispirited convention, Gore tossed them a bone. The candidate's ever-changing personae had become a running joke—and a fitting symbol for his party's perpetual search for an appealing identity. But in Los Angeles, reading a plain-talking speech he'd written himself, the cocreator of the DLC transformed into Populist Al, the natural-born son of a rabble-rousing senator from Tennessee who lost his seat by opposing the Vietnam War. Gone were his tight-lipped calls for fiscal responsibility and bureaucratic downsizing. Gone was the emphasis on "personal responsibility." Gone were the words "New Democrat." For the first time in years, a Democratic nominee was giving a Democratic speech. "They're for the powerful, and we're for the people," Gore declared. He vowed to "stand up and say no" to "big tobacco, big oil, the big polluters, the pharmaceutical companies, the HMOs."

Gore's populist pitch rocketed him ahead of George W. Bush in the polls—where he stayed, until his first disastrous debate performance a little more than a month later. Gore surged again at the end of the campaign when he returned to his "people vs. the powerful" theme, but it wasn't quite enough—partly because his campaign had bypassed the South and ceded "populism," in its very stronghold, to the swaggering fakery of Bush.

"Gore's message—when he had one—was pretty much tailor-made for Southern voters," said Pete MacDowell. "It seemed to come from his gut, too, which appeals to Southerners. They don't like mealy-mouthed types, which is one big reason that the Democrats' triangulation never won any hearts down here. So Gore had the message, potentially, to win North Carolina, Tennessee, Arkansas, Louisiana—and he didn't run a campaign in any of them!"

★

Bright and early on a steamy August Saturday in 2003, the Democrats of Oconee County, South Carolina, gathered for their monthly breakfast in a windowless Rotary Club meeting room, way in back of the Community Restaurant in the mill village of Seneca. Thirty-five of them turned out that day, a record crowd in recent years. Mostly senior citizens, mostly white, these folks carried vivid memories of the fine old days, not so long ago, when Republicans were the ones huddled in the back rooms of diners all across Dixie, looking like some quaint, outmoded social club that just keeps meeting out of habit. Nowadays, the Oconee County Republicans owned their own meeting place, a spacious former showroom two blocks up North First Street. It was the once-omnipotent Democrats who sat under the royal-blue Rotary banners, forking spongy scrambled eggs, staring at the yellowing wall mural of Lake Keowee, and urging one another not to give up.

"Now, some of you folks have *got* to run for office," said county chairman Charles Hamby, a vigorous veteran bluegrass picker who was once a protégé of the legendary Bill Monroe. Folks looked down at their plates, waved their coffee cups meditatively, and sheepishly peeked around the long table to see if anybody else was volunteering. No takers. "Y'all keep thinking about it," Hamby said. "We need to be on the ballot, now, stay in the game."

Five decades of economic upheaval had transformed the piney hills of upstate South Carolina into a jumble of shuttered-and-rusted mills and clapboard mill houses running to ruin, sitting side by side with high-tech business parks and massive lakefront McMansions occupied by Republican émigrés. As in almost every part of the South, folks here now voted routinely for Republicans in "Washington elections" for president and Congress. But, while in most of the South Democrats still competed on a more-or-less even basis locally, Oconee had gone whole-hog Republican, up and down the ballot, from state senator to county coroner. It was getting tough to find Democrats intrepid enough to tilt at the electoral windmills.

But getting talked into running for office was not what had brought out three dozen Democrats that morning. The main order of business was the following February's presidential primary— a high-profile event, soon after the contests in Iowa and New Hampshire, that was supposed to lift the sagging spirits of Palmetto State Democrats. The early South Carolina primary was also supposed to help the national Democrats scare up a candidate who could compete for at least a few of the South's 173 electoral votes.

The White House had never been occupied by a Democrat who failed to win at least five Southern states. In 2000, Al Gore had found out just how difficult it was to buck that history. If Gore could have held on to his home state, a whole lot of things would have looked different in 2003. But Gore's poll-watchers convinced him the best strategic move was to shut down his campaign in every Southern state but Florida after Labor Day; that way, they could load resources into key swing states outside the Democrats' terra incognita—aka Dixie. "It just about killed me to pull out of North Carolina and Virginia and Arkansas," said Gore's campaign manager, Louisiana native Donna Brazile. "But the poll numbers were telling us we couldn't keep spending money there and win elsewhere."

The whole world knows what happened in Florida. But Gore also lost his home state, along with Arkansas and West Virginia, narrowly. A few campaign stops here, a TV ad buy there, a few get-out-the-vote organizers in Nashville and Little Rock and Wheeling, and the Democrats of Oconee County might have been spared the trouble of grilling a series of presidential candidates and their flacks at their monthly meetings in 2003. No such luck.

"We were supposed to have a guy from the Kerry campaign," Chairman Hamby had explained. "But he had to fly off to Washington. Guess we'll excuse him for that." Instead, Connecticut senator Joe Lieberman's South Carolina chairman addressed the group. "As you've seen in the papers, we've lost a lot of textile jobs here," Barry Butler informed them. His listeners had not seen it in the papers, of course; they had lived it. They had passed by boarded-up mills and rust-eaten warehouses on their way to the breakfast. When somebody chimed in and asked whether Butler's candidate would be showing up in person at some point, Butler replied, "We're trying to get him out into all these rural counties." *All these rural counties.* With that, Butler, albeit unwittingly, summed up the national Democrats' troublesome attitude toward Southern voters in one neat phrase.

To compete in "these rural counties," the non-Southern "experts" have long been unshakably convinced, Democrats must make Faustian bargains, selling their progressive souls in the process. This is nonsense, as Lieberman's guy was finding out. The Oconee Democrats kept firing off sharp questions, questions that rural Southerners are not supposed to ask. Like, "How does Senator Lieberman think he has a right to criticize what the president's doing in Iraq when he voted for a blank check to let Bush do whatever he wanted to do?" Or, "You said something about the mills shutting down. Didn't your candidate vote to give China favored-nation trade status?"

The Oconee Democrats' breakfast meeting broke up after Hamby made one last appeal for office seekers. As folks milled around the Rotary room, Maxie Duke, the group's seventy-six-year-old secretary-treasurer, tallied up the morning's proceeds: $240, not bad. Accounting done, Duke rested her elbows on the table and allowed herself a sigh. "I feel inferior sometimes," she said. "I feel like people don't think I'm an important person, you know, because, 'She's a Democrat.'"

It had not always been like that. While Duke taught high school, her late husband, a druggist in Seneca, had served as county sheriff for sixteen years. Democratic, of course. "You've got to understand: Oconee County has *always* been Democratic." Duke corrected herself: "*Was* always Democratic. Till about 1980, the Reagan years. The religious right started controlling things then, and all of a sudden if you didn't espouse the Bible all the time, you were immoral and you couldn't win."

But Duke knew the Bible-thumpers hadn't changed the Southern political landscape all by themselves. Nor had the Republicans' Southern strategy. When the defections began, South Carolina Democrats had no clue how to respond, Duke said. As in most Southern states, the Democrats had been the only viable party for so long there had been no need to build a functioning party structure. "If you won the Democratic primary here, you couldn't lose a general election if you tried," Duke recalled. "We had it so easy. So when the Republicans started to crest, we weren't ready for it. We didn't know what to do or how to do it."

Even so, it took three decades for registered Republicans to finally outnumber registered Democrats in South Carolina. "It was drip, drip, drip," said Don Aiesi, a Massachusetts native who teaches political science at Furman University, just down the road, in Greenville, South Carolina. "Slow, steady, and unstaunched." While Republicans were building professional party organizations from scratch across the South, national Democrats watched their state and local parties run to rot. These parties needed help, especially in Deep South states, where half the parties were suddenly black, and the old white guard tried desperately to hold on to its power. "The

DNC stood back and watched as Democrats became the minority party of the South," Aeisi said. "Apparently they were content to see it happen."

As their numbers slowly dwindled, Dixie Democrats grew more and more disconnected from the national party—and in many cases, downright resentful. "We need to get connected with the national party," Duke said. "That's where the big money comes from. You sure can't win Washington elections without them. But they just don't seem to care." Or care to listen. "When they do show up out here, you see how little they understand who they're talking to. They think we're all religious right people. If you noticed, the Lieberman man didn't even say he was pro-choice, though he is. Bet he mentions it when he's up north."

★

While the Republican Lite approach helped win some statewide victories in Dixie in the 1980s and '90s, the strategy tamped down the enthusiasm of the Democratic base. Over time, it paid predictably diminishing returns at the polls. "After a while," said former North Carolina senator and presidential contender John Edwards, "it got to the point where voters couldn't tell any difference. Why could people choose Democrats when they could vote for Republicans who really believed what they were saying?"

While the Democrats pursued their me-too strategy in the South, the gap between Southerners' social views and those of the rest of the country continued to narrow. By 2003, pollster Scott Keeter found Southerners tilting to the right of other Americans on issues of race, immigration, and the use of military force—but the tilt was nowhere near as dramatic as it had been twenty years earlier. Meanwhile, Southerners were as likely to support government regulation of business, social welfare, and strong environmental protections as non-Southerners were. They were pro-choice, too, though by a narrow margin, and on another contentious cultural issue, gay civil unions, were only 3 percent less supportive than other Americans.

None of that registered with Democratic strategists. As the 2004 election approached, political scientist Thomas Schaller wrote an influential *Washington Post* op-ed, calling for a "non-Southern" Democratic strategy (hardly a new idea). "Bowing and scraping to salvage a few southern votes here and there only leads to the kind of ideological schizophrenia that . . . muddies the party's image," he noted in his subsequent book, *Whistling Past Dixie*. Writing off the South, agreed Ryan Lizza in the *New York Times,* "lets Democrats be Democrats." While no one had ever been elected president without winning at least a sizable chunk of Dixie, the time had come, in the minds of many non-Southerners, to officially kiss off the region. They soon found their ideal candidate.

On the doleful morning of January 20, 2004, my Alabama friend and hair stylist, Todd Taylor, had just one question: "What are the Democrats smoking this time? 'Cause whatever it is, if it can make you that oblivious to reality, I want some."

The night before, Iowans had held their quadrennial caucuses and made Senator John Kerry the overwhelming favorite for the Democratic nomination. I was living then in the heart of old Dixie, Montgomery, "cradle" of both the Confederacy and the civil rights movement, and getting a taste of how unaccountably strange—and remote—national Democratic politics looked from the vast swath of America that the party had sworn off. I worked for a civil rights group housed just a couple of downtown blocks from the state capitol, that gleaming symbol of white supremacy where Jefferson Davis was sworn in as Confederate president and George Wallace spat out his "segregation forever" speech in 1963. At the bottom of the long marble steps, the great Selma-to-Montgomery voting rights march of 1965 reached its destination—a little short of it, actually, thanks to hundreds of riot-ready state troopers blocking those tired feet from trodding the hallowed ground. Not far away is the humble old brown-brick church, Dexter Avenue Baptist, where the young Dr. Martin Luther King Jr. revved up a movement that stifled the racist claptrap up the hill. Another two blocks down Dexter and you reach the Alabama Judicial Building, where the most pernicious contemporary threat to American democracy, the theocratic movement, pitched a fit throughout the summer of 2002 on behalf of a 360-ton monument to the Ten Commandments installed by soon-to-be-deposed Chief Justice Roy Moore.

"It's sort of the ultimate Southern street when you think about it," remarked Georgette Norman, who runs the Rosa Parks Museum a few blocks farther up Dexter. She's right—except that it's also the ultimate American street. You can stand on those capitol steps and drink in potent emblems of the finest and ugliest aspects of the American political character, piled right on top of one another. It's a microcosm of the South for sure—or, as Norman says, "a big damn contradictory mess." Which is the single best summation of Southern political and social realities that I have ever come across.

For Southern liberals like Taylor and Norman, the Democrats' simplistic misreading of the South falls somewhere between a bad joke and a tragedy. Since the late '60s, most Southerners' image of the two parties had flipped, even if their voting habits had not. Now it was Democrats who entered every campaign suspected of being wine-and-edamame elitists out to screw, or at least disdain, the folks. Kerry was the very personification of that image. "You only have to listen to the man for thirty seconds," Todd said, "to know that's somebody who'd be afraid to even dip a toe in Alabama."

If there were any doubt about that, Kerry quickly dispelled it. "Everybody always makes the mistake of looking south," he tut-tutted to a Dartmouth College crowd just three days after his Iowa win. "Al Gore proved that he could have been president of the United States without winning one Southern state." As an ABC reporter archly noted on air, this was a singularly odd interpretation of events, since Gore's surrender of the South had ended in defeat. Besides, as political scientist Merle Black, coauthor of *The Rise of Southern Republicans,* noted, "Usually, if you write off a group or a region, you don't say it. It's against all the rules of politics." But Kerry, who spelled out his non-Southern intentions twice more as he rode his momentum to victory in the New Hampshire primary, was eager to advertise his plans to replicate Gore's losing strategy, no matter if it further alienated Southern Democrats. The blue-state pundits cheered him on. Others foresaw both short- and long-term disaster.

"Presidential campaigns are the primary vehicle for selling a party's identity," argued Steve Jarding, who helped steer Mark Warner and Jim Webb to upset victories in Virginia, for governor and senator, in 2001 and 2006. "When John Kerry says, 'I'm not going south,' that means that there's some forty to fifty million dollars in Democratic investments not going south, either. It means digging a deeper and deeper hole in those states." This was not simply a question of getting to 270, as Ruy Teixeira noted in November 2003. Writing off the South, he warned, "would imply that we see all Southerners as a culturally alien mass that we don't know how to talk to. And that would further skew our image, identifying us even more with upscale social liberalism—which is a tendency we already have."

There were other ways to see it. "Democrats keep losing," said Democratic strategist Dave "Mudcat" Saunders of Virginia, "because they can't fucking count." Indeed, the math was clear enough for most third-graders to parse. After three decades as the country's fastest-growing region, the South in 2004 accounted for more than one-third of all electoral votes. Kerry's only chance to beat incumbent president George W. Bush was a clean sweep of every large state (and just about every medium-sized and small state) in the Northeast, Midwest, and West. Even if they managed a narrow victory in the presidential election, the Democrats stood to lose more seats in Congress with their non-Southern campaign, especially in a year with five Democratic-held Senate seats up for grabs in Dixie.

In the summer, Kerry's math skills appeared to have sharpened a tad, as he reluctantly bowed to popular sentiment and tapped John Edwards for vice president. The genial North Carolinian had crafted a fresh populist pitch that might help the Democrats speak to working-class and middle-class voters in the South and Midwest. His background as a mill-worker's son lent a down-home credibility to the Democratic ticket. At the very least, Edwards's presence on the ticket meant that Republicans would have to spend some time and money to defend Dixie, making it tougher for Bush adviser Karl Rove to shovel resources into big swing states like Ohio and Pennsylvania as planned.

But shortly after the Democratic convention, just as the campaign began to crank up in earnest, Kerry waved a big white hanky, officially "suspending operations" in Virginia, Louisiana, Arkansas, and the border state of Missouri (along with Nevada, Arizona, and Colorado, three equally competitive states out west). No new "operations" were going to start up even in Edwards's home state of North Carolina (where the Democrats, with little help from party campaign committees, would ultimately lose his Senate seat in a close race). In all, even before the traditional kickoff of election season on Labor Day, Kerry and the Democrats had, for all practical purposes, conceded twenty-seven states and 227 electoral votes to Bush. Neither Kerry nor Edwards set foot in the South, outside of Florida and Edwards's trips home to North Carolina, in the last two months of the campaign. In the process, Kerry neutralized his own vice-presidential choice. Thanks to his obliging opposition, Bush needed just 43 more electoral votes—from the remaining twenty-three states of the union—to become the least popular president in U.S. history to win reelection.

Once again, Republicans were left to preach, unchallenged, their divisive cultural populism to Southerners, making hay with emotionally charged issues like gay marriage. The Democratic presidential campaign—and whatever its message might have been—was little more than a distant rumor in Dixie. While the Democrats were spending more than twenty-five million dollars on television ads in Ohio alone, yellow-dog Southerners, even in majority-Democratic areas like Montgomery, couldn't even scare up Kerry/Edwards yard signs or bumper stickers at state headquarters. (A friend of mine finally drove the ninety minutes up to Birmingham to buy a bundle.) "In the South, and in most of the country for that matter," Edwards told me after the election, "you couldn't hardly tell we were running. It's tough to convince people you're right when you can't be bothered to talk to them."

3

DIXIEPHOBIA

"The actual history of the South too often rests in an unmarked grave, while the celebratory lies and politically convenient distortions march into immortality."

—TIMOTHY B. TYSON,
Blood Done Sign My Name (2004)

WHEN THE INEVITABLE came down on November 2, 2004, with Republicans riding another Southern sweep back to Washington, it looked like the occasion for something beyond the quadrennial butt-covering, finger-pointing, "soul-searching" ritual undergone by the losing party. "We had the money," said a shell-shocked Harold M. Ickes, the longtime Democratic operative and Clinton crony who had raised much of it himself as the head of two of the 527 groups that helped the party match Republican spending for the first time in modern history. "We had a ground operation the likes of which has never been seen, and we had a good candidate who stood toe-to-toe with the president and bested him in three debates. We had all that, and we still lost."

The Democrats' non-Southern strategy had come a cropper in two straight national elections. In both, they had enjoyed historic political advantages: the popularity of the Clinton administration in 2000 and the subterranean approval ratings of Bush in 2004. But the party had hemorrhaged white working-class votes, with John

Kerry losing them nationwide by 23 percent. Hispanic voters had swung "red" in the South and tilted "purple" in the rest of the country. The Democrats lost five Senate seats from the Southern states, where the national party spent only chump change. The magnitude of the Southern wipeout was seen most vividly on a county-by-county map: of 1,154 majority-white counties in the old Confederate states, Kerry won just 90; eight years earlier, Bill Clinton had carried 510. Kerry's decision to write off the South had not "freed" him to run as a reformist liberal; instead, he had crafted tepidly moderate positions on every major issue, from the Iraq War to health care, sounding like the DLC. "The illusion that George W. Bush 'understands' the struggles of working-class people was only made possible by the unintentional assistance of the Democratic campaign," wrote Thomas Frank. "Once again, the 'party of the people' chose to sacrifice the liberal economic policies that used to connect them to such voters on the altar of centrism."

The Democrats had whistled past Dixie like never before, and the results were bleak: a "mandate" for the most radically destructive right-wing administration in American history. But anyone hoping for a sober recognition of these facts was sorely and swiftly disappointed. When politics and sectionalism collide, there is precious little rationality involved.

"Fuck the South. Fuck 'em," began the most popular in a parade of blue-state blogs, books, and op-eds blaming the benighted denizens of Dixie for Bush's unconscionable victory. "We should have let them go when they wanted to leave," ranted the anonymous (and possibly parodic) blogger, whose "Fuck the South" page attracted more than fourteen million visits. "But no, we had to kill half a million people so they'd stay part of our special Union. Fighting for the right to keep slaves—yeah, those are the states we want to keep."

The Dixiephobic rhetoric was by no means limited to the blogosphere. The morning after the election, Bob Beckel, a veteran

Democratic strategist, went on *FOX and Friends* to declare, "I think now that slavery is taken care of, I'm for letting the South form its own nation." *West Wing* writer and former Bill Clinton speechwriter Lawrence O'Donnell seconded the notion. "Some would say, 'Oh, poor Alabama, it's cut off from the wealth infusion it gets from New York and California,'" O'Donnell mock-whined on *The McLaughlin Group*. "But the more this political condition goes on . . . the more you're testing the inclination of the blue states to say, 'So what?'" In other words: if Southerners don't shape up and start voting for candidates who don't campaign among them, for a party that does not even ask for their votes, the recriminations are going to have to begin.

Conveniently forgotten was that Democrats had chosen a presidential candidate whose idea of "relating" to regular Americans consisted of donning camouflage and bagging some turkeys in southern Ohio. Maybe the most disheartening thing about the "blame the South" response was how it made even Zell Miller, the cranky Old Democrat from Georgia who had endorsed Bush at the Republican convention and challenged MSNBC's Chris Matthews to a duel, sound halfway reasonable—on one point, anyway. "Once upon a time," Miller had written in his 2003 screed, *A National Party No More: The Conscience of a Conservative Democrat,* "the most successful Democratic leader of them all, FDR, looked south and said, 'I see one-third of a nation ill-housed, ill-clad, ill-nourished.' Today, our Democratic leaders look south and say, 'I see one-third of a nation and it can go to hell.'"

But as hard as the right-wing media tried to fan the flames of a new civil war ("Blue States Buzz Over Secession," crowed the *Washington Times*), Yankee secessionism never really caught fire. The Democratic bounce-back in the 2006 midterms largely quelled the civil-war chatter. But it did nothing to put a damper on "strategic" calls for Democrats to step up their Southern retreat and relegate the South to a Republican backwater as punishment for its electoral sins.

The urge to set the South adrift is understandable, God knows. The political predilections of Dixie are frustrating even to those of us who love it. "You see your neighbors standing in line to vote," said Valerie Downes, a left-wing activist in Montgomery, "and you just want to go up and shake them all and say, 'Do you *really* know what's at stake here? God*damn* y'all!'" But Southern progressives know better than to chalk up Republican votes to cultural backwardness and willful ignorance. They know the South better than to believe that it's somehow stuck in 1965—or 1865, for that matter. They know how sweepingly, surprisingly, and dramatically the South has transformed itself. And they know that the Democratic Party doesn't see it.

★

The South has long amounted to little more than a swirl of stereotypes in the national mind—some flattering, most derogatory. When pundits, bloggers, and Democratic strategists talk about "the South," everybody knows just what they mean: a dank, magnolia-scented otherworld where prehistoric obsessions with "God, guns, blacks, and babies," in the words of Republican strategist Jeff Roe of Missouri, hold white voters together in an unbreakable sway, making it hopeless terrain for planting any politics to the left of Jefferson Davis or Jerry Falwell.

"The Southern mystique" is what liberal historian Howard Zinn called it in his 1964 book of the same title. It's that false "notion that the South is more than just 'different,' that it is distinct from the rest of the nation . . . an inexplicable variant from the national norm." This notion "feeds self-righteousness in the North," Zinn wrote, and "it stands so firmly and so high on a ledge of truth that one must strain to see the glitter of deception in its eye."

Jacob Levenson found the mystique still thriving in media coverage of the South during the 2004 campaign—four decades after the South's great "variant," its *de jure* system of racial apartheid, was peacefully dismantled. "[T]he country and, by natural extension, the press, often use the South as a convenient box to contain all sorts of problems, situations, and conditions that are national in scope: race, white poverty, the cultural rift forming between the religious and the secular, guns, abortion, gay marriage . . . the contours of American morality, and the identity of the major political parties."

The Southern "box" once had an undeniable basis in reality—"not quite a nation within a nation," wrote W. J. Cash, in his flawed-but-fascinating rumination on *The Mind of the South,* "but the next thing to it." But that was 1941, and even then, it was hyperbole, particularly when it came to politics. There is truth to the rumor that Southerners are still culturally distinctive in some unmistakable ways. "Like most stereotypes," said John Shelton Reed, a sociologist specializing in Southern culture at the University of North Carolina, "it's exaggerated, undiscriminating, resistant to change—all the usual bad things about stereotypes. But there's a grain of truth, if not a bushel or a peck, at the bottom of it." For instance, "People say Southerners are more religious. Well, we go to church more often than other Americans, and maybe we are. More patriotic? Well, look at our enlistment rates. More polite? Hard to get good data on that, but I think we are. These are people's attempts to make sense of what they experience, and what they see. Laziness? Well, in the days when you had ninety-eight degrees without air-conditioning, it was certainly true that people weren't moving very fast." True, too, that Southerners themselves—from Erskine Caldwell and D. W. Griffith to Lewis Grizzard and Jeff Foxworthy ("you know you're a redneck if . . .")—have contributed their share to the cultural typecasting. But while Southerners are somewhat rightly seen as distinct, "what's distinct about them keeps changing. People keep inventing new 'Southern' things," Reed said. "NASCAR didn't exist a hundred years ago. Country music didn't exist a hundred years ago; it's now becoming American white working-class music."

Even as the cultural markers keep moving, the political diversity of Dixie has multiplied exponentially in the six decades since Cash's observations. By any measure you choose—economic, educational, ideological, cultural—Southerners have merged pretty seamlessly into the American mainstream. More than thirty years ago, journalist John Egerton in his landmark book, *The Americanization of Dixie: The Southernization of America,* pronounced the South "just about over as a separate and distinct place." Drive through it today and you can see how right he was. More recently, Don Fowler, the former DNC chairman from South Carolina, barked at a reporter who kept asking stereotypical questions about Southern politics: "There ain't no South anymore!"

Why has the perception of Southern distinctiveness so long outlived its relevance? Partly because "once you've seen a film like *Mississippi Burning,* it's hard to have any other kind of perception," said Richard Howorth, the mayor of Oxford, Mississippi, and proprietor of the city's famous Square Books. "And it's hard to think that Southerners could change in such a short time. They have changed, but it's hard to believe in the extent of it unless you live here." But that's not the only reason. Stereotyping is simply intrinsic to human nature; Southerners do their share, too. "Every Arkansas likes to have a Mississippi," is how Howorth put it. And every North likes to have a South.

"The South is everything its revilers have charged, and more than its defenders have claimed," Zinn wrote in 1964. "It is racist, violent, hypocritically pious, xenophobic, false in its elevation of women, nationalistic, conservative, and it harbors extreme poverty in the midst of ostentatious wealth. The only point I have to add is that the United States, as a civilization, embodies all of these same qualities. That the South possesses them with more intensity makes it easier for the nation to pass off its characteristics to the South, leaving itself innocent and righteous." Perhaps the most disturbing aspect of the boxing-in of the South is the way it inoculates non-Southerners. "Talking about race in the South," Levenson wrote, "becomes a way of *not* talking about race in the rest of the country."

Ever since the buildup to the Civil War, the supposedly unmatched racism of the white South has offered Northern whites a flattering measure of comparison and contrast. In his masterful study of Civil War literature, *Patriotic Gore,* Edmund Wilson seconded Robert Penn Warren's observation that the Civil War victory left the North with a "Treasury of Virtue," a sort of cleansing effect that "has enabled us to carry along in all our subsequent wars . . . the insufferable attitudes that appeared to us first justified by our victory over the Confederacy in 1865." Legend had it, wrote the great Southern historical revisionist C. Vann Woodward, "that the Mason and Dixon line not only divided slavery from freedom in antebellum America, but . . . also set apart racial inhumanity in the South from benevolence, liberality and tolerance in the North."

Southern stereotypes are the North's contribution to what Martin Luther King Jr. called the "thingification" of human beings. From the beginning Northerners were suspicious of Southerners who acted too, well, *Southern.* Whether Thomas Jefferson was appearing publicly in faded overalls, egregiously flouting formal convention at state dinners with first-come, first-served seating, or extolling radical populism—he recommended a revolution every twenty years or so to flush out the political system—it triggered anger and fear. Jefferson's government of Southern "blockheads and knaves," proper Yankee Theodore Dwight thundered three months after the Virginian's inauguration, was out to "destroy every trace of civilization in the world, and to force mankind back into a savage state."

The most powerful egalitarian populists ever since—Andrew Jackson, William Jennings Bryan, Huey Long—have come in for similar treatment. The attitude has never been better exemplified than by Franklin Roosevelt's interior secretary, Harold Ickes (the elder), who huffed that Long, who attacked FDR's economic policies from the left, suffered from "halitosis of the intellect."

In the nineteenth century, even many of the region's most vociferous critics rejected the idea that Southerners were uniquely ignorant and hateful and the North inherently righteous and virtuous. Northern abolitionists like the thundering prophet William Lloyd Garrison, who took the "evil" slave South to the woodshed without remorse, didn't give the white North a free pass; after Frederick Douglass wowed a group of Northern abolitionists in 1841, Garrison called it a "stunning blow . . . inflicted on northern prejudice against a colored complexion." Alexis de Tocqueville believed that "the prejudice of race appears to be stronger in the states that have abolished slavery than in those where it still exists." In the North, Tocqueville wrote, "the Negro is free, but he cannot share the rights, pleasures, labors, griefs, or even the tomb of him whose equal he has been declared; there is nowhere where he can meet him neither in life nor in death." (More than a century later that observation would reverberate in James Baldwin's arch opinion that, "for the negro, there's no difference between North and South. There's only a difference in the way they castrate you.")

In the 1920s, *Baltimore Sun* columnist H. L. Mencken, an admirer of the (largely mythical) Old South aristocracy, popularized his vision of the New South as a "stupendous region of worn-out farms, shoddy cities and paralyzed cerebrums." The portrait was never more savage, or hilarious, than in his accounts of the 1925 Scopes trial in Dayton, Tennessee, where a schoolteacher was convicted of teaching evolution. Mencken imprinted the indelible image of gape-jawed, holy-rolling rubes—the "local primates," he called them—onto the American brain as the quintessence of small-town Southernness. Mencken's famous denunciation of Southern culture, "Sahara of the Bozart" still resonates as well, having barged into the twenty-first century when, in 2004, *Slate* columnist Timothy

Noah praised Kerry's disinterest in Southern votes with the words, "For Democrats, the South has become the Sahara of the Electoral College."

Contemporary pundits like Noah might feel free to borrow freely from Mencken's catchiest aphorisms about Southern culture in the 1920s, but they ignore Mencken's *real* reporting from Dayton, which was more nuanced than the cartoon replica of the trial popularized by the play and movie *Inherit the Wind*.

"The town, I confess, greatly surprised me," Mencken wrote. "I expected to find a squalid Southern village, with darkies snoozing on the horse-blocks, pigs rooting under the houses and the inhabitants full of hookworm and malaria. What I found was a country town full of charm and even beauty." And devoid of the kind of frothing hatred he'd come to expose. "Nor is there any evidence in the town of that poisonous spirit that usually shows itself when Christian men gather to defend the great doctrine of their faith. I have heard absolutely no whisper that Scopes is in the pay of the Jesuits, or that the whisky trust is backing him, or that he is egged on by the Jews who manufacture lascivious moving pictures. On the contrary, the Evolutionists and the Anti-Evolutionists seem to be on the best of terms, and it is hard in a group to distinguish one from another." With an unmistakable tone of disappointment, Mencken concluded, "There is absolutely no bitterness on tap."

Except for that of Mencken himself, when he turned his attentions to William Jennings Bryan. Mencken's sketch of the populist-champion-cum-creationist was intended to savage the old Democrat—and there was plenty in Bryan's testimony on behalf of Genesis to pike him with. But it wasn't just Bryan's patent irrationality on the subjects of evolution and Biblical literalism that got under Mencken's skin, it was the unbearable spectacle of the populist entering a Southern town in triumph. Daytonites might have turned out to be nice, respectable, tolerant folks—but they loved Bryan. That was enough to turn Mencken's account into a sort of primer on

Dixiephobia: "There was something particularly fitting in the fact that his last days were spent in a one-horse Tennessee village, and that death found him there," Mencken wrote after Bryan died, just days after the trial ended.

> The man felt at home in such scenes. He liked people who sweated freely, and were not debauched by the refinements of the toilet. Making his progress up and down the Main Street of little Dayton, surrounded by gaping primates from the upland valleys of the Cumberland Range, his coat laid aside, his bare arms and hairy chest shining damply, his bald head sprinkled with dust—so accoutred and on display he was obviously happy. He liked getting up early in the morning, to the tune of cocks crowing on the dunghill. He liked the heavy, greasy victuals of the farmhouse kitchen. He liked country lawyers, country pastors, all country people. . . . The simian gabble of a country town was not gabble to him, but wisdom of an occult and superior sort. In the presence of city folks he was palpably uneasy. Their clothes, I suspect, annoyed him, and he was suspicious of their too delicate manners. He knew all the while that they were laughing at him—if not at his baroque theology, then at least at his alpaca pantaloons. But the yokels never laughed at him.

You can't help imagining, though, that they had a few giggles at Mencken's expense.

By the time of the civil rights revolution, the notion of Northern superiority was so well entrenched—and so dismally reinforced by some Southern whites' gusty defense of their racial caste system—that Dixie had become a kind of all-purpose national dump. Even though historians such as the Marxist Eugene Genovese began to provide a corrective to historical Dixiephobia in the 1960s, detailing the economic circumstances that undergirded the practice of slavery and the maintenance of Jim Crow, the dominant historical fashion endured: "whatever appeared retrograde in national history," C. Vann Woodward wrote, was "somehow attributable to Southern votes or influence."

During the 1960s and '70s, the systematic degradation of blacks in the urban North became impossible to ignore—and their frustrations impossible to tamp down. Meanwhile, the South—legal segregation no longer possible—began to mimic the North's de facto patterns of segregation, like neighborhood "redlining," in which black neighborhoods were shut out of mortgages and other economic investments. As the racial patterns in the regions grew more similar and as Northern racism became more obvious, the need to draw distinctions between white Northerners and Southerners was newly urgent. "To explain or account for any and all of the ills that beset the black people in the Northern ghettoes," Woodward wrote, "the answer was always the same: 'Look away! look away! look away! Dixie Land!'"

The South embodies a whole spectrum of anti-liberal evils beyond racism. The *American Prospect* published a stellar specimen in 2007, when veteran political reporter Harold Meyerson wrote a story called "Wal-Mart Comes North: The Continuation of the Civil War by Other Means." Decrying the "casual barbarities" of "the nation's most backward region," Meyerson linked the rise and menace of Wal-Mart's discount empire to the South and attributed all that is good in opposing the chain's expansion to the North. "Wal-Mart couldn't keep to the backwaters," he wrote, gloating over the fact that the company had recently met with staunch opponents in many a northeastern and west coast burg. "Wal-Mart's drive northward may be the event that clarifies what the entire conservative revolution of the past 30 years truly is; not just the rolling back of the New Deal but the imposition of the grotesquely stunted economic and moral norms of the South on the rest of the nation."

As usual when Dixiephobia infests the brain of an otherwise

intelligent Northerner, Meyerson overlooked a few facts about the South's history of addressing economic inequalities. He failed to note that the New Deal was actually more popular in the South than in the North; that Wal-Mart and its labor practices were opposed and protested in numerous Southern towns and exurbs; that the labor patterns he decried were invented in the Industrial North and exported down South after the Civil War by such industrial moguls as Andrew Carnegie, who built up Birmingham as a factory town for U.S. Steel; and that, around the time Myerson wrote his article, a Pew Center study had found that 81 percent of Northeasterners said they found Wal-Mart a "good place for you and your family to shop." In Meyerson's mythic version of the controversy over Wal-Mart, "[N]orthern workers have mobilized their political power to keep a southern labor system from coming north." He continued, "Wal-Mart and Republicanism share a common commitment to traditionalist morality and patriarchy, to the degradation of labor, to enriching the rich, and to the global expansion of their power. Refitted for our time, these are the same southern values that this nation once, at immense cost in blood, rightfully crushed."

The Treasury of Virtue just keeps on giving, and no contemporary entity does more to keep it alive than the Democratic Party. The party actively exacerbates and justifies a nation divided—right along the old Mason-Dixon, between the enlightened and the unwashed, the liberal and the conservative, the American and the Southern. Zinn's set of "Southern characteristics," from 1964, are remarkably similar to the catalog of "pathologies" attributed to the region forty-two years later by Tom Schaller in *Whistling Past Dixie*: "The South is a place where racial animosities run deepest and xenophobia toward outsiders—foreign or domestic—is most palpable," he wrote. (Peculiar qualities for the region with the highest rate of domestic in-migration.) Southerners have "among" the highest bankruptcy rates in the nation, even though they live in a "welfare-addled South," which "receives more in federal outlays and subsidies than it sends to Washington in taxes." The region "is home to some of the most conspicuous overconsumption of commodities like beef, oil, and tobacco," we are informed, "which in turn lead to greater dependence on domestic water resources, scarce foreign oil reserves, and scarce health-care services." Schaller warned further that "the South is the most militarized region of the country." Even worse, "Evangelicals are many and libertarians are few in the South." (In fact, while it's true that most of the nation's evangelicals—52 percent—live in the South, it's also true that almost as many Southerners say they're libertarians as do Westerners—31 percent and 32 percent respectively.)

Campaigning in Iowa in October 2007, Senator Hillary Clinton added an item to the inventory: sexism. When a *Des Moines Register* reporter asked about the Hawkeye State and Mississippi being the only states never to have elected a woman to Congress or the governorship, Clinton replied: "[H]ow can Iowa be ranked with Mississippi? That's not what I see. That's not the quality. That's not the communitarianism; that's not the openness I see in Iowa." Democratic Dixiephobia shunts aside responsibility for the immense damage that racism, religious fanaticism, and sexism continue to inflict. The non-Southern strategy represents a deep, only partly conscious, desire on the part of liberals and non-Southern Democrats to "box" backwardness into the South. By viewing the South as hopelessly, stubbornly, unchangeably "red," the superior hearts and brains of non-Southern liberals can rest assured, once again, that American evils are not theirs to confront—or to overcome.

★

Most of the black folks sitting in the atrium-style dining area of the Beacon Drive-In in Spartanburg, South Carolina, in March 2003 neither knew nor cared who Howard Dean was. They had seen plenty of politicians snaking their way through this mostly black small city. They were intent on their Sliced Pork-a-Plentys and chicken stew and wedges of gummy pecan pie, politely applauding the little-known Northerner until he got around to saying something they hadn't heard before. "You know all those white guys riding around with Confederate flags in the back of their pickup trucks?" he asked. "Well, their kids don't have health insurance either!" That perked people up. As *Newsday* reported: "This blunt appeal to the commonality of racial interests won the moment and a burst of applause."

Dean had won the moment with a different crowd a month earlier, when he told the Democratic National Committee at its winter meeting in Washington, "I intend to talk about race during this election in the South because the Republicans have been talking about it since 1968 in order to divide us. . . . White folks in the South who drive pickup trucks with Confederate decals in the back ought to be voting for us and not them, because their kids don't have health insurance either, and their kids need better schools, too." The party leaders stood and cheered. After the meeting, Donna Brazile called Dean's remarks "the medicine to cure my depression." Former mayor Maynard Jackson of Atlanta was equally impressed. "Dean blew the roof off today," he said. "There was no mealy-mouth wishy-washiness about it. It was very gutsy."

Nine months later, after the Vermont governor's unstinting anti-war rhetoric and innovative Netroots campaign had rocketed him to the top of the polls, Dean told the *Des Moines Register,* "I still want to be the candidate for guys with Confederate flags in their pickup trucks. We can't beat George W. Bush unless we appeal to a broad cross-section of Democrats." Suddenly, with the Iowa caucuses just two months away, the plaudits turned into brickbats. Rather than stimulate a much-needed debate about how Democrats might appeal to white working-class voters, Dean's words set off a hailstorm of nonsensical controversy that not only began his campaign's slide into oblivion, but crippled the party's viability in the South.

"I recently read a comment that you made," a young man said at a Democratic forum in Boston on November 4, "where you said that you wanted to be the candidate for guys with Confederate flags on their pickup trucks. When I read that comment, I was extremely offended." After Dean haltingly attempted to explain what he meant, without apologizing for the "offense" he had given, his presidential rivals smelled blood and commenced a feeding frenzy.

John Edwards, whose campaign hinged on winning white working-class votes, accused Dean of stereotyping Southerners, snapping, "The last thing we need in the South is somebody like you coming down and telling us what we need to do. The people that I grew up with . . . they didn't drive around with Confederate flags on their pickup trucks." Al Sharpton, whose campaign hinged on winning African American votes in the South, did his best to portray Dean as the next grand cyclops of the Ku Klux Klan, opining that the governor's "insensitive" invocation of the Confederate flag sounded "more like Stonewall Jackson than Jesse Jackson." Sharpton even invoked one of the Democratic luminaries who had earlier applauded Dean's candor (but who had since died): "Maynard Jackson said that the Confederate flag is America's swastika." John Kerry, accusing Dean of pandering to gun enthusiasts—apparently every pickup with a Confederate flag comes equipped with a loaded gun rack as well—sniffed, "I'd rather be the candidate of the NAACP than the NRA." Missouri congressman Richard Gephardt, locked in a fierce pissing-match with Dean in Iowa, struck an equally pious note: "I will be the candidate for guys with American flags," he bravely announced.

Notably absent from the chorus of denunciation were those people Dean had supposedly offended. "The Democratic candidates and party leadership should bear in mind that black voters think for themselves as they stand on their soapboxes to castigate Dr. Dean's remarks," wrote the Reverend Joe Darby, an NAACP officer in Charleston, South Carolina. "I appreciate the substance of what he said—that the problems faced by many citizens of modest means are 'people problems' that cross color lines."

Southern Democratic consultant Steve Jarding thought Dean "could've found a better way to phrase it. But this is what Southern Democrats—black and white—had been waiting to hear for a long time. When he said it, I thought, 'Well, I'll be damned. Here's a Democrat saying we're not going to keep leaving 110 million Americans [in the South] behind, who recognizes we have to start speaking again to working-class voters.'"

While speaking in friendly terms about the Confederate flag was hardly something that a campaign consultant would recommend—whether you're running for president of the United States or sheriff of Coosa County, Alabama—Dean's intentions were clear to anyone not out to smear him for political gain. "I was really mad about how Dean got hammered for the Confederate flag comment," said *Jackson Free Press* editor Donna Ladd. "I was like, 'Either you don't know what you're saying, or this is just a political tar and feathering.' Which is worse, I don't know." "He wasn't condoning racism," wrote *Slate* columnist William Saletan. "He was saying that his party shouldn't write off people who share its economic philosophy just because they don't yet share its understanding of civil rights. . . . He wants the votes of these people *despite* their fondness for the Confederate flag, not because of it." Yet Dean's once-popular remarks fueled the fast-developing campaign narrative that he was a reckless shoot-from-the-hipster who would make a disastrous nominee.

When Dean attempted to defuse the Confederate flag nuttiness by apologizing and elaborating at New York's Cooper Union, he expressed "regret" for the "pain that I may have caused either to African American or Southern white voters," then tried in vain to revive the substance of his argument. "I do believe that this country needs to engage in a serious discussion about race," he said. "Today in America, you have a better chance of being called back for a job interview if you're white with a criminal record than you do if you're black with a clean record. . . . Institutional racism exists in this country not because institutions are run by bigots or racists, but because of our unconscious bias."

Dean's effort collapsed after the Iowa caucuses, leaving the Democratic field to the very politicians who had huddled behind the flimsy mask of political correctness rather than challenge the "color-blind" pretense of contemporary Republicanism. For the white working class, the Democrats were once again coming across as Ivy League elitists more concerned with policing speech than fighting for economic justice. For black Southerners, the party's white leadership was once again displaying its racial paternalism.

"What hurts Democrats most in such charades," wrote the liberal, pickup-driving, deer-hunting Arkansas journalist Gene Lyons, "is the absurd ritual of forcing somebody like Dean to apologize for a remark everybody knows wasn't offensive in the first place. It feeds the perception that they're fakers and panderers to trumped-up, phony grievances in a party dominated by sissies and snobs."

And, of course, it also fed the perception that Democrats are Dixiephobes—the sorts of people who instinctively recoil at the mere suggestion of asking for the vote of a white, blue-collar Southerner.

The most powerful leaders of the Congressional Black Caucus endorsed Dean smack in the middle of the controversy, but it was not enough to heal the damage. "The thing that impresses me is Dean talks about race to white people and black people," said CBC chairman Elijah Cummings of Maryland. Vice chairwoman Sheila Jackson Lee of Texas stumped for Dean. Jesse Jackson Jr., the congressman from Illinois, made the case for Dean in a strongly worded *Roll Call* op-ed. "Democrats know the divide in the South is race," Jackson wrote. "Republicans have exploited it. Democrats have evaded it," by "imitating Republicans on social and cultural issues, and failing to challenge around economic issues. . . . Rather than repeating this stereotypical and condescending approach of appealing to whites in the South with a 'balanced ticket' and 'social conservatism,' Dean dares a new approach—to join whites and blacks around a common economic agenda of good schools and health care."

There is no other way to win back the South, Jackson noted. But as he must surely have known, even as he wrote his endorsement, winning back the South was no higher a priority for the Democratic leadership in 2004 than delivering on decades of false promises to its African American constituents was. Once again, while stumbling toward defeat, the Democrats were boring a few feet deeper the trench of division they have dug around the South.

★

After Al Gore lost the White House in 2000, blue state Democrats blamed the defeat on DLC-style pandering to Southern conservatives—even though Gore had not tried to win those votes. The DLC, meanwhile, blamed populism. "Gore chose a populist rather than a New Democrat message," complained Al From, the DLC's head honcho. "As a result, voters viewed him as too liberal and identified him as an advocate of big government. . . . By emphasizing class warfare, he seemed to be talking to Industrial Age America, not Information Age America." DLC strategist Mark Penn, the microtargeting whiz who would eventually steer much of Hillary Clinton's campaign for president, claimed that Gore had lost because he didn't appeal to "wired workers," those "middle-class, white suburban males" who had supposedly put Bill Clinton over the top.

But Gore had lost neither the suburbs nor the middle class. Where he lost ground, in close states like Missouri, Ohio, Florida, Arkansas, West Virginia, and Kentucky that Clinton had carried in 1996, was among the white working class. It wasn't populist fist-waving that lost Gore those votes; a more insistent class appeal would almost certainly have put him over the top. The biggest factor in Gore's loss, according to later polls, was the perception that he was "untrustworthy"—something that had to do with his Clinton association, for sure, but also with his varying campaign personalities and themes. It had something powerful to do, too, with being the candidate of a party that increasingly, like the *Seinfeld* series, was about nothing: nothing but trying to get to 270.

The bitter outcome of the 2000 election spawned a new backlash. Blue state Democrats had grown fed up with the DLC-inspired centrist compromises that had been justified by the need to win white Southern votes. If selling the party's soul wasn't going to win elections, even with an incumbent vice president running on a record of peace and prosperity, how could it be justified? It was a question well worth asking. But the debate was sidetracked, once again, by anti-Southern animus. The culprit angry progressives fingered was not the national Democratic cabal, not the lack of a forward-looking progressive vision for the country, not the superior ground game of the GOP, not the Gore campaign's narrow targeting of "swing states" outside the South. The trouble lay squarely with the Democrats' supposedly "ceaseless courtship of Southern votes," as *Slate* columnist Timothy Noah put it. After all, Noah wrote, "Gore lost *every Southern state* [his italics], including his home state of Tennessee. Thus *Lesson 1:* Southerners won't vote for you just because you're a Good Ole Boy. But Gore still came within four electoral votes of winning. If he'd taken Florida, which in many ways is not really a Southern state, he'd be president. . . . Thus *Lesson 2:* Democrats don't really need those Southern votes."

The image of Gore—the Washington-bred, Harvard-educated king of Democratic power geeks—as a "good ole boy" showed exactly how in touch blue state pundits were. Noah also conveniently omitted the rather pertinent fact that there was no Gore campaign in the South outside of Florida. Yet the logic went that because folks in Tennessee, Virginia, and Arkansas rejected a Democrat who never asked for their votes, they would never in the future vote for a Democrat who *did*.

Confronted with this kind of thinking, it's difficult not to catch a powerful whiff of Dixiephobia. Particularly when the blue staters take it a step further, blaming the Democrats' failure to advance a progressive agenda on the fact that—as with the Gore campaign, apparently—the party thinks about nothing but appealing to right-wingers in Dixie twenty-four hours a day. "When Democrats give the president authority to start a preemptive war in Iraq, they accede to Southern bellicosity," wrote Tom Schaller. "When Democrats go soft on defending social policies, they lend credence to the south-ernized, 'starve the beast' mentality of governance. When Democrats scramble around to declare that they, too, have moral values, they kneel in the pews of Southern evangelicalism. This absurdist catering to the worst fitting, least supportive component of the Democratic coalition must cease."

Armed with such ironclad analyses, the blue staters began to forge a new, non-Southern trail to the presidency. Both Schaller and Kevin Phillips, an architect of the Republicans' Southern strategy in his 1969 Nixon handbook, *The Emerging Republican Majority,* called on Democrats to not simply run away from the South but to run *against* it.

"The Democrats need their own 'them,'" Schaller argued, "and the social conservatives who are the bedrock of southern politics provide the most obvious and burdensome stone to hang around the Republicans' necks." After all, Schaller wrote, the Republicans have their "'liberal elite' that is somehow blamed for orchestrat-ing America's cultural and spiritual demise." If it works for them, Schaller insisted, it's high time that the Democrats—in the name of returning to the party's own "bedrock values"—start vilifying people unfairly, too. "If the GOP can build a national majority by ostracizing an entire region of the country, the Democrats should be able to run *outside* the South by running *against* the conservative South."

Phillips's Northern strategy was a bit less mercenary and more idealistic—but no less suicidal. In a *Washington Post* op-ed in 2004, and again in his 2006 warning shot of a book *American Theocracy:*

The Perils and Politics of Radical Religion, Oil, and Borrowed Money in the 21st Century, Phillips urged Democrats to declare war on the Republicans' "excessive domination by evangelicals and fundamentalists, unilateralist foreign policy and preemptive war (verging on Armageddonism) and extremist Texas economics in the Tom DeLay mode." But Phillips pointed only at evangelical extremists from the South (Jerry Falwell, Pat Robertson, and Bob Jones Jr.), ignoring the movement's power centers outside the South (James Dobson in Colorado, Rod Parsley in Ohio). And he ignored the evidence, becoming clear in 2006, that the influence of religious right politics had already peaked.

Phillips and Schaller both argued that the Democrats should continue to compete in "marginal" Southern states—those that they deem to be "not really Southern," such as Virginia, Florida, and West Virginia. But it's hard to imagine how an anti-Southern strategy would not prove just as disastrous in Richmond and Jacksonville as it would in Birmingham and Charleston. A Democratic Party that attempts to unite the rest of the country by demonizing Southerners would alienate not just the right-wingers Schaller and Phillips have in their sights, but substantial numbers of moderate white, African American, and Hispanic voters as well. Democrats' proclaiming their party the "voice of reason" would only further their image—which is hardly limited to Southerners—as bloodless elitists who consider themselves superior to regular Americans.

The one sure outcome of an anti-Southern strategy would be to drive increasing numbers of Southerners into an even more formidable Republican bloc—a real "solid South." Its effect would be similar to that of the aftermath of the Civil War, when the idea of "Southernness" was not strangled, as the Yankees anticipated, but instead grew heartier. "If this war had smashed the Southern world," wrote W. J. Cash, "it had left the essential Southern mind and will . . . entirely unshaken. Rather, after the manner of defensive wars in general and particularly those fought against the odds and with great stubbornness, it had operated enormously to fortify and confirm that mind and will."

It is remarkable—remarkably depressing—that at a time when the tectonic plates are shifting ominously under the Republicans' Southern and Western bases, many Democratic thinkers are not looking to build a new politics of national reconciliation, but instead to reinvigorate sectional prejudices and resentments. "The trick of effective politics," journalist Marc Cooper wrote in 2005, "is to unite people with different views, values and families around programs, candidates and campaigns on which they can reach some consensus, however minimal. Before liberals and progressives dash out with their new vocabulary to try to convince others of the righteousness of their values, they might consider spending some time listening to others instead." Liberalism never flourishes in an atmosphere of division and disunity. You might expect the party of "the big tent" to look at the coming crack-up of the GOP as a chance to tweeze the sectional divisions out of American politics. But you'd be discounting the malignant influence of Dixiephobia.

★

The first non-Southern strategy was cooked up by the post–Civil War Republican Party. The GOP pursued a "Lincoln strategy" of running against Dixie for a century, collaborating with the Southern Democratic Party's white supremacists to make partisan politics a primary conduit for North-South vitriol.

In an overheated but prescient 1891 essay in the *North American Review,* the New South apostle and legendary Kentucky journalist Henry Watterson railed against the Republicans' lust for a "Solid North," an indestructible voter base that would win them national elections by creating a "perpetual ascendancy of sectional passions" and boxing Democrats into a minority South. "To this end the politicians and journalists of the Republican party have set themselves the task of educating the Northern mind; and no occasion is missed for establishing and enforcing the assumptions on which the native white people of the South are to be subverted." The Republicans developed a catalog of stereotypes pernicious enough to convince non-Southerners that "if the whole power of the North is not consolidated to check their progress, they will presently control the Government, overthrow the national credit, and disgrace the national honor."

How far we have *not* come. The parties have changed places, but the politics of Dixiephobia remain largely intact. The demonization of Dixie, Watterson wrote, was "persisted in all along the Republican line with an ardor which never loses its self-glorifying righteousness. . . . Every utterance which can be misquoted or misconceived is tortured into treason. Every fisticuff is elevated to the dignity of rebellion. Everything, in short, that passes in the South is wrested from its surroundings, and lugged off Northward to do duty as an informer against the humanity and opinions of the Southern people, to whom are assigned baser motives and a different standard of morality than prevail at the North."

Like many a defender of Dixie's honor, Watterson certainly allowed his defensiveness to blow up his rhetoric. But his cry against sectional partisan warfare resonates at this transitional moment in American politics. The Mason-Dixoning of elections continues to cleave the country into artificial camps—and to make progressive politics, which thrives on common purpose rather than mutual animosities, a difficult proposition. The South was once held back from progressivism by white people's addiction to segregation. It is a bleak irony that non-Southern progressives are now holding the South back because of their addiction to the region as the source and expression of national ills. Anti-Southern Democrats may see a new Lincoln strategy as their best chance to sway the country in a progressive direction. It would accomplish precisely the opposite. As the writer and rock musician Neal Pollack wrote, "If you fuck the South, you're fucking yourselves."

The most glaring practical flaw in a non-Southern strategy is that it can give Democrats, at best, only a narrow victory margin. In the words of Senator Joe Biden, there is "not a single, solitary problem out there that can be solved with a 51 percent solution." Without a national strategy that embraces the South—its economic populism, its embrace of patriotism, its moral tenor, its suspicion of wealth and greed—the Democrats are dooming themselves to a 51 percent solution (when, that is, they manage to win). There will be no durable, workable progressive governing majority in America without Southerners making up part of it. It's true, "mathematically" speaking, that the Democrats could win the presidency without a single Southern electoral vote. But it is also true that such a victory would be slender and would not produce a working majority in Congress. And within a few years, demographic shifts will shake up the congressional map and hand several more Electoral College votes to Southern states, leaving the Dixiephobic Democrats with even longer odds.

The Democrats' non-Southern strategy is wrong on both principle and pragmatics. By surrendering the region, Democrats have passively allowed right-wingers to build a mighty fortress for the defense of free-market excess in a region full of economic populists. They have let cultural, racial, and religious divisions fester and expand. Now, even with the Republicans' Southern strategy wearing thin, they are lurching toward an even more dramatic break with the South. As Chris Kromm, the director of the liberal Institute for Southern Studies in Durham, North Carolina, has eloquently argued, "For Democrats to turn their backs on a region that half of all African Americans and a growing number of Latinos call home, a place devastated by Hurricane Katrina, plant closings, poverty and other indignities—in short, for progressives to give up on the very place where they could argue they are needed most—would rightfully be viewed as a historic retreat from the party's commitment to justice for all."

4

THE DONKEY BUCKS

★

"This fellow told me last time, 'My daddy would roll over in his grave if I didn't vote Republican.' And I said, 'Well, roll him over.'"

—ROBERT ERVIN, retired coal miner,
Castlewood, Virginia, 2006

A BIT PAST five o'clock on a mid-September Wednesday in 2006, one month after the miraculous resurrection of his moribund Senate campaign, Jim Webb came busting out of the Democratic Senatorial Campaign Committee's Call Room One, where "viable" candidates are held captive for hours and forced to plead for cash. He barked ahead in his rumbling bass, "We've got to be in Alexandria, don't we?" His feet, shod in combat boots belonging to his son, Jimmy, who had just gone on active duty in Iraq, pounded down the narrow walk-up toward his ride—a small SUV, painted in camouflage, with a "Jim Webb—Born Fighting" sign fixed to the side. Behind the wheel was "Mac" McGarvey, who had served and lost an arm in Vietnam under Webb's command. When his best pal decided to challenge wildly popular Republican senator George Allen, Mac had left his job running a bar in Nashville and volunteered to spend the rest of the year being directed—and misdirected—across the interstates and back roads of Virginia.

"I have no earthly idea where we're going," Mac said, more

amused than concerned as Webb jumped into the front seat, dead-panning, "That *could* be taken as a symbolic statement about this campaign." Indeed, Webb was driving a campaign with no political road map—following, partly by instinct, the uncertain paths of an inchoate Democratic South. Virginia, long one of the most deeply Republican of Southern states—not only in presidential elections, which Democrats have not carried there since 1964, but also in the state house of delegates races—was suddenly on the leading edge of a blue tide washing into Dixie.

The political shift in Virginia first became apparent in 2001, when a genial Internet entrepreneur named Mark Warner won the governorship by galvanizing the swelling progressive (and largely nonnative) population of upscale northern Virginia and, simultaneously, winning back Reagan Democrats in the socially conservative, rural Republican stronghold of the state's southwest. Warner's campaign gurus, Dave "Mudcat" Saunders and Steve Jarding, used a strong dose of cultural populism: he stumped with a bluegrass band, sponsored a race-car team, and organized "Sportsmen for Warner" clubs across the state to emphasize his support for "gun rights." This hokum was designed to gain a hearing for Warner's forward-looking economic pitch. Like so many successful Southern Democrats before him, Warner preached modernization—broadband access, education to prepare students for the new "idea economy," better infrastructure to attract better jobs. And once he got into office, Warner took advantage of a Republican assembly split between religious right and big business Republicans to get most of it done. His successor, Democrat Tim Kaine, has continued Warner's economic initiatives and muted the Republicans' cultural advantages by tying his progressive views—his opposition to the death penalty, for instance—to his deep convictions as a former Catholic missionary.

Yet, despite the Democratic trend in Virginia—which pollster John Zogby had taken to calling "the next Ohio"—Webb looked like a sure loser in 2006. Senator George Allen had mastered the

Southern strategy trick of convincing working-class voters he was a
regular guy while carrying water for big money. The Southern California native's blend of Reaganesque optimism, easygoing geniality,
and tough-guy talk had made him one of the most popular political
figures in modern Virginia history. "It was no surprise," said political scientist Mark Rozell, that Allen entered 2006 as "Republican
conservatives' first choice for president in 2008."

On the other hand, nobody knew what to think of Webb. What
could one think about a Democratic candidate who had served in
Ronald Reagan's cabinet and had bitterly denounced Vietnam War
protesters, civil rights activists, '60s liberals, affirmative action policies, and women in combat? Seemingly overnight, Webb had transformed himself from a cranky Republican traditionalist into a gonzo
antiwar Democrat. His campaign—chaotic, underfunded, and featuring a candidate who refused to pander or even, at many appear-
ances, to so much as crack a smile—grew out of his exasperation
with Allen's unwavering (and, to Webb, unthinking) support for
President Bush's Middle East misadventures. But by the time he
announced his run, Webb's ambitions had broadened. Far from
being merely a frustrated Republican, Webb entered the race with an
eye toward rehabilitating the Democratic Party.

"I think both parties have been taken over by elites," Webb said
as the Born Fighting SUV barreled south. "The natural base of the
Democratic Party, working-class folks, looked at both parties back
in the '80s and saw they weren't going to get any help on economic
issues. The one place they thought they could make a difference was
on these divisive social issues, so that's how they've been voting. But
I think that has run its course." So, he said, has the "cultural
Marxism" of the '60s that he believed dominated the national
Democrats. "We're in a sea change with political terminology and
identities," he said. "The terms 'conservative' and 'liberal' have been
rendered meaningless. What is right and what is left anymore? What
is conservative and what is liberal?"

Because of his past, Webb was consistently characterized as a "conservative" Democrat, though he was pro-choice and staunchly opposed the anti–gay marriage amendment on the 2006 Virginia ballot. The main thrust of his campaign was gut-bucket economic populism. "This race is a test," Webb had said. "If we can get a number of these people to come back to the Democratic Party based on economic populism and fairness, rather than the way they've been maneuvered on issues like flag burning, God, guts, guns, gays— if they can be reached out to with respect, and in terms of fundamental fairness, I think a lot of them will come back to the Democratic Party."

But in August, Webb was a forgotten candidate, trailing by double digits in the polls and facing an ominous sixteen-to-one fund-raising deficit. Then Allen, sticking to the tried-and-true Southern strategy script, pointed out the lone person of color at one of his southwest Virginia rallies—a Webb volunteer, S. R. Sidarth, who'd been videotaping Allen's summer "listening tour"—and called him "Macaca," adding, "Welcome to the real world of Virginia." The moment rippled across the Web and displayed how, at least in the blue-trending South of Virginia, racist wisecracks long popular on the Republican Dixie circuit would no longer be shrugged off, winked at, or openly cheered. Allen's attempts to paint his Democratic foe as an out-of-touch elitist—a *writer,* of all suspicious things!—fell equally flat. That was no surprise since it has partly been the booming population of highly educated left-leaning nonnatives in northern Virginia that have made Virginia a "purple state."

While the old Southern strategy was unraveling for Allen, Webb was fighting for the votes of Reagan Democrats in the more traditional regions of southern and eastern Virginia. Like practically every sixty-year-old white person with family roots in southwest Virginia, Webb had been born into a blue-collar clan of ardent Democrats. As he came to political consciousness in the '60s, Webb was offended by the attitude civil rights activists—"liberal

Yankees," in particular—took toward working-class whites in the South. "[T]he fight over ending legal racial segregation," he wrote in *Born Fighting*, "ended up demonizing people who had shared the same social and economic dilemma as the blacks themselves." The venom should have been directed, Webb believes, at the small class of wealthy Southern (and Northern) whites who had always controlled Dixie's economy and ensured the continuation of Jim Crow and anti-union "right to work" laws. When he came back from Vietnam, he was equally dismayed by the cold shoulder returning soldiers received from those who opposed the war. The combination sent him scurrying into the waiting arms of the GOP. "I was generally comfortable with the Republicans, until the neoconservatives took over," Webb told me. "But the one issue that always bothered me was economic fairness."

He wasn't alone. At the local United Mine Workers' annual fish fry in tiny Castlewood, in the heart of George Allen's "real world of Virginia," the scene turned into a rally of sorts for Webb, who delivered a speech virtually identical to the one he'd given the day before in liberal northern Virginia—right down to the Marx and Engels references. The message: Bush and Allen's war was a disaster, and working Americans were getting shafted while corporations and CEOs raked in record profits. In southwest Virginia, Webb's laconic delivery, far from being a liability with blue-collar folks, testified in shorthand that he was not another slick politician. Perched in a lawn chair nearby and clutching his cane, Robert Ervin—who left the mines in 1979 after thirty-eight years—didn't mince words about Webb's charming opponent. "George Allen? He's a big old fake, that's all."

Whatever the folks in Castlewood might have thought about gay marriage or abortion rights—not much, in most cases—the Republican stewardship of the economy had left them with a higher priority. "Young people are really suffering here," said Jimmy Taylor, a gregarious young truck driver. "Old people, too." While Taylor and his girlfriend, Brittany Brading, both had steady jobs, neither one had health insurance. "Most people my age don't have it," Taylor said. It was getting hard for him to make any kind of living off his truck, too, he said. "With gas prices, it's five hundred to six hundred dollars a day to haul a load. There ain't much left after that."

Without the Rural Medical Assistance program Governor Warner had pushed through the state legislature, Brading said, "people would really be in terrible shape around here." Warner, the Democrats' candidate for U.S. Senate in 2008, got Brading fired up about politics—so much so that, just as Southerners used to do with FDR, she keeps a picture of the former governor on her bedroom wall.

"Mark Warner has a place in my heart," her boyfriend joked. "I have to wake up and see him every morning."

Webb's ultimate victory over the seemingly invincible Allen offered more proof that Virginia, with its combination of upscale out-of-staters in the north and fed-up military and working folks downstate, is swinging. With Allen's unintentional assistance, Webb had pulled off something few thought was possible: making the Republican in a Southern race look unreal, elitist, and out of touch with regular folks. It was 1972 in reverse. Meanwhile, in other parts of the region, Democrats were blazing different—and equally unorthodox—populist trails.

★

With the Iraq War more bloody and dubious by the day, with bombshell sex scandals and lobbying revelations ripping the "moral values" sheen off Washington Republicans, and with President George W. Bush's approval ratings hovering somewhere around those of the Prince of Darkness, Democrats expected to see many happy returns in the 2006 midterms. But none of them was supposed to involve John Yarmuth. Not even in a Louisville district with a sizable core of organized and agitated labor, and the liveliest grassroots peace movement this side of San Francisco. Not even against a congresswoman who had become intimately associated with Bush's Iraq fiasco. Not even in a congressional district where Democrats outnumbered Republicans by double digits. Not even with Yarmuth's notoriety as the founder of the local alternative weekly, *Louisville Eccentric Observer,* and his familiarity as a friendly, unrepentantly liberal TV and radio pundit and columnist.

That liberal part was the problem. Liberals weren't supposed to win congressional seats in Kentucky. "Nobody believed this guy could win," said Mark Nickolas, a longtime Democratic strategist and creator of the Bluegrass Reports blog, which documents political shenanigans in Kentucky. "I mean—*nobody.* Except John, apparently." The pessimism seemed warranted. Louisville's best-known "L"-word was running against five-term congresswoman Anne Northup, who had a famous knack for courting crossover Democrats and reducing her opponents to rubble with brass-knuckles offensives. A staunch "values" conservative described by Nickolas as "an animal in the trenches," there was no question Northup would use Yarmuth's columns to make her opponent look, in Yarmuth's own words, like "the craziest person who's ever run for office."

Illinois congressman Rahm Emanuel, head teller of that cash machine known as the Democratic Congressional Campaign Committee (DCCC), certainly thought so. Democrats were feeling snakebitten in the urban Third District, where an edge of more than a hundred thousand in party registration had led them to sink millions into three promising (and moderate) challenges against Northup, only to come up short every time. In the adjacent Fourth District, the party had gotten behind Nick Clooney, liberal father of the famous actor, in 2004, but Clooney's published writings bit him.

"They killed Nick Clooney with his columns," Yarmuth said Emanuel told him in the summer of 2006, when the candidate pleaded for DCCC support in person. "I tried to tell him the districts are worlds apart," Yarmuth said.

The DCCC had supported Yarmuth's less liberal opponent, Iraq veteran Lt. Col. Andrew Horne, in the Democratic primary, though Horne was largely unknown. It then stiffed Yarmuth until just two weeks before the general election, when the party finally kicked in an attack ad and some spare change. The Democrats had chosen to hitch their Kentucky wagon to the Fourth District and the "fiscally conservative" and genteel moderate Ken Lucas, and to the Second District and Col. Mike Weaver, a military veteran so conservative, Nickolas said, that "he could easily be a Republican and he wouldn't have to alter a stance."

To the national Democrats, Lucas and Weaver's "me too" politics were the only way to go in Kentucky. To Yarmuth, it looked like the same old losing formula. "The mistake Democrats have made over the years is that they never provided a sharp contrast," he said. "I said from day one, 'Anne and I are a hundred and eighty degrees apart. If she believes something, I don't.' I was that clear. The last few Democrats had not done that. They'd tried to play three degrees of separation, to do that triangulation thing that's been the norm for Democrats for so long. I wanted the voters to have a real choice and see where they'd go."

They went with the liberal—while Lucas, the recipient of almost three million dollars in DCCC ad money, and Weaver went down (albeit in districts with more conservatives). "They didn't give voters a reason to kick out the Republicans," Nickolas said. "Yarmuth gave people a reason. He didn't offer a 20 percent difference; he offered a 100 percent difference. Voters respect principled candidates regardless of what their principles are."

Yarmuth agreed. "The whole idea that a candidate was willing to say what he or she believed without calculating the political consequences was a huge factor," he said. "If somebody asked me about the Military Tribunals Act, I said, 'That's just wrong.' It came up in a debate. I said, 'This thing allows Donald Rumsfeld to decide that an American citizen is a suspected agent, and he could put him or her away without any recourse to legal rights.' And I loved Anne's recourse to that: 'Yeah, but that's just one section of the bill.' The audience laughed."

Yarmuth had also spun a strong populist narrative through the years. "When I sold my paper, it was the year they had reduced the capital gains tax. So I did nothing different, but the government gave me a 5 percent extra break. I didn't deserve that," he said. During the 2004 presidential campaign, "I took some of that capital gains money and ran ads saying, 'Here's how wacked-out it's gotten. People like me are benefiting, thanks to George W. Bush, while most people are struggling. . . . So I decided to spend the money I saved to urge you to vote for John Kerry.'" Kerry won the district, barely. "I had people walk up on the street and say, 'Thank you for doing that.' I had a waiter say, 'I'm buying you lunch.' People feel ignored."

Yarmuth's cheerful campaign exuded much the same spirit. When Northup came out swinging in September, with a snarling press conference and a sixty-second ad using the expected, out-of-context "radical" quotes from the *LEO* columns, Yarmuth ignored strategists' advice to strike back fast and mean. Instead, he developed a sly thirty-second response: The exaggeratedly ominous bass voice of a negative-ad announcer intoned, "John Yarmuth: He plays golf with Saddam Hussein and snatches toys away from little children." After a beat, Yarmuth's own smooth voice piped up: "Ridiculous? No more so than Anne Northup's deceptive TV ads." As Nickolas said, "John went against conventional wisdom and it worked. He showed more political smarts than most of us who do it for a living."

But even with the polls showing his race neck and neck throughout the summer and fall, Yarmuth could hardly get the DCCC to return his calls. The Kentucky Democratic Party, historically as timidly moderate as most Democratic parties in the South, had no interest in assisting him, either. Fortunately for him, Yarmuth is wealthy, the co-owner of the Sonny's Bar-B-Que chain and a regional golf magazine among other enterprises, so he could easily afford to kick $700,000 into the campaign. Yarmuth believed that he knew something the party decision makers didn't. Before he decided to run, he had sat down with local union leaders and with Democratic leaders in the more conservative chunks of the district. "I asked them, 'Are these culture war issues going to be predominant this year? If so I'm probably dead.' They said no. Everybody pretty much said the same thing: The people are worried about Iraq, and they're worried about a government being sold out to corporate interests." There were signs everywhere of burnout in the culture war launched by the Moral Majority in 1979 and pitchforked by Pat Buchanan in 1992. "The [Iraq] war, of course, has contributed to that," Yarmuth said. "You can't look at the television every night and think gay marriage is that important."

No, not even in Kentucky.

★

After the 2004 wipeout in Dixie, many blue state Democrats were pleased to think that the party's long-running debate—can we win in the South, and should we even try?—had been settled. Settled in the negative, of course. But on November 7, 2006, Southern Democrats showed some new life, and not just in Kentucky and Virginia. The party took five House seats previously occupied by Republicans—two in Florida, one each in Texas and North Carolina along with Kentucky—and lost two other challenges by minuscule margins. In the border state of Missouri, Claire McCaskill, an economic populist who ran energetically in the working-class, heavily Republican southern part of the state, upset Republican incumbent Jim Talent. Democrats won back the governorship in Arkansas and built bigger majorities in eight of the South's state legislatures.

Digging beneath those results uncovers the potential for a long-term Democratic tilt. It wasn't just the war and scandals that opened the door to Southern Democrats in 2006. A majority of young Southerners, who had swayed rightward throughout the 1980s and

'90s, voted Democratic. In a dramatic shift from their support of George W. Bush in 2004, 55 percent of Southerners making less than fifty thousand dollars a year voted Democratic for Congress. Even among the sturdiest core of Republican voters, evangelicals, the Democratic cut of the vote rose from 19 percent to 27 percent. Despite the use of faith-based funds to make black evangelicals friendlier to the GOP, 87 percent of African Americans in the South voted Democratic.

Taken together, said Chris Kromm of the Institute for Southern Studies, a picture emerges of a Southern Republican Party that is "increasingly the party not of 'the South' in general, as some pundits claim, but of *older, wealthy, and white Southern voters*—a base that puts the GOP on the wrong side of all the key demographic trends unfolding in the South." For the Democrats, the question "isn't whether to cut and run, but how to capitalize on constituencies and trends that clearly work in their favor."

The question, after 2006, was whether the Democratic Party could see the South's populist and progressive trendlines clearly enough to take advantage of them. In 2006, it sunk more than five million dollars into what Democratic strategists considered the "perfect" Southern campaign, Congressman Harold Ford Jr.'s run for an open Senate seat in Tennessee. The thirty-six-year-old former prodigy, who had been a moderately progressive congressman for most of his eight years in Washington, decided that despite the recent trend toward Democrats statewide, the way to win in Tennessee was to out-Republican his Republican opponent. Anticipating his run, Ford shifted his positions in Congress, voting in favor of the NRA (raising his grade from "F" to "B"), the Iraq War, and pretty much anything else that might be termed "conservative." In the summer of 2006, Ford began airing radio spots bashing "illegals," a big issue since Tennessee is home to the nation's fourth-fastest-growing immigrant population. In the fall, he filmed a commercial in the sanctuary of the First Baptist Church in Memphis. Radiant with stained-glass sunlight, the movie-star-handsome Ford edged up the aisle, smilingly recounting how he had "started in church the old-fashioned way—I was forced to. And I'm better for it." Dead-eyeing the camera, he solemnly proclaimed, "I voted for the Patriot Act, five trillion in defense, and against amnesty for illegals. I approved this message because I won't let them make me somebody I'm not. And I'll always fight for you."

Rocketing back and forth across the green hills of Tennessee with an unflagging energy that his opponent, former Chattanooga mayor Bob Corker, called "frantic," Ford wooed white conservatives with a mash-up of high-voltage star power, earthy eloquence, and a contrarian right-wingery that always seemed to surprise and delight. "I get in trouble with Democrats," Ford confessed to the Rotary Club in the tiny town of Cleveland, "because I like President Bush." In a year when even most Republican candidates wouldn't touch their commander-in-chief with a ten-foot pole, Ford hugged him—and almost all his policies—tight. He took hard lines on gay marriage, guns, national defense, and affirmative action, while wielding an array of Bible quotes that could have whipped John Ashcroft in a holiness contest any day. "They say I don't look like you," he assured another all-white crowd at the Catfish Place in Camden, "but I share your values."

The trouble was that, unlike Webb or Yarmuth, Ford, a DLC apostle, was pretty obviously running as "somebody I'm not"—and doing it with all the contagious enthusiasm that Bill Clinton once brought to the task. But the appeal of the act, even from its finest practitioners, had worn thin.

It was Democrats who offered Southerners a frank, unqualified brand of economic populism who broke through in 2006. That was true even in the case of Heath Shuler, the former Washington Redskins quarterback who captured a long-held Republican seat in western North Carolina. Shuler, who had strong backing from the national Democrats, was recruited by Emanuel for the seat mostly because of his rigidly conservative Christian beliefs. But it wasn't until he stopped emphasizing his cultural views and started preaching an economic and environmental gospel—"Mountain Values," he called it—that his candidacy took off among Democrats. "At first," said historian Dan Carter, author of *The Politics of Rage: George Wallace, the Origins of the New Conservatism, and the Transformation of American Politics,* "a lot of the real committed Democrats said, 'Can I really commit myself to this, to putting out the sixty hours a week between now and the election?' But once he started campaigning, Shuler didn't press the social issues. He started talking about more bread-and-butter things. I heard him three different times, and there was a clear progression from 'I defend your right to have your guns' and 'make sure you don't kill babies' to, by the third speech, none of that. When he was asked about it, he ultimately would just say, 'You know where I stand on that. These are not the pressing issues.'" As Shuler and the other winning Democrats recognized, voters were more invested in such tangible matters as a minimum wage hike; more than 86 percent of Southerners were in favor, and minimum-wage initiatives passed in Florida, Texas, Virginia, and Missouri.

In Tennessee, Ford's loss to Corker was chalked up to a race-baiting campaign from the Republican National Committee that culminated in the infamous ad featuring a blond bombshell recounting how she'd supposedly "met Harold at the Playboy mansion"—at a big Super Bowl party given by Hugh Hefner in 2005—and climaxed with her cleavage leaning into the camera and a whispered, "Harold—*call me!*" But Ford's decision, in a good Democratic year, to build his campaign around a '90-style renunciation of his own party played a large role in his demise. "The irony is that if he'd run as a Democrat," said Vanderbilt professor and African American scholar Carol Swain, "he'd probably have won."

While the Democrats were investing their hopes—in the form of cash—in Ford's approach, the party overlooked a chance to take another congressional seat in neighboring North Carolina. In a textile-manufacturing district hit hard with job losses over the past decade, blue-collar populist Larry Kissell, a high school history teacher and twenty-seven-year-old veteran of the textile mills, mounted a creative grassroots challenge to four-term Republican Robin Hayes. The national Democrats should have recognized the potential: not only was Hayes the sixth-richest person in Congress and the deciding vote in favor of the controversial Central America Free Trade Agreement, he owed his fortune to the textile mills that had been laying off his constituents.

With help from a small army of young volunteers, Kissell pedaled his message relentlessly from door to door: "Hello, I'm Larry Kissell. I'm from Montgomery County and I worked in textiles for twenty-seven years and five years as a teacher. I believe things are broken in Washington and we need a change." Kissell highlighted his populist message in a host of ways, including selling gas for a day in his hometown of Biscoe for $1.22 a gallon—the price when Hayes was first elected to Congress. He even managed to turn bad news upside-down, as when a campaign finance report heading into the home stretch of the campaign showed Hayes with $1.1 million cash on hand—and Kissell with a grand total of $88.94. "I'm sure my bank balance looks a lot more like the typical Eighth District voter than Hayes's," Kissell quipped.

But all the populist energy and folksy charm in the world couldn't make up for Kissell's lack of funds. He got some help from the Netroots, from former senator John Edwards, and from the state party, but ultimately Kissell came up 329 votes short as the DCCC, which gave Shuler more than $1.4 million in his campaign next door, could never bring itself to believe that Kissell stood a chance. (After the election, Rahm Emanuel apologized to Kissell, and for his second joust at Hayes, in 2008, the party ponied up.)

The progressive populist resurgence of 2006 suggested a way past the false dilemma Democrats have long believed they faced: either run away from the South or try to compete there with a Republican

Lite message. Rather than focus on neutralizing the Republicans' Southern strategy by mimicking it on cultural issues, candidates like Webb, Yarmuth, and Kissell reasserted economic fairness as the central moral issue of politics. That will be key in the long term not only to attracting moderate evangelicals fed up with the narrowness and corruption of Republican "values," but also to firing up the South's black voters, who take a backseat to no one as strong Bible believers but tend to vote above all for their economic interests. A new "moral populism" could also help bring a lasting majority of Hispanics into the Democratic fold.

"It's a toss-up at this point whether people will go Democratic or Republican," said former Georgia state senator Sam Zamarripa, a leading advocate for that state's booming immigrant population. "On the one side, a lot of people are going evangelical. But a lot are also seeing that the politics that prevail in Republican America are not working to their benefit."

A plainspoken progressive message on economics will go a long way toward convincing Southerners that the Democrats are, once again, on their side. But Democrats will also have to learn to compete with the precinct-by-precinct, church-by-church grassroots framework Republicans have painstakingly built in Dixie. Fortunately, at the same time that a feisty new breed of Southern Democratic populists rose to the surface, the South's progressive grassroots were sprouting like never before.

★

"Welcome to red-hot Republican territory," said Dick Sloop, a career-military retiree who was about to become the new chair of the Wilkes County Democrats. "We've been like the homeless around here: silent and invisible. The best we ever did in my lifetime, we had two Democrats once on a five-seat county commission." So what on God's green earth had gotten into these western North Carolina Democrats? On the first pretty April Saturday of 2007, after a snowy, blowy winter, there were yards to mow, balls to toss, plants to plant, Blue Ridge Mountains to hike, ice-cold Buds in the fridge—all of them very tempting on Democratic convention day in a place where Republicans have nearly a two-to-one edge. Instead, a previously unfathomable number of Democrats were streaming up the steps of the old county courthouse, past bobbing balloons and "Welcome, Democrats!" signs.

As Wilkes's old main courtroom filled up, three new Democratic spirits bustled around, chatting folks up and laying plans for the day. One of them was trim Clyde Ingle, a one-time Hubert Humphrey campaign worker who, in 2004, "finally just got tired of sitting up there in Deep Gap"—the small town where he'd retired from teaching at the University of Tennessee—"and complaining." Ingle and his wife, Marcia, had spent a couple of years cajoling shy Wilkes County Democrats to "come out of the closet," get organized, and get active. To help them there was Mark Hufford, a young, tow-headed bundle of energy who was lighting a spark under western North Carolina Democrats as one of the field organizers funded by the Democratic National Committee's fifty-state strategy. Hustling the room with them was the white-haired, wisecracking Bob Johnston, known to one and all as "Uncle Bob," who had retired to Wilkes County from upstate New York four years earlier and had been promptly talked into the party chairmanship. "You've got to be in trouble when you're asking an eighty-year-old Yankee to run things," he said.

Yet, things actually *are* running these days, after a couple of decades of fire-and-brimstone conservatism. "The county has twenty-two precincts," Johnston informed the assembled Democrats, "and I'm proud to announce that every one of them is organized as of just the other day, when we finally got Trap Hill 2 up and running." It might sound dull as dirt, but this was just the kind of meticulous organizing—and pride taken in it—that had underpinned the Republicans' dominance in places like Wilkes County. The fifty-state strategy, kicked off in 2005 by another Yankee, Howard Dean, had rapidly begun to level the playing field—nowhere more strikingly than in North Carolina.

The new ground strategy was not the only reason record numbers were turning out to the South's county conventions, precinct barbecues, and Jefferson-Jackson Day shindigs. A heaping helping of progressive and populist frustration—and fury—was fueling the Democratic resurrection across "red America." That morning in North Wilkesboro, the booming drawl of Seth Chapman, the long-time clerk of courts in neighboring Alexander County, welcomed everyone. "Isn't this something—in Wilkes County of all places! I'll tell you what: I've been over here before when there was maybe six of us. This is great. How on fire the Democratic Party must be in Wilkes County—and rightfully so: You have suffered for centuries!"

Amen! shouted several voices as Chapman, a plain-looking, middle-aged fellow in a dark suit ideal for funerals, surveyed the crowd with a gimlet eye and then, rather than work himself up to it, flat-out hollered into the superfluous microphone. "This hard work that we've got going on here, and the only thing the opposition is working for is their own sorry hides! Staying in there with the rats, looking out for nobody but their own selves and their own political agenda. And I for one am about fed up with it!"

Mmmm! rose a woman's voice from the second row. *Tell it!*

"*Heard* all the rhetoric. *Heard* everything they said they was going to do. What have they done? Bankrupted this country. Got us into a war needlessly! And doing nothing but telling us everything's all right. I'm going to go into a little more detail about that." Chapman paused to shuffle his notes dramatically, Baptist preacher–style, then brandished a copy of resolutions passed at the GOP's recent district convention. "Do you *believe* their resolution said, 'Listen to the people of their district, not special-interest groups?' Republicans talking about cleaning up governmental corruption is just like saying that Lucifer will suddenly become the angel of light again!"

You know that's right! It seemed impossible, but Chapman just got louder, jowls swinging, sweat beading, as folks alternated between *mmm*s and *amen*s and *whoop*s.

"We're fighting a war" right here at home, Chapman said. "Let's see . . . what should we call it? A war against *radical Republicanism*!" And from there he swelled toward one final crescendo, the Wilkes County Democrats themselves having gotten pretty red-faced and sweaty by now. "The day of Republican smoke-screening and hiding under the outward righteousness of Pharisitical Rome is *ovahhhh*! America has seen, America has witnessed, your party's lip service to values, and we're tired of it. We will tolerate it no more! The Republican Party has no more claim on values and principles and especially God than those crazy Jihadists over there! Your party's reign of terror values is *ov-ahhhhh*!"

Back in the day when Chapman's style of Democratic preachment was a popular form of entertainment in the South, people would have started filtering away after "the speaking" and the barbecue lunch. But the South's emerging progressive movement involves more than rabble-rousing and officer elections. The day's events included a "practice canvass," in which novices peeled out across local neighborhoods, each accompanied by an experienced canvasser, to knock on the doors of fellow party members, identified by an online voter file, and urge them to funnel their own frustrations into political action.

"Practice, practice, practice," Ingle said. "We're going to take back the halls of Congress *and* city hall." He pointed up the road to three formerly Republican western North Carolina counties. They had done it, with Democrats going from dormant to dominant, and so could Wilkes County. But only if Washington Democrats fanned their flames instead of reverting to old form and dousing them.

★

For beleaguered Southern Democrats, Howard Dean's election as chairman of the Democratic National Committee in 2005 had flashed a flicker of hope. In launching the fifty-state strategy, he argued—contra the strategists who had been steering the party for decades—that "people will vote for Democrats in Texas, in Utah, in West Virginia if we knock on their doors." Alone among Democratic leaders, Dean had shown some understanding of the price his party was paying for neglecting the South. The region's DNC members supported him overwhelmingly over two "viable" Southern candidates.

Dean's fifty-state plan was hardly a hit with other party leaders, who complained bitterly about the expense of "hiring a bunch of staff people," in the words of former Bill Clinton adviser Paul Begala, to "wander around Utah and Mississippi and pick their nose." Little did Begala know that Mississippi was among the earliest success stories in the fifty-state effort. Long a mere skeleton of a party, the Mississippi Democrats had hired two field organizers, a political director, and a communications director and begun to revive their county operations. Florida's Democrats, who cracked up after the retirement of the beloved governor Lawton Chiles in 1998 and fell into despair after the 2000 presidential election recount mania, bounced back to retake two congressional seats and the state house in 2006. In West Virginia, the party got half its counties organized within a year.

"The Republicans sat down thirty years ago and figured out how to do this," Dean told me. "Through disciplined organization they were able to take over the country"—precinct by precinct. One critical component, said Donna Brazile, Al Gore's 2000 campaign manager, was that Republicans never rest. "They start the next campaign the day after an election, win or lose," said the Louisianan, who advised Senator Mary Landrieu on her way to a narrow reelection victory in 2002. "They don't wait to have a nominee before they start putting together a battle plan. Same on down the line, state and local. Democrats have started the day the nominee is selected, which is just bass-ackwards. We haven't had a party; we've had candidates and campaigns."

The DNC's belated catch-up effort paid off quickly, in at least two tangible ways: it exponentially multiplied grassroots party involvement and—in a short-term benefit not even envisioned by its architects—it helped win an impressive number of state, local, and congressional elections in 2006. The intangible benefits of fanning out 180 Democratic organizers, fund-raisers, and communications specialists across the map will be felt for years. Many of them were assigned to places like western North Carolina, where, one local activist put it, "a lot of Democrats think of the national party as the devil itself." As the Democratic Party chairman of the most overwhelmingly Republican of states, Utah's Wayne Holland, wrote, "Democrats have become outsiders who do things to us, not insiders who do things for us. The fifty-state strategy is one way to turn that around."

Yet, it might not outlive Dean's DNC tenure, which ends in 2009. Why? For starters, look no further than the other modifier often attached to the effort: "*Howard Dean's* fifty-state strategy." From the moment the former Vermont governor launched his campaign for DNC chair in 2004, Washington's Democratic establishment—that shadowy claque of high-paid consultants, big-money donors, lobbyists, pundits, Clintonites, and congressional leaders—went out of its way to paint the fifty-state vision as another manifestation of the screaming radicalism and out-of-control tendencies they fretted about—and whispered so gainfully to the media about—when Dean ran for president. Dean's campaign for party chair was an outsider's run at the ultimate insider's job, spurred by a meeting he had at the 2004 national convention with disgruntled party leaders from eighteen long-neglected "red" states in the South, Midwest, and interior West. They urged him to run on a fifty-state platform and change the DNC's laserlike focus on narrowly targeted presidential campaigns. Dean had also studied the national rise of Republicanism, finding lessons the Democratic sages had long ignored—including the way the GOP built from the ground up.

"The Republicans sat down thirty years ago and figured out how to do this," Dean said. "It's been a problem that presidential campaigns are the places where our themes are developed. Presidential campaigns are risk-averse by their nature, and it's not the best place to be developing your message and thinking big-picture about where your party stands."

Dean's analysis ran directly contrary to the entrenched interests and comfort levels of those who had long dictated the DNC approach. "If you make your living buying and making TV ads, then you're not really very wild about a change in technology that said, 'Let's hire organizers,'" said Elaine C. Kamarck, a Harvard public-policy lecturer and highly unlikely "Deaniac" best known for encouraging the party's move away from New Deal liberalism as a DLC strategist in the 1980s and '90s. "The whole political-consultant industry has been built on ads. But with cable TV and the diffusion of media, what the hell good is an ad? The fifty-state strategy takes a generation of consultants and kind of says, 'Let's put you out to pasture.'"

Despite opposition from the party establishment, Dean set out speedily to make good on his promises. In 2005, he dispatched assessment teams to meet with leaders of every state party. The first state was North Carolina, where a progressive thirty-four-year-old chair, Jerry Meek, had recently been elected—stunning the favored candidate of traditional party leaders—after pledging to revitalize local parties and precincts in all the state's one hundred counties. A former state vice chair and president of the National Teen Democrats (at seventeen, he'd been the youngest delegate ever to a national convention), Meek was familiar enough with the old national apparatus to be pleasantly flabbergasted by the DNC team's new attitude. "They came down here and said, basically, 'What do you need? What is it that we can do to help build the state party in North Carolina?'"

These were jaw-dropping questions. As Dean said, "Washington's idea of accountability is that you ask people in the states to

jump and they'll ask, 'How high?'" Meek recovered quickly enough
from the shock to ask the DNC to pay the salaries of three regional
organizers he was already planning to bring on board. "A lot of
state parties weren't as fortunate as we were, in terms of already
having some fund-raising staff, a communications director, an
administrative director," Meek said. "But what we lacked were these
field operatives." They got them. And they weren't sent down from
Washington; the state parties made their own hires, on Dean's wild
theory that "the closer you can get to neighbors talking to neighbors, the better you can reach people with the Democratic message
in a way they'll understand."

What North Carolina needed from the fifty-state strategy was a
world away from, say, Idaho and South Carolina, where once-proud
Democratic parties had been pretty well plowed under by the
Republicans' superior organizing and culture war politics. Below the
ballot lines for president and Congress, North Carolina was overwhelmingly blue: Democrats held the governorship and virtually
every statewide office, huge majorities in the state house and senate,
and, in most places, practically everything down to the sewer
boards. In the 2004 election cycle, the state party outraised the N.C.
GOP almost five to one. With no need to build back up from scratch,
the North Carolina Democrats deployed the fifty-state staffers to
turn purplish areas blue—and, as a result, elect more genuine progressives—while tackling Republican terrain with down-home vigor.

North Carolina's first hire, Mark Hufford, had managed an
unorthodox, grassroots-fueled campaign in 2004 against the powerful western North Carolina Republican congressman Charles Taylor
that came surprisingly close to scoring an upset. He knew the "WNC"
turf. He also knew that Democrats in a few of these mountain counties had already begun to dig themselves out of the doldrums—particularly in Watauga County, where a band of progressives had taken over
the party apparatus in the 1990s and, despite a sizable Republican
majority among registered voters, slowly built toward dominance in

local elections. As Watauga County chair Diane Tilson happily recalled, "We were the first county in the nation to do a countywide canvass. Yes, we were! It was freezing cold, but we did it. Jerry and Mark both came, and we sent them out to the boonies. I think Jerry was a little surprised at the way people live," she said, laughing.

"The canvasses have been such a good learning experience," Tilson said. "We go out and listen. There's no hard sell; you start by talking to people about whatever you have in common, and ask them what they're concerned about." Those concerns are duly noted and entered in an online voter file. Often, even when hardcore Republicans answered their doors, they turned out to have issues on their minds that ran right up the Democratic alley. "There's so many people that really don't realize the relationship between elections and whether or not they're going to be able to get their drugs, or how expensive gas is." While new canvassers often braced themselves for a barrage of questions about abortion and gay marriage, they soon found that wasn't foremost on most folks' minds. "They're thinking about whether they'll have heat this winter," Tilson said. "How they're going to get themselves to the grocery store and work."

Meanwhile, Hufford and Meek got together a group of WNC Democrats to devise creative ways to win over their most troublesome demographic. "We had a problem reaching out to rural, older voters," Meek said. "Those were the ones who were abandoning us and going Republican." The group came up with a low-cost ad campaign that their targets couldn't miss: six different series of rotating signs, addressing issues of special concern in these mountains— environmental destruction, gas prices, health care—and based on the regionally famous "jingles" that advertised Burma Shave cream from the 1930s to the '60s. Like the old Burma Shave signs, they were put up in sequences along the roadways that added up to a kind of poem, with the "brand" and message at the end. One read: "My future grandchildren/Are destined for strife/With Republican budgets/They're debtors for life/WNC Democrats/Demand fiscal responsibility." The signs changed every two weeks to form a new jingle and generated not only considerable publicity but an unexpected bonus: unsolicited donations to local parties from Democrats delighted to see that the party, as one put it, "finally stands for something."

Then, in November 2006, for the first time any living body can remember, Democrats won every single election on the ballot in Watauga County. They won big down the road in Ashe County, another Republican stronghold with a newly energized Democratic grassroots. Congressman Taylor was dethroned by Heath Shuler and his Mountain Values. And the Democrats made a clean sweep in Polk County, where registered Republicans outnumbered Democrats by 6 percent. Polk County chair Margaret Johnson chalked it up not only to better organizing, but to "walking the talk about what it means to be a Democrat." Where grassroots Republicans stuck together around religious issues when it wasn't election time, the Polk and Watauga County Democrats had turned themselves into quasi-civic groups year-round, organizing roadside cleanups, planting gardens at Habitat for Humanity homes, helping the needy, and putting on fund-raising walks to benefit the environment. "Even Republicans come up to me," Johnson said, "and say, 'I may not agree with your politics, but I sure like what you're doing.'"

Here was what the South had so long lacked: a progressive movement nurtured from the bottom up, rather than the same old stick-your-toe-in-at-election-time campaigning. Here, in its crib, was a new people's party waiting to be born.

★

It didn't take the fifty-state strategy to light a fire under progressive Kentuckians. The Bluegrass State's antiwar movement announced its presence in November 2002, when President Bush came to Louisville for a speech—ostensibly on behalf of incumbent congresswoman Anne Northup—in which he rolled out the rationale for invading Iraq. Upwards of four hundred peace supporters came out on a wild, windy night, their drums and chants so unnerving to the local police that some officers charged the protesters on horseback, driving them back, scaring them to death, arresting nine of them for leaving the "protest zone," and sending a handful to the nearest emergency room.

Despite the South's reputation for being reflexively "promilitary," Southern Democrats have opposed the Iraq War strongly—by 2003, even more so than non-Southern Democrats. The Kentucky peace movement is a politically charged, vibrant microcosm of the nontraditional mix of pacifists, military veterans and families, blue-collar hard hats, and college professors who were spurred to action by the war in Iraq. It has been particularly creative when it comes to getting under the skin of pro-war Republicans. When Representative Anne Northup refused to meet with her antiwar constituents in 2003, activists posted "Missing" posters with smiling images of Northup around the city, noting that she "Answers to Bush." They staked out her Louisville home for seventy-three straight Sundays with "a variety of signs you can't even imagine," said Judy Munro-Leighton, a local teacher who helped organized the Louisville Peace Action Community. "We had a cardboard Bush with a bubble to show he was speaking, and we changed the message weekly to 'I Love Anne' or 'My War's Going Great!' or 'I Sold the Country.'"

When Northup, tarred by her unflagging support for Bush and the war, lost her seat to John Yarmuth in 2006, the Kentucky peace brigade laid plans to fry an even bigger fish: Republican Senate minority leader Mitch McConnell, the Senate's wiliest and most powerful backer of Bush and the war. Matt Gunterman, a twenty-nine-year-old rural Kentucky native and Yale University graduate student, launched the Ditch Mitch blog, bringing together grassroots bloggers from across the state. In June 2007, two young native Kentuckians and a navy veteran opened an "Iraq Summer" headquarters in Louisville, part of a national campaign by labor unions, veterans' groups, and the Netroots powerhouse MoveOn.org to target key members of Congress with a home-grown antiwar message.

By mid-August, McConnell was sending out fund-raising letters complaining about being dogged by "the radical '60s antiwar movement on steroids." But as he well knew, the reality of what the senator faced was something altogether different from that old stereotype—and considerably more formidable. Because it wasn't just traditional peace activists and young bloggers who were banding together around their opposition to Iraq and McConnell. Take Jim Pence: a sixty-eight-year-old, Salem-smoking, pickup-driving, self-proclaimed hillbilly from economically devastated Hardin County, retired after thirty-five years in the factory at the American Synthetic Rubber Corporation. He was politically inactive until 2004, but President Bush's reelection and the war in Iraq led him to "vow to fight with every ounce of my strength from then on." From that point forward, Pence has devoted himself with around-the-clock intensity to making antiwar and political videos from locations all across Kentucky—and sometimes from the front porch of an outbuilding in his backyard. Linking from his own Hillbilly Report Web site to YouTube and Ditch Mitch, Pence posts snappy videos of peace rallies, along with hard-hitting exposés like his series on liquor-industry fund-raising by Ron Lewis, the holy-rolling congressman from Pence's district.

Ditch Mitch creator Gunterman sees Pence as a prime example of the passion and wit that generally go untapped by Democrats and urban progressives. "He is very much a hillbilly, and he's reinvigorated the term," said Gunterman, whose goal is to fire up an Internet-based "ruralution," connecting rural progressives. "What we want to do is create a progressive movement in rural America by combining the 10 to 20 percent who are there with the expatriate rural community—people like me who still have intimacy and affection and concern for the places we come from. The majority of rural Americans would classify themselves as moderates, but they've been swayed by the right wing into adapting and accepting conservative postures."

Gunterman settled on the Internet route after he tried another, harder one in 2005, running for county judge/executive—the equivalent of a mayor—in his tiny, dirt-poor county of McLean (median household income: sixteen thousand dollars). "The good old boys came after me with everything they had," he said. For one thing, "They sued me, claiming I was a resident of Connecticut because I have a P.O. box here. But I won the primary, against the former mayor"—Gunterman chuckled—"saying, 'I don't have any experience but I'd like your vote.' And getting them." He came up short against the Republican incumbent by a mere forty-eight votes. "In the end," he said, "I'm happier having lost by forty-eight rather than having won by forty-eight votes, because the good old boys would have made my life a living hell with a margin of support that small." He has his consolation: "We still scared the living shit out of them."

Gunterman grew up in a deeply religious household and was introduced to politics in 1988, when an elderly Democrat from church took him along to see Democratic vice presidential candidate Lloyd Bentsen in Owensboro. But Gunterman didn't wind up in the more conservative, Bentsen wing of the Democratic Party. "I don't think we should run away from our beliefs to win," he said. "The technocrats are concerned about getting power, and they're not concerned about building a progressive majority in the long run." The state Democratic chairman, a religious progressive and former state treasurer named Jonathan Miller, agreed. The party, he said, has long been split between "those who are out to change the world, and those who are in office to game the system."

The world changers are asserting themselves anew in Southern states like Kentucky—and Florida, North Carolina, Virginia, and Arkansas—where the Democratic parties stood reasonably solid through the earthquakes of 1980s and '90s Republicanism. In

Kentucky, moderate Democrat Steve Beshear trounced scandal-haunted incumbent governor Ernie Fletcher, who had been hand-picked for the job by McConnell, with 60 percent of the vote in 2007.

It helps tremendously that while Gunterman and other activists have inspired Kentucky progressives, they have also pushed the state's more established media to take notice. "Ditch Mitch gives us the power to hold the media accountable in Kentucky for the first time," said twenty-four-year-old Shawn Dixon, a native of rural western Kentucky now studying at NYU Law School. In 2004, when Dixon was working as deputy policy and communications director for Democrat Daniel Mongiardo's uphill Senate challenge to Republican Jim Bunning, he spent much of the campaign in a state of frustration over Kentucky newspapers' assumption that the incumbent would cruise to victory. "There was no recognition that this would be a competitive election and this guy was beatable, until about a month before the election, when it was impossible to ignore." Bunning wobbled back to Washington with a slender twenty-thousand-vote victory, but with Ditch Mitch documenting the anti-McConnell movement, "the media don't have a choice anymore," Dixon said. On the day in August 2007 that the *Lexington Herald-Leader* ran a story about McConnell's dip in popularity (below 50 percent approval), Louisville's *Courier-Journal* ran an editorial, fifteen months before the election, head-lined "McConnell Vulnerable."

5

COLOR CODES

"[T]here is nothing indestructible, nothing frozen, nothing 'natural,' in the Southern pattern of race relations. If racial integration in some form could persist in the South, not only during the Radical Reconstruction period with its forced situation but for decades after that, then racial separation is no mysterious necessity of Southern life but rather the product of historical circumstance. And man can change historical circumstance."

—HOWARD ZINN,
The Southern Mystique (1964)

ON A DAMP South Carolina Low Country night in the spring of 2007, the stage was set for Democratic presidential contenders to do something they have rarely managed: talk about race in a way that can be heard by blacks and whites alike. The moment demanded it: Just the summer before, the aftermath of Hurricane Katrina had stripped away, all too vividly, any pretense of a color-blind New South—or a color-blind America, for that matter. Just a few months earlier, the Republican National Committee had unleashed one of the rawest race-baiting campaigns in recent memory against Congressman Harold Ford Jr. of Tennessee in his bid for the Senate. And a week before the debate, one of South Carolina's most famous figures, USC football coach Steve Spurrier, had denounced "that dang, damn Confederate flag" that still flaps over the state capitol in

Columbia, kicking off a spirited renewal of the state's ongoing symbolic battle. The setting demanded some plain talk about race, too: the year's first Democratic face-off was happening at South Carolina State University, the historically black school in largely black Orangeburg where, in February 1968, South Carolina Highway Patrol officers opened fire on black students protesting a segregated bowling alley. Three were shot dead; twenty-seven more were wounded. Every officer was acquitted; the only person convicted was Cleveland Sellers, a civil rights activist and student who is now a professor at the University of South Carolina. But the story was quickly buried beneath the series of atrocities that plagued that year.

On this night, at the Democratic debate, it was forgotten again. There was not so much as a nod to the Orangeburg Massacre. Not a word, for that matter, about the shame of New Orleans, the evils of racially divisive politics, or the racial underpinnings of the two economic Americas. In a part of the country where African Americans fought bravely and sometimes violently to turn the Civil Rights and Voting Rights acts into practical realities just four decades ago; in a place where most white people vote in Republican blocs; in a place where the Confederate flag is still a symbolically potent issue; in a place where a burgeoning population of Hispanics faces even deeper poverty and greater segregation than blacks now do; here, even here, the subject of race was uncomfortably shooed away by the Democrats.

Senator Barack Obama had his chances. Lobbed a softball question by the moderator, NBC anchor Brian Williams, about the strange persistence of the Confederate flag, Obama responded with a dispassionate remark about putting the rebel flag in a museum for good, then quickly transitioned to another issue he preferred to address. You couldn't blame Obama for wanting to pooh-pooh a symbolic firecracker of an issue like the Stars and Bars, perhaps, but in the process, an opportunity was lost to address the freight carried by that flag, the new page that might be turned with a biracial president, and the crying need for blacks and whites to learn to vote together in a place where they otherwise coexist with, by and large, a remarkable degree of equanimity. The other candidates had their chances in the debate, too, when they were asked about Iraq and the economy and health care—all subjects through which race runs, swift and sure as poison. But you wouldn't have known it on this night.

The contrast between what the candidates were putting forward and what black Southerners, in particular, were longing to hear was stark. One of the most startling statistics, as the American public turned sharply against the Iraq War in 2005 and 2006, was the number of Southern blacks calling for immediate withdrawal: 90 percent. They were fired up about the increasingly tenuous business of trying to make a living, too. Just the week before, the country (or at least the newspaper-reading public) had learned that a full one-eighth of Americans—and one in seven Southerners—were now officially living in poverty, just as the Dow Jones was ding-dinging its way to a record-high thirteen thousand.

Black voters, especially in the South, often find themselves wondering about where the Democratic Party really comes down on these matters. Of course, there is no larger or more loyal core of Democratic voters; Southern black voters went for Al Gore at a 93 percent clip in 2000, and John Kerry got 90 percent in 2004. It is no wonder that non-Southern strategists like Thomas Schaller casually expect black folks to continue supporting the absent party, even if it starts rallying the rest of the country against Southern evangelicals. Addressing the amazing fidelity of black voters in Dixie, Schaller sees no reason that it won't continue without any care and feeding from the party—after all, *why would they not vote for Democrats?*

This attitude from the national Democrats—and the obvious stereotyping of black voters in Dixie, where candidates seem to think there is nowhere to find African Americans but in churches or historically black colleges—has led to disquiet under the surface of what looks like as "solid" a Democratic vote as it gets. Polled in the summer of 2007, blacks in South Carolina still overwhelmingly identified with the Democrats. But a majority also said they felt the national Democratic Party was taking black voters for granted. And a rapidly growing chunk of the black population in South Carolina— almost 20 percent—was registering independent. Meanwhile, African Americans in the state were turning out to vote at about 15 percent below the level of whites.

That trend away from the Democrats—and away from *enthusiasm* for the Democrats—is most pronounced among young African Americans; nationally, almost 35 percent of those under thirty are bypassing the Democrats and registering as independents. Part of the reason, according to Cornell Belcher, the influential Washington pollster, is an ongoing effort by Republicans to "assert that African Americans are taken for granted and Democrats are out of touch with the values of the community." In the 2002 midterms, Republican and right-wing groups spent more than seven million dollars on black media; the Associated Press reported that a mysterious Christian right outfit called the Council for Better Government had ordered black radio ads worth $1.5 million in twelve states, including Arkansas, Florida, Georgia, and North Carolina. In 2006, in the six states in Dixie with gay marriage referenda, much of the money was devoted to stirring up socially conservative black voters—which is to say, the majority of Southern black voters. Still, while most blacks voted against gay marriage, they still supported the Democrats who opposed the constitutional restrictions (including Jim Webb in Virginia). It's not easy to find common ground between Republicans and black Southerners on any issues outside the "moral" realm, but the Republicans' outreach was not all about the gay-marriage wedge; most of the ad money went to ballyhooing the GOP's support for private-school vouchers, which the majority of Southern blacks favor, and the claim that blacks are shortchanged in the Social Security system. As demographic changes weaken their white Southern bloc over the next few decades, the GOP will surely step up such efforts.

At Orangeburg, a couple of thousand students and local folks—about 80 percent black—who couldn't get into the media-saturated debate hall packed into the S.C. State gym for a "community celebration," watching the proceedings on a big screen and cheering each candidate in turn afterward. But they weren't finding much to celebrate whenever the "viable" candidates gave their carefully hedged pitches. The loudest cheers were mostly for the two dark-horse liberals, Congressman Dennis Kucinich and former senator Mike Gravel, when they spoke their minds—especially about the war. Like most Americans, many of these folks were surely unaware of these two fellows' candidacies before the debate. But they had come to hear some unvarnished talk. They had not come to hear Senator Hillary Clinton offer sunny assurance that hedge funds are perfectly fine because "we know how to regulate them so nobody gets an unfair advantage." They had not come to hear Obama's platitude about "organizing ordinary people to do extraordinary things." They *had* come in hopes, hot and high and pressing hopes, of hearing some exceptionally smart and well-informed people speak some truth—*finally!*—about the world in which they live and struggle.

Maybe next time.

Pete Henderson, an elderly South Carolina State alumnus, had driven down to Orangeburg from his coastal home of Georgetown to scrutinize the candidates up close. He was turned out crisply in a camel-colored suit with a sharp tie; perched a little incongruously atop his head was a mesh baseball cap that announced, "Retiree, Air Force." With impeccable Southern politeness he first said he thought that the evening had gone "very well, very well." But Henderson had to admit to not being exactly bowled over by the candidates. "The first thing I wanted to hear was how we're going to get out of Iraq," he said. "I understand a lot about these wars. I served in Korea and

I served two tours in Vietnam." Twenty-eight years, in all, before he came back to the Low Country for good. "To me it's abominable to see us sending young troops over there to be killed," he declared, folding his arms.

Young black men, he said, are "lost," largely due to a dearth of hope. "Every day, I see in this country, people are *destitute,*" he said, as if he just can't emphasize it enough. "It bothers me so much. *Destitute,* right *here.*" Did he hear the appropriate outrage from the Democrats? Henderson took a drag on his cigarette and gazed skyward. "Not really. A little bit. I expected more. But I always expect more," he said with a little smile. "And at least they came here. Twenty years ago, they wouldn't have. That's *something,* you know." But for black Democrats in the South, gestures like debating in Orangeburg are nothing especially new. Follow-up is another matter.

★

Eight months after that first debate, on the springlike second Sunday in December, Barack Obama emerged triumphantly from the same tunnel where Steve Spurrier's Gamecocks spill out on fall Saturdays. Amid the foot-stomps and hollered blessings of the biggest campaign crowd of the year, with Oprah Winfrey hallooing above the din, it looked as though the black South—at least this big chunk of it—had found itself a candidate after all.

"I'm so grateful to be here today," Obama beamed, soaking up the adulation and sliding into half-baked dialect. "Givin' all praise and honor unto *Gahd.* Look at the day the Lord has made!" The twenty-nine-thousand-strong congregation, many of whom had driven straight from church, let up a happy whoop. "I would be blessed even if I was in Chicago," Obama went on, "but I don't mind being in seventy-degree weather." He paused for another round of cheers, then broke in with a chuckle: "Michelle said, 'Praise the Lord! It's been *coooold* up in Chicago!'"

For most of 2007 Obama had felt a chill in the South. South

Carolina's contest, coming on the heels of the almost-all-white elec-
torates in Iowa and New Hampshire, featured the first all-out fight
for African American votes in the campaign—and black voters
across the country were watching closely. The primary was widely
portrayed as a Clinton-Obama battle, particularly for black women,
who were reportedly torn between their enthusiasm for electing a
sister versus a brother. But the real focus, from the get-go, was
relentlessly on Obama. When black South Carolinians looked at the
biracial Illinois senator, they saw not flesh and blood but symbol—a
symbol of both defeat and promise. When they weighed whether to
back him, they were also weighing the future of African American
politics. Obama was supposed to be part of a "post–civil rights
movement" generation of new black leaders, a group that included
"blue dog" Harold Ford Jr. and Massachusetts governor Deval
Patrick. Which made a lot of South Carolinians wonder just when,
exactly, they had stopped needing a movement.

In the state where the Reverend Jesse Jackson's wildly successful
1988 uprising still stood as a high-water mark for black political
aspirations, Obama's cool style and "postracial" rhetoric had initially gone over like a lead balloon. In April, he had given the state's
legislative black caucus a speech, offering his joking opinion that "a
good economic development plan for our community would be if
we make sure folks weren't throwing garbage out of their cars."
To black South Carolinians like Kevin Alexander Gray, who ran
Jackson's campaign in the state, this smacked not of fresh, "postracial" thinking but of "the oldest stereotypes. Translation: Black people
are dirty and lazy." Obama's middle-of-the-aisle message and delivery kept reinforcing black South Carolinians' doubts about whether
he was sufficiently one of them. "I've heard people say, and I've probably said it myself, 'He's a white boy,'" Gray told me. "Or he's what
some working-class black people perceive as a middle-class Negro.
Anyway, let's face it: You don't get a revolution from Harvard"—
Obama's alma mater.

The tide began to turn in the summer of 2007, when Obama and his surrogates started to recast his image from that of a brainy harbinger of a new "color-blind" politics to—in South Carolina, if not in white Iowa—a latter-day extension of the civil rights movement. The wonk was redrawn as a kind of political savior, adding down-home, preacherly populism to his message and proclaiming, "I'm running because of what Dr. King called 'the fierce urgency of now.'" Black voters' doubts were explained as sad examples of what Michelle Obama, speaking in the majority-black upstate town of Anderson in September, called "that veil of impossibility that keeps us down and keeps our children down . . . the bitter legacy of racism and discrimination and oppression in this country." The only proper response, she said, was to "dig deep in our souls, confront our own self-doubt, and recognize that our destiny is in our hands." Or, more to the point, in the hands of Barack Obama.

"You know," Oprah had said as she introduced him in Columbia, "Dr. King dreamed the dream. But we don't just have to dream the dream anymore. We get to vote that dream into reality."

Many of the folks who came out to cheer Obama had clearly embraced that message. "I believe anything is possible," said Obama volunteer Josie Barton. "If you say that it's not going to happen, and don't do anything about it, then nothing will change. You have to step up to the plate. Words without works is dead." But the doubts had hardly been dispelled.

"I've heard a lot of black people saying they don't want to vote for Barack," Barton's daughter Michelle told me, "because they don't believe it would make a difference. They feel that even if a lot of white people voted for him, somebody in a higher-up position would still find a way for him not to win." When asked if white people would vote for a black candidate, Barton and two fellow Obama volunteers chorused back with an emphatic "no."

The South Carolina campaign cracked open a unique window into the fractured state of racial politics in the twenty-first-century

South—a gumbo of bleak cynicism, wary pragmatism, frustrated progressive aspirations, and messianic longings. Early on, Hillary Clinton's support among African Americans in South Carolina proved surprisingly strong, giving her a stunning 57 percent in CNN polls as late as October 2007. Clinton was the fall-back candidate for African Americans—the safe, traditional choice. She did every expected thing to woo black voters in South Carolina: held forth in black colleges and churches; called for removing the Confederate flag from the statehouse; lined up endorsements from preachers and politicians; and deployed her popular husband to the state with increasing urgency. She talked about the Bible (favorite book: James, especially when congressional majority whip Jim Clyburn, the state's most powerful black pol, was nearby), and she winced over the "Corridor of Shame," a particularly desperate and heavily black stretch of I-95 that was the subject of a 2007 documentary. It was a familiar routine, complete with symbolic photo ops like the one in Spartanburg in early December 2007: a beaming Hillary, flanked by more than sixty applauding African Americans in nice suits, under the *Spartanburg Herald-Journal* front-page headline "Black Pastors Stand Behind Clinton."

On Hillary's left in that photo, smiling along with the rest, stood one of the most familiar figures in the local religious and civil rights community, the Reverend J. W. Sanders, the longtime pastor of two churches. Introducing Clinton, Sanders called her "the right choice," a "lady who has proven herself to do exactly what should be done." While Sanders told me that he had endorsed her for her "proven leadership," he could not deny that it gave him qualms to bypass Obama. "It does have a tinge of conscience on our part. . . . But," he added, getting back on message, "we've been trying to move beyond that. We don't want to be pigeonholed or put in a box."

Even less comfortable was state representative Harold Mitchell, an early Obama supporter who had defected to Clinton and helped organize the event. "I was originally caught up in the hoopla" over

Obama, Mitchell explained. "I tuned her out because here was somebody exciting." But then, around the time Clinton invited him to testify at the first-ever Senate hearing on environmental justice, Mitchell had begun to believe that it was more important to find someone who "we know we can win the general election with." He worried that "right now, we don't have time for experimentation."

Another black Clinton supporter in South Carolina, state senator Robert Ford, put it more bluntly: "Every Democrat running on that ticket next year would lose because he's black and he's on top of the ticket," Ford told the AP. "We'd lose the House and the Senate and the governors and everything."

Meanwhile, Obama's growing ranks of South Carolina supporters were convinced that the time for "experimentation" had come—in part because of the candidate's biracial appeal. Where the Clinton backers called for careful pragmatism (and political butt covering), Obama's faithful believed they had found their long-sought leader. In Obama's cramped and bustling Spartanburg office—a converted attic upstairs from Democratic Party headquarters—super-volunteer Carolyn Reed-Smith, an elementary school teacher, invited me to "pull up a chair, honey" while she took a break from calling local folks who had pledged to work for Obama. "I had really been drawn to Hillary at first," she explained, "because I voted for her husband. I thought, 'Wow! Now we'll have him *and* her.'" But when Obama came to Reed-Smith's church, Mount Moriah Baptist, he made a convert. "He had such a calming presence," she said. "It's sort of biblical, but I believe in men having dominion and having some sort of mystical power that God gave them. I believe Barack has acquired that."

A native of Waterloo, Iowa, Reed-Smith sports dreadlocks and teaches reading to local elementary students who "don't make the basics." She moved to South Carolina in 1986, where she learned some hard lessons about the everyday realities of race in a place where black people weren't as exotic as they had been in the heartland.

"When I started teaching at an elementary school here, I would drive every morning past a crossing guard, an older white guy. . . . Every morning I was going to school and this crossing guard would just be waving at people. For a whole year, I'd come up close and try to wave to him and he would turn his head. I thought, 'Maybe it's the car.' I got a different car and then I tried waving at him again and he would never wave back. I just wanted to change his mind about African Americans in some way. I said, 'If I could do something, if I could fix just one thing, it'd be this.'" She thought Obama could fix it. To Reed-Smith, the questions about Obama's "blackness" actually pointed to one of his most important assets. "I believe that he has the best of two cultures within him."

Reed-Smith signed up to be one of some fifteen thousand volunteers fueling Obama's unconventional campaign in South Carolina. While her candidate snagged his share of endorsements and sweet-talked his share of preachers—and by the fall had matched Clinton's top-level staffing—on the ground, the focus was more on person-to-person contact. That made it easier for Obama's campaign to calibrate its appeals to the complicated mix of black politics in South Carolina.

"The mistake Democrats always make," said Winthrop University political scientist Scott Huffmon, "is seeing blacks here as monolithic and as more liberal than they are. Conversely, they see white Southern Democrats as being much more conservative than they are. Obama's campaign hasn't organized around the stereotypes." Along with the usual church network, Obama's people put together a Main Street machine of more than nine hundred black barber and beauty shops.

"There's not been retail politics in the past here, at least not like in Iowa or New Hampshire," said Amaya Smith, Obama's South Carolina press secretary. "People still get their information from their churches, but here they're getting it directly from folks like this."

★

Later, after Obama's overwhelming black support in South Carolina was repeated in state after state—lifting him to strong wins in Virginia, Georgia, Alabama, North Carolina, and Mississippi, among others—the value of these votes was routinely shrugged off. Obama's two-to-one margin over Clinton in South Carolina was thoroughly unexpected, but the pundits reacted as though his black vote had been a given. The story became Obama's difficulty winning white votes (although he won a majority of under-thirty whites in South Carolina and in North Carolina); the morning after Obama won Mississippi, the headline on Real Clear Politics was typical: "Race defines vote in Mississippi." The idea that African American votes in Dixie were anything but purely and mindlessly "race-based" was apparently beyond considering. And the idea that their votes were as important as those of whites seemed to be implicitly, repeatedly, dismissed. "The press has scoured every exit poll for the latest evidence of racial polarization," Obama said in his March 2008 speech on race and religion. But Obama had not only overcome the early favorite among black voters—Hillary Clinton—but also a candidate who had won a plurality of black South Carolinians' votes in 2004—John Edwards. Black support was anything but automatic; Obama's primary campaign was, for African American Southerners, an extended exercise in political soul-searching, right up until voting day.

While the grassroots orientation of Obama's South Carolina campaign recalled the glories of Jackson's run in 1988, when he registered thousands of new black voters and got white progressives fired up, the Illinois senator's candidacy still hadn't clicked with progressive blacks as voting day approached. At the big rally in Columbia, Oprah Winfrey had notched up the Holy Obama rhetoric, referencing a scene from *The Autobiography of Miss Jane*

Pittman. "I remember Miss Pittman, her body all worn and withered and bent over. As she would approach the children, she would say to each one, 'Are you the one? Are you the one?'" Oprah hadn't mentioned that Miss Pittman was looking for a black messiah, or that folks used to use this very same language to refer to the Reverend Dr. Martin Luther King Jr. She didn't have to. "I watched that movie many years ago, but I do believe today I have the answer to Miss Pittman's question. . . . South Carolina, I do believe he's the one."

For Efia Nwangaza, a lifelong activist and onetime Green Party candidate for the Senate, the Sunday spectacle just left her with the question: "He's the one for who, and what?" Obama's fresh-faced moderation did not appeal to her, but she was impressed by the jubilant energy of his fans. "I was really moved by it," she said. "By the yearning of the people who were there to have someone representing them and their interests."

Other progressives remained skeptical. Kevin Gray, the author of *The Decline of Black Politics: From Malcolm X to Barack Obama,* echoed Nwangaza's sentiments. "People say they're voting for Obama because they want a change. This is people thinking that the cosmetic is more important than the structural. Obama is a candidate who happens to be black. That's his prerogative, and it's fine. But it's not what we need. Obama's campaign is not a movement. It is someone running for office."

Anything that smacked of go-along politics was simply a waste of time. In Obama's special case, Gray feared it also offered an open invitation for white Democrats to congratulate themselves on having been enlightened enough to vote outside of their own race—and to congratulate themselves, just like the Republicans, on their color-blindness. "To the extent that the Democratic Party is using Obama to cancel its debt to the African American community, I am concerned," said Gray. Even so, Gray was having trouble shaking off one nagging fact: "The brother is black." While he preferred Kucinich's liberalism and Edwards's populism, Gray admitted that he just might "end up being guilted into voting for the brother." He frowned, debating himself out loud. "A movement has to be about something. I have my problem with Reverend Jackson, but when you look at the construction of that campaign, the way the elements came together—*that* was a movement."

★

The Jackson campaign was the last time Marjorie Hammock, a long-time social worker who does expert defense testimony in death-penalty cases, allowed herself to get swept up in politics. Hammock's first campaign was Adlai Stevenson, she told me, laughing. Originally from Brooklyn, she worked in the inner circle of Shirley Chisholm's pathbreaking 1972 run for president. And then she became part of the large remigration of blacks to the South, moving to Columbia, "a whole new planet," where Jackson's 1988 insurgency came along not a moment too soon. "That was exciting," she said, and "it paved the way for a number of people to get active in politics. By the same token, though, another kind of apathy developed as a response to the fact that Jackson didn't win. That maybe if we had someone who was that powerful, with that much organization, and he didn't win, it was hopeless."

Hammock had been drawn to Edwards. She appreciated the former North Carolina senator's unusual attention to New Orleans during the campaign, which he had kicked off from the backyard of a black family trying to rebuild from the flooding that followed Hurricane Katrina. But she had also attended an Obama focus group to see what was what. "I must say, there are a number of African Americans here who are terribly excited about Obama," she said. "He's viable, in many kinds of ways. He's got some good positions on things that are important. He's not a black candidate. He truly is a candidate of the people, and that's good." What made Obama not a black candidate in her mind? "I think his life," Hammock said. "I think he's interested in black people, no question about it. He demonstrated that in terms of his work in Chicago. But for me, in part, and this may sound petty, but who do you cite when you talk about things? Frederick Douglass? DuBois? Ida B. Wells? No. We hear from Kennedy a lot. And it ain't bad. It's just not what I would call a black candidate."

Regardless of her own feelings, Hammock nodded her head when I asked about Obama's boast that, as Democratic nominee, he would bring out 30 percent more black voters (not to mention 25 to 30 percent more young voters) and put states like Mississippi and North Carolina into play. "I can see that," she said. "We can sometimes get real loyal." But, she noted, a black candidate on the ballot also has had a tendency, in the past, to draw out more white folks, too; on average, both black and white turnout rises 2 to 3 percent when black candidates run in general elections, and as a result, white turnout is numerically bigger. Hammock remained unpersuaded that black turnout—the great hope of the Jackson movement—would make it possible to elect a black president. In South Carolina, Obama would need 35 percent of the white vote to win in a general election. "As we've seen time and time again," Hammock said, "a lot of people will say, 'I'm with you.'" But "when they get behind those curtains, they change their minds. And unfortunately it appears that in many instances they vote race."

★

A driving tour of Richmond, Virginia, is almost enough to make a person wonder whether the rebels actually won the war. While it's now a moderate, racially mixed city with a popular black mayor, former governor Douglas Wilder, and a swelling white-collar population, the erstwhile capital of the Confederacy still teems with plaques, statues, streets, museums, and monuments honoring the Southern cause. Downtown, there's the historically comical Museum of the Confederacy and the nearby Confederate White House, where Jefferson Davis and his family dwelt. At Hollywood Cemetery, a hilly boneyard containing eighteen thousand dead rebels, a bronze memorial to Davis presides over the roaring James River. In the central city, along busy Monument Avenue, traffic islands feature massive tributes to Confederate luminaries, led off by Gen. Robert E. Lee. Standing sixty-one feet high, with the general tall in the saddle of his famous horse, Traveler, Lee's statue is the spitting image of heroic triumph.

In December 2002, the Richmond-based United States Historical Society announced that it was donating a small measure of historical balance to its hometown: a statue of Abraham Lincoln. Next to the elaborate homages to Davis, Lee, General Stonewall Jackson, and so many other Confederates, this nod to Lincoln would be decidedly modest, anything but triumphal. The sculptor, David French, was creating a likeness of Lincoln during the president's "healing visit" to Richmond on April 4 and 5, 1865, right after the city fell to Union forces and right before he was assassinated by that renowned Confederate thespian, John Wilkes Booth. While Lee's towering bronze looked eternally raring for battle, French's life-sized Lincoln rested on a bench, looking weighed-down and spent by four years of war, above a conciliatory fragment of Lincoln's second inaugural address inscribed on the statue's base: "to bind up the nation's wounds."

As soon as the plans for the Lincoln statue were announced, a ragged clamor of rebel yells rose up. Outraged letters piled up at local newspapers, likening Lincoln to Adolf Hitler, Saddam Hussein, and Osama bin Laden. Protesters from white supremacist hate groups handed out anti-Lincoln propaganda; thousands signed an online petition organized by neo-Confederate blogger Ron Holland, a prominent member of the white supremacist League of the South. Many petition signers took the opportunity to vent their splenetic feelings about the man who consistently tops polls as the nation's, and the South's, most widely admired president.

"Just say NO to America's greatest WAR CRIMINAL—the murderer of 600,000!!" exclaimed Robert G. Patrick. "Not even with a rope around his neck," declared Dewey Lee Martin. "Why not put up a statue of Osama Bin Laden at Ground Zero?" wondered Mary Looney. "It's the equivalent, to Southerners, of what's proposed for Richmond." Ken E. Neff suggested an alternative to the Lincoln memorial: "Build a John Wilkes Booth statue instead." Protesters, many organized by the local Sons of Confederate Veterans, held signs with slogans like: "Lincoln killed 5 of my ancestors."

The issue was larger than Lincoln, of course—just as Confederate flag battles are only tangentially about the Stars and Bars. While organized white supremacists are an aging, increasingly pathetic crowd in the South—protesters always outnumber white hoods on the rare occasions when a Ku Klux Klan group marches in Dixie—they still speak, as always, for a larger group of more respectable whites who wouldn't dare stand on a street corner holding a "Saddam Bin Lincoln" sign.

"Some white people feel like their history is disregarded and neglected, if not scorned," said UNC-Charlotte historian David Goldfield, author of the prize-winning *Still Fighting the Civil War: The American South and Southern History*. "They realize the tide of history is rolling very heavily."

In Richmond, it rolled right over the anti-Lincoln brigade. On the overcast afternoon of April 5, 2003, a gaggle of children and dignitaries pulled back a green cloth, unveiling French's pensive rendering of the president. The sight of Lincoln in Richmond was greeted with enthusiastic cheers from the audience of 850 inside the American Civil War Center, and even more enthusiastic jeers from the estimated one hundred protesters outside. But the pro-Lincoln blasphemies went forward uninterrupted, with Democratic governor Tim Kaine proclaiming on behalf of the state, "Abraham Lincoln is one of us."

Mayor Wilder, taking note of the hapless protesters, proclaimed, "Times marches on, and leaves many in its wake. But that wake lessens with the passing of the years."

Trying to prove him wrong, unreconstructed Southerners massed in force the next afternoon for a march honoring Confederate Heritage and History Month. At least, they massed in such force as they can muster in today's South. Led off by a platoon of bikers with rebel flags fixed to their Harleys, an estimated 1,500 to 1,800—many of them decked out in butternut Confederate uniforms and mushroomlike black hoop skirts of mourning—paraded past the Confederate tributes on Monument Avenue and wound their way toward an afternoon of glum festivities at Hollywood Cemetery. Intended as a show of defiance, the spectacle ended up highlighting the marginality of those few remaining white Southerners who continue to cling to the South's racial and cultural (and largely fictional) past. Lined up sparsely along the parade route, both black and white spectators found themselves more amused than offended by the procession. "Kill the time machine!" bellowed one unimpressed Richmonder.

The time machine of Confederate nostalgia, and old-style Yankee paranoia, is certainly headed for the grave. But there is still one arena where white solidarity prevails in the South to an extraordinary degree: politics. If there is a "race problem" in Southern politics, it has pretty much everything to do with whites. (The pundits have that right, at least.) Since the Voting Rights Act "normalized" Southern elections, two things have distinguished Southern politics from what's practiced in the rest of the country: the sheer voting muscle of African Americans and the unparalleled tendency of white people, especially in Deep South states like Mississippi and South Carolina, to vote in counterblocs almost as solid. While 90 percent of Southern blacks voted for John Kerry in 2004, right in line with African Americans elsewhere, 70 percent of whites went with George W. Bush—way out of whack with the rest of the country. While 75 percent of black Southerners say they are Democrats, only 33.5 percent of whites identify with the party. Forty-six percent of white Southerners call themselves conservatives—and 19 percent liberal—while blacks are considerably more likely to call themselves liberal or moderate.

Nowhere in the country do blacks and whites vote so differently, especially in federal elections. But when it gets down to issues, the gulf mostly disappears. Black Southerners are more liberal than white Southerners when it comes to economic questions, but a strong majority of whites support the same populist and interventionist policies. While 67 percent of whites believe government should be spending money to improve people's standards of living, 89 percent of blacks agree. Similarly, 67 percent of whites favor government action to reduce inequities in wealth—along with 78 percent of Southern blacks. Sixty-four percent of whites say government spends too little on education, compared to 83 percent of blacks. They agree that too little is spent on Social Security, too little on crime. And too little on health—according to 75 percent of Southern whites and 85 percent of blacks. Yet, while the government should be spending more, according to Southerners, it should also be restricting more: banning gay marriage (say 65 percent of Southern whites and 70 percent of blacks) and abolishing affirmative action (90 percent of whites and 59 percent of blacks). Blacks are nearly as conservative as whites on most social issues. One of the few on which black and white Southerners disagree, in fact, is capital punishment, which most blacks (54 percent) oppose, while most whites (54 percent) support.

All of which means that issues, as they're commonly understood, are not at the root of the way blacks and whites vote in Dixie. Southern blacks and whites share an ideology—or, at least, a similar mix of liberal and conservative viewpoints—but they make their political calls on drastically different grounds and with vastly different historical frameworks. While Southern blacks tend to overlook their qualms about Democrats on "moral" issues and vote on the basis of kitchen-table economics and post-1964 loyalty, white Southerners tend to exemplify the phenomenon chronicled by Thomas Frank in

What's the Matter with Kansas?: middle Americans voting against their economic interests.

This is nothing new. For business boosters in the South, the passive fealty of white workers to their white masters has always been a key selling point for Northern investors. The great *Atlanta Journal-Constitution* editor Ralph McGill quotes one such pitch from an "industrial promoter" in his 1963 book, *The South and the Southerner*: "The white laboring classes here are separated from the Negroes . . . by an innate consciousness of race superiority. This excites a sentiment of sympathy and equality on their part with the classes above them and in this way becomes a wholesome social leavener." And a guarantee, too, of political solidarity—a "coalition of the rich and the credulous," as W. J. Cash put it.

For almost one hundred years, Southern whites had consistently backed Democrats to ensure Jim Crow's continued reign, preventing most Southern states from having anything resembling competitive party politics. "The destruction of the normal party system," wrote W. J. Cash in *The Mind of the South*, "signalizes the completion of the divorce from what I have called a part of the proper business of politics—that is, the resolution of the inevitable conflict of interest between the classes, and the securing of a reasonable degree of social equity—and the arrival of the final stage of that irresponsibility which had belonged to the politics of the Old South." Dixie's racial politics precluded the development of a healthy class politics, making it easy to avoid close scrutiny of economic issues when it came time to vote. Voting became for many white Southerners an expression of cultural unity—of racial unity, before civil rights, and more recently of moral and "patriotic" unity.

Even as their racial views have liberalized, white Southerners' bloc-voting habit has died hard in the past four decades—partly because it has always involved something beyond race. "Southern white identity was created out of conflict with the North," said Alabama native Sheldon Hackney, former chairman of the National

Endowment for the Humanities. "It was a social construction invented to fashion a consciousness of commonality among whites living in a slave society and therefore affected by the antislavery movement," despite the fact that fewer than one-third of Southern families owned slaves. "Thus was invented a mythological people whose mission was to protect a besieged social order."

This sense of siege still courses powerfully through the cultural veins of many native white Southerners. One reason is the ghostly flare-ups of old times not forgotten—such as the Confederate flag tussles of the 1990s and early '00s. The rebel flag first rose again in the South in an outbreak of viral nostalgia following the *Brown v. Board of Education* shocker in 1954. Far removed from that time of racial panic, popular New South Democratic governors—Roy Barnes of Georgia, Dick Riley of South Carolina, and Ronnie Musgrove of Mississippi—considered the lingering Stars and Bars primarily as a brass-tacks issue: they were simply removing an impediment to the relocation of factories from tax-heavier points north. Moderate chamber-of-commerce types, a key swing vote in the suburbs like Jackson, Columbia, and Atlanta, seemed eager to support their efforts to dispatch the Confederate flag.

Black voters, the majority of Democrats in all three states, were assumed to have a deep stake in the issue. Many did. But many others did not get quite so fired up about the issue as white people, most of whom claimed they were simply honoring their "heritage" rather than asserting white supremacy. In Mississippi, black turnout for the 2001 flag referendum was one-half that in the 1999 gubernatorial election. In South Carolina, an NAACP-backed effort to remove the battle flag roused significant numbers of African Americans; an estimated fifty thousand turned out for an anti-flag rally in Columbia. But whites voted in greater numbers, and they voted overwhelmingly to keep the flag, business interests be damned. In Georgia, the legislature changed the flag without a referendum, infuriating enough folks to cost Barnes his reelection. Musgrove and Riley also lost. As historian James C. Cobb wrote, "Power over the past, after all, is but a reflection of power over the present."

Part of the problem, some progressives felt, was the defensive and bloodless way in which flag reformers made their case. "They didn't want to talk about the symbolism, about the pain being symbolized for many people," said Willie Legette of the campaign in South Carolina. "They wanted to talk about how it was good for business. They weren't trying to do right by black people. . . . They were just trying to bring in more money and jobs."

It was much the same in Georgia and Mississippi. "They tried to trick it past the voters," reported Donna Ladd. "The way they ran the campaign was that they were trying very hard not to offend. It was all about business. They were afraid. They should have used morality and religion and storytelling—go right into it." It's possible that the direct approach wouldn't have been enough to carry the referendum, Ladd said, but it would have prompted some honest and sorely needed debate.

In Mississippi, Musgrove's Republican challenger in 2003, the former Washington super-lobbyist and RNC chairman Haley Barbour, appeared publicly with the Council of Conservative Citizens, a white supremacist group descended from the White Citizens Councils, and then refused to denounce the group's views (which, among other things, equate blacks with "apes" and accuse immigrants of turning America into a "slimy brown mass of glop"). Like his hero, Ronald Reagan, Barbour talked like a racial moderate while symbolically demonstrating his fidelity to white privilege. "I'd love to hear a Democrat, in our state, say to people, 'They're assuming you're racist. Can you believe that?'" Ladd said. "Put it out there. I wouldn't be surprised if we'd start to see much less Southern strategy rhetoric after that."

In his March 2008 speech on race and religion addressing the controversy over "anti-American" remarks by his pastor, the Reverend Jeremiah Wright, Barack Obama made a first tentative step toward a new racial message that might speak to whites. In his rant about white political evils and how "Hillary's never been called a nigger," Obama said, Wright had "expressed a profoundly distorted view of this country—a view that sees white racism as endemic." Instead, Obama cast racial divisiveness as "a part of our union that we have yet to perfect." He spoke with understanding of the roots of black anger like Wright's—an unusual enough thing to hear on a national political stage—but the most surprising moment came when Obama acknowledged that "a similar anger exists within segments of the white community. Most working- and middle-class white Americans don't feel that they have been particularly privileged by their race. Their experience is the immigrant experience—as far as they're concerned, no one's handed them anything, they've built it from scratch." In the face of increasing economic anxiety, these whites also "feel their dreams slipping away; in an era of stagnant wages and global competition, opportunity comes to be seen as a zero-sum game, in which your dreams come at my expense. So when they are told to bus their children to a school across town; when they hear that an African American is getting an advantage in landing a good job or a spot in a good college because of an injustice that they themselves never committed; when they're told that their fears about crime in urban neighborhoods are somehow prejudiced, resentment builds over time." Those resentments, he acknowledged, "have helped shape the political landscape for at least a generation." Obama had, of course, been forced to make the speech by the controversy over his former pastor. But, whether by choice or not, his bracing eloquence in Philadelphia offered the promise of transforming his "postracial" politics from a tactic to skirt around race to one that tackled it head-on and with extraordinary insight. These insights were often hard to hear against the static of campaign gossip and innuendo. But emerging from the wreckage of the 2008 Democratic primaries, it was a message with the potential to knock down the political walls between black and white Southerners.

★

Most Americans would be perplexed to find themselves sitting in a sunny living room in Philadelphia, Mississippi, talking about racial reconciliation with a tight-knit group of local whites and blacks. But that's because most Americans know only a couple of things about this small outpost of southeast Mississippi—neither of them suggestive of much racial harmony. Everybody knows Philadelphia as the place where, in June 1964, at the bloody dawn of the Freedom Summer, three young civil rights workers were mowed down by local Klansmen who, until 2005, escaped justice (atrocities fictionalized, with more heat than light, by the Hollywood film *Mississippi Burning*). And everybody with the smallest curiosity about politics knows that Ronald Reagan launched his 1980 general election campaign just outside Philadelphia at the annual political hoedown of white Mississippi, the Neshoba County Fair, returning to the scene of the notorious hate murders to declare in well-worn code his undying devotion to the cause of "states' rights."

"Neshoba County is the Mississippi of Mississippi," said Donna Ladd, who grew up there. With a sizable black and Chocktaw Indian population—about 30 percent each—and with only light manufacturing and the Chocktaws' Pearl River Resort casino providing jobs, Neshoba is one of Mississippi's hardest-scrabble counties outside the heavily black Delta. All of which, combined with its history, makes it nothing short of "astonishing," as Ladd said, that Philadelphia has become a model for Southern towns trying to come honestly to terms with the ghosts of racial violence that continue to haunt them, stifle them, and divide them into warring political clans.

Before the biracial Philadelphia Coalition got cranking in 2003, the events that made the town infamous had been whispered about—but rarely talked aloud about—for thirty-nine long years. One notable exception had come in 1989, when the twenty-fifth anniversary commemoration of the murders was rocked by Secretary of State

Dick Molpus, then the Democrats' fair-haired, progressive hope for governor, who gave what amounted to an official apology to the families of Michael Schwerner, James Chaney, and Andrew Goodman. "We deeply regret what happened here twenty-five years ago," Molpus said simply. "We wish we could undo it. We are profoundly sorry that they are gone. We wish we could bring them back. Every decent person in Philadelphia and Neshoba County and Mississippi feels that way." Rather optimistically, he expressed the hope that if Schwerner, Chaney, and Goodman "were to return today, they would see a Philadelphia and Mississippi that, while far from perfect, are closer to being the kind of place the God who put us here wants them to be. And they would find—perhaps to their surprise— that our trials and difficulties have given Mississippi a special understanding of the need for redemption and reconciliation."

Molpus's stirring words sounded to many like a harbinger of Mississippi's much-awaited, long-delayed "second Reconstruction," which was supposed to have commenced with civil rights. To others, Molpus sounded like just another liberal blaming white people for everything. During his campaign for governor, he promised to lift Mississippi into the New South but won too few white votes. "There are a lot of people who believe he lost the governor's race because he stood up there and said that we deeply regretted what happened," said Stanley Dearman, the longtime editor of the *Neshoba Democrat* and a founding member of the Philadelphia Coalition. "It was the first time somebody had apologized."

Some whites were not convinced that apologies were needed. The day after the event, Dearman recalled, "I went to work and had 'KKK' in spray paint on the columns of our building." That sort of thing persuaded most folks in Neshoba—and most Democratic politicians in Mississippi—to clam up again and relegate the past to the past. "It's only been since the late '90s, coming to a head with the trial of Edgar Ray Killen"—the Klan chief who organized the killings, finally convicted in 2005—"that the town has settled down and come to grips with it," Dearman said.

For blacks, including Jewel McDonald, a nurse and activist, the intervening silence was deep. Like many black families, McDonald's had been caught up in the "commotion that started in June of '64," as she called it. "I had grown up here. It wasn't the greatest place to live, but you were used to it. We lived out in the country. We farmed. We really didn't have a lot of people bothering us. But that changed over the years." She turned eighteen on June 10, 1964, and eight days later her mother and brother were savagely assaulted by Klansmen when they went to the monthly financial meeting of the Mount Zion Church, which the Klan and local authorities considered a civil rights "hot spot." (Unbeknownst to McDonald's family, the three young civil rights workers had visited the church earlier in the day.) Five nights later, the civil rights workers disappeared after being detained on a bogus traffic charge by a deputy sheriff who was in cahoots with the Klan. Forty-four days after that, their bodies were found in an earthen dam just outside Philadelphia.

"That particular Sunday, when these young men disappeared, they had come by our house," McDonald remembered. "They were looking for my mother, wanting to talk with her about the beating." That evening, "the news came on the television, they had this bulletin that these boys were missing. . . . My mother said, 'Oh my God,' and we just looked at each other and said, 'If they're missing, they're dead.'" McDonald left Neshoba County that November, bound for upstate New York with her new husband, joining the last leg of the great Northern migration of Southern blacks that had begun in the 1920s.

When McDonald returned, in 2002, to take care of her ailing mother, she joined the more recent remigration south. Surprisingly, she said she had few qualms about returning. "I didn't think about the racial thing," she said. "Never really crossed my mind. When you go away, you find there's prejudice everywhere." But even if she wasn't frightened about coming back to Neshoba, McDonald was jolted—pleasantly—by what she found. "Going to the stores and stuff and seeing different people, it was quite different from the way it was when I grew up. Then, blacks always communicated. Whites wouldn't talk to you, unless they knew you. I was a little bit surprised when I came back. 'Well, they all open the door for you. They'll say thank you.' We didn't have that before."

The Klan hasn't been heard from here in years, and the Citizens Council that sprung up in the 1960s has aged and atrophied. In 1970, when school integration came, the national media flocked to Philadelphia to watch the violence erupt; there was none. "I've often wondered," said Stanley Dearman, "how much of that peaceful transition was due to what happened in '64. I think people were ready for nothing to happen. They were ready to show they could be law-abiding Americans." Molpus's 1989 apology was another step. Then, during the fortieth anniversary of the murders, in 2004, even Republican governor Haley Barbour joined in.

"Here's this big Southern strategy guy not only acknowledging but apologizing for these murders," Ladd noted. "Right down the road from where Reagan had exemplified the whole strategy twenty-four years before that." For the outsiders in attendance, the Philadelphia Coalition printed a glossy brochure, spearheaded by local chamber of commerce president David Vowell, detailing the murders, complete with a map of local movement churches and the murder site. The chamber even offered free tours on specially chartered buses.

"We wanted to tell our own story," said local NAACP president Leroy Clemons, a founding coalition member. "We saw the change. You know, people talk about integration this and integration that, but it was one of the best things that could have happened here. People can be friends now. It's casual." The younger people are, he said, the more casual they are about it. All of which, he realized, would surprise the bejesus out of most everybody who lives elsewhere.

"I remember a group of teenagers from New York came here one time," Clemons recalled. "They asked me, said, 'Aren't you afraid to walk the streets at night?' I said, 'No, I'm more afraid of New York than I am of here!' They were just amazed. In their minds, blacks didn't walk the street at night in Mississippi."

For Clemons, it's not just Yankees who get Philadelphia and Mississippi wrong. It's also the '60s-vintage civil rights leadership, which he believes was unwilling to let go of a symbol of hate. "Every year on the anniversary of the murders, people would come into town from outside who didn't live here, speak for us, tell what a terrible place this was, and after the ceremonies were over, get back in their cars and back on their buses and leave. And the media would write what they said, because local people didn't want to talk. That's how we came up with the idea of forming the coalition. It was time for us to speak."

This kind of reconciliation process is taking place, slowly and painfully, in a handful of other Mississippi towns that became notorious for civil-rights atrocities. In Tallahatchie, the Delta county where Emmett Till was lynched in 1955, Susan Glisson, a civil rights historian who runs the William Winter Institute for Racial Reconciliation at Ole Miss, and Philadelphia Coalition members nursed along a group to save the courthouse where the famous trial took place—and to get people talking, finally, about what it all meant. "The first meeting we went to," Glisson said, "the group was all black. So the first thing we did was identify potential white allies and get them to a meeting. Then we opened it up to the community." Later, they fought over whether to call in the Reverend Jesse Jackson to help promote their effort. (They didn't.) The patience paid off. One of the state's poorest counties, Tallahatchie boasts not a single stoplight, but its biracial coalition has now created a youth center and put up markers for an Emmett Till civil rights trail.

Dearman, who had the unenviable task of integrating Neshoba's Democratic executive committee in the 1970s, believes that breaking silence across the Deep South about the enduring toll of racism will ultimately help break up the white Republican bloc. "Race is the reason the Republican Party is white," he said. "It's all got very subtle, very unspoken and unsaid. But it's still out there. The Republicans are so skilled at stirring up race without being obvious about it. But that's also because nobody's been calling them on it. The Democrats here have just tried to survive the white exodus, which has almost shaken out now. They haven't been so successful at bringing people together."

★

When Casey Hughes heard about Drinking Liberally, part of a national Internet-based effort to bring together progressives, particularly in "red" parts of the country where they're often lonely and isolated, she figured Natchez, Mississippi, was a perfect candidate. In the late 1990s, Hughes had moved back from Chicago to Mississippi's miniature version of pre-Katrina New Orleans—not only in spirit but in demographics, with nearly an even split between blacks and whites. But as in New Orleans (or Chicago, for that matter), the diversity implied by that number is deceptive. For the most part, blacks live on the east end of Natchez and whites on the west, which created a dilemma for Hughes. It wasn't that black and white liberals weren't willing to hoist a brew together. The trouble was, there was nowhere for them to comfortably do so. "Natchez is a partying town," said Hughes, "but there are black bars and white bars."

This didn't come as a total surprise. Returning to Mississippi, Hughes saw changes, but not all were positive in her eyes. "I discovered that 'Democrat' is now a euphemism for 'black.' I'd be talking about somebody and say, 'He's a Democrat,' and people would say, 'Oh, no, he's *white*.' It's not socially acceptable to be white and a Democrat." She found it a little ironic that Natchez has a "thriving and accepted gay community," while the races remained so rigidly segregated, even within the Democratic Party. Ultimately, Hughes found "a black bar in a white part of town" that was acceptable to everybody, and about thirty people came out for the first session of liberal drinking on election night 2004. Some were recent relocators to town; others were "longtime Democrats who finally came out of the closet." But after the outcome that night, the folks "crawled back in the woodwork" until the 2006 midterms reawakened their fragile sense of hope.

By then, the fifty-state strategy had begun to revive Mississippi's moribund state Democratic Party. While Democrats still win most local elections in Mississippi, and still control the state house, it's been loss after loss statewide for the increasingly black-dominated Democrats ever since Reagan's turn at the Neshoba County Fair— even though, as of 2007, the party needed only about 31 percent of white votes to win statewide elections. "Mississippi ought to be in the game," said Donna Ladd. "Mississippi ought to be taken seriously. We have such potential because of having the highest percentage of African Americans, and also having young voters who went 63 percent for John Kerry in 2004"—one of the highest margins in the country among under-thirty voters. (A large majority of young whites also supported Obama in the 2008 Mississippi primary.) "The problem is that so many people don't vote. We ought to be beating the street for votes."

That's what Rita Royals, a forty-seven-year-old native of mostly white northern Mississippi, and DeMiktric "Mike" Biggs, a twenty-six-year-old computer whiz from a small black town on the Gulf Coast, were hired by the Democrats to do. Like many progressive whites in the South, Royals was stirred from a long political slumber by 9/11, Iraq, and the 2004 election. A former rape-crisis-center director, she said, "I had been a Democrat all of my life and I had not really paid much attention to what had happened to the party. I went to see John Kerry at Tougaloo College, the only time I think he came to

Mississippi." She found him "infinitely superior" to George W. Bush, and organized Democratic women to work for Kerry/Edwards. "I knew nothing about campaigns," she said with a laugh. "I just thought if we worked hard enough, we could get him elected." But she began to spot trouble when she drove to state headquarters to pick up yard signs. "I talked to the one half-time staff person that worked here then, and it was, 'No, we don't have any signs.' I was stunned. I finally had to buy some. When Kerry lost, I thought, 'No, this is totally wrong. The Democratic Party needs to be strong in Mississippi.'"

Royals already knew the main obstacle to reclaiming that strength: the notion that Democrats had become "the black party."

"It's a status deal," she said. "It's a country club mentality; you're in the club if you're in the Republican Party. It's not said, but it's there. I have been told, 'You need to go to the Republican Party'—not just from the white side, but also from the black side. We're not always wanted in the Democratic Party." As Royals and Biggs criss-crossed the state, working to reorganize and rekindle the state's eighty-two county organizations, they had to deal firsthand with old resentments and entrenched suspicions between black and white Democrats. "I've really had to work" to win over many black county leaders, Royals said. "There's some county chairs that won't talk to me; they'd much rather talk to Mike."

"And vice versa," Biggs said. "They'll call and ask for Rita and I'll say, 'She's not in—can I help you with something?' I've gotten pretty good with voices, and I'll know it's a county chair. They'll say, 'Uh, no . . . I'll try back shortly.' And when they do, they'll talk with her and we'll find out they wanted a list or something that I was eventually going to have to help them with anyway."

Beginning in the 1970s, Mississippi Democrats had been split by race into two different parties—a fissure far deeper than in most of the South. For years, there were black and white cochairs statewide,

and many counties had exclusively black or white executive committees. The divisions stemmed from the 1960s, when most whites who'd
historically dominated the party refused to accept black Democrats
into the fold—a refusal symbolized by the standoffs over delegations
at the national conventions in '64 and '68.

Freedom Democrats, an "alternate" delegation made up of blacks
and whites, demanded admittance to the 1964 Democratic
Convention in Atlantic City, New Jersey, with Fannie Lou Hamer
famously testifying about being pulled from a bus in Mississippi and
beaten for trying to assert her rights. On the convention floor, locked
arm in arm with other Freedom Democrats, was Emma Sanders,
grandmother of the current Democratic executive director in
Mississippi. She had believed, before she found herself forcibly
thrown off the convention floor amid the threats of a white mob, that
the national Democrats and President Johnson would "do what was
right." Instead, "they tried to break us." They didn't. "We were more
determined than ever to become involved in the process," Sanders
said. "We came back and worked hard to get the Democratic nominee elected, so they could not say we were disloyal to the party. But
the regular Democratic Party was not ready to accept us. Blacks were
not allowed to run for office at all, you know."

Until Sanders herself ran, that is. "In 1966, I filed suit against the
state of Mississippi to get myself on the ballot," running for
Congress against segregationist John Bell Williams. Three other
blacks joined her on the ballots that year. Sanders received numerous
threats throughout the campaign, and once had her car chased by
the Klan. She and the other black candidates lost, but, "We ran
strong, and that was a revelation. The year after, in 1967, we were
able to elect blacks in local elections."

Today, Mississippi has more African American elected officials
than any other state. Yet by the mid-1990s, the Democrats were stumbling, losing the big statewide elections with some regularity. "The

party was broke, in more ways than one," Sanders said. "When things like that happen, you go to the person you can depend on who won't require pay!" That was her. When she volunteered to run the party, Sanders found the Democrats had "a little over one hundred dollars" in the bank. "We started pulling it back up," with fund-raisers and a bit more attention to the needs of the long-neglected county parties.

The paid staffers of today run into the same old obstacles, but they are finally able to clear many of them. There are still a handful of counties where whites and blacks won't meet together. Royals and Biggs have, at times, had to resort to sneakiness. "You may have a committee where only blacks usually show up, or only whites," said Biggs. "But what has happened, as we've traveled and done trainings, is that the county chairs will agree to have the meeting not realizing what's going to happen when we invite everybody from our database. . . . You'll have them all show up at the county courthouse—everybody meets in the courthouse—and things go surprisingly fine."

By 2007, all but a few counties were meeting regularly, with "the black-white thing," as Biggs called it, no longer cleaving them apart. That spring, there was another healthy sign of progress: Democracy for America, the progressive group spawned by Howard Dean's campaign that trains candidates and activists across the country, held a training weekend in Pearl, Mississippi. Ninety-one people showed up, the largest crowd ever for a DFA training. Better yet, the crowd was equal parts black and white, with folks blending familiarly as they learned about "persuadable voters," targets, and Democratic Performance Indexes. But throughout the weekend, racial issues kept cropping up—with the trainers at a loss about how to respond.

At one point, a cigar-chewing older white man, named Albert Gore Jr., raised his hand and declared, "I left here in 1954 not intending to return to Mississippi," referring to the white supremacist organizing and violence that broke out after *Brown v. Board of*

Education and alienated moderate white folks like Gore. But he then proceeded to ask a question that stiffened the spines of the black Democrats in the room. Referring to a candidate he was supporting for supervisor in his mostly black district of Smallville, he asked, "Is it true that the people in that district already know who's going to be elected?" It was the kind of conspiratorial thinking that the black-white political divide had created. But when local radio host and civil rights advocate Renee Shakespeare started to set him straight, the DFA trainers swiftly intervened. "That's not something we can help you with," one of them said, briskly moving on.

Later, in a "developing a message" breakout session with advertising whiz John Rowley of Nashville, the subject reared up again as folks watched a series of commercials designed to speak to Southern Democrats. In one, Louisiana state senate candidate Nick Gautreaux was featured, casually dressed, in his "office."

"I work in my truck," he declared, as the message flashed on screen: "One of us—Nick Gautreaux." Shakespeare raised her hand. "In the African American population of the South, when you say 'one of us,' what that means is 'one of them.'" Rowley quickly moved on to the next ad. During a break, Shakespeare said, "My cousin moved down from Detroit a couple of years ago, and he was talking about dumb Southerners this, dumb Southerners that. I said, 'You better understand that people are not stupid here; they're savvy. You start talking to them like you do and they'll turn your head around so fast you won't know what's happened.'"

The kind of healing that Mississippi Democrats need doesn't happen overnight. In one striking example, the majority-black state executive committee voted to disqualify longtime state insurance commissioner George Dale from seeking reelection on the grounds that he publicly supported George W. Bush for president in 2004. Challenged in court, the decision was nullified, but Dale lost in the Democratic primary. The attempt to force conservative whites off the ballot was seen as a strong-arm tactic by black Democrats hoping to brush aside the few remaining vestiges of the old Mississippi party.

So was a lawsuit, instigated by Delta "party boss" Ike Brown, that ended up mandating partisan registration in Mississippi as of 2008. Conservative whites who had continued to call themselves "Democrats" without having to actually declare it on a registration form would now be forced to decide where their allegiances fell— which may, in the short term, mean even fewer white Democrats statewide. But it could also portend the removal of the most stubborn impediments to a party with a stronger, more coherent, and more progressive message that might increasingly appeal to younger white Mississippians for whom the racial past is, quite literally, history.

Ladd is looking forward to a future in which Democrats like Musgrove, the party's candidate for U.S. Senate in 2008, no longer waver and waffle over such issues as the Confederate flag. "We see him support the flag change, and then weasel around it. We see a party that is too weak and too scared. They won't step up and be strong." But Republicans, she said, "play to white people's worst instincts. And if you don't want to play that game, so often our young people feel like there's no place for them here. The Republicans are so dominant, culturally as well as politically. So as soon as they graduate, they're going to leave. It's almost part of the game."

It wouldn't take a whole lot of white votes in Mississippi to change the game completely. "When you think about it that way, it shows the potential," said Ladd. But it also shows the depth of the racial divisions in the state when you consider how rarely that 31 percent threshold is achieved. In the 2007 statewide elections, Democrats barely held on to their once-huge advantage in the state house. They lost the state senate and most statewide offices (with predominately white candidates), and Barbour won reelection with 59 percent—including more than 80 percent of the white vote. Tellingly, black turnout was low. The Republicans' "biggest goal has always been to divide," said Ladd. "They've succeeded for so long because there just weren't enough white people who said no, who would just draw the line in the sand."

That, Ladd thinks, is changing—and she is part of the change, the progressive white youngster who goes off for an education, starts her career, and comes back home. When she has been invited to speak to mostly white groups in Jackson, Ladd said she loves to start by saying, "I left the South and got to New York and learned that racism is everywhere." That opener, she said, warms things up: "You can watch the shoulders relax about an inch or two. Everyone's surprised. They think they're going to get a liberal lecture. And then I say, 'But that doesn't excuse racism anywhere. It doesn't make any difference in what we still have to do.'"

6

BIG BANG

"I'm 'overqualified' for everything. I can't find a job in
this town. There's nothing here. Not if you're legal. I've
been paying into this system since I was fourteen years old.
I can't get insurance. I can't get health care."

—ROBIN LOWE, Morristown, Tennessee, 2007

IF DEMOCRATS CAN'T put a dent in the political potency of
white Southern Republicanism, demographics soon enough will.

From 1990 to 2005, the white population percentage fell in every
Southern state but West Virginia (the region's only state to become
more homogeneous, partly because of its sagging economy). In
Georgia, the drop was especially dramatic—from more than 70 percent white to less than 60. Over the next few decades, large swaths
of the South will become minority white, as the state of Texas
already is. One result: the Democrats' "threshold" of white votes
needed to win statewide will fall steadily—at the same time that a
new generation of more progressive whites displaces the '60s backlash generation.

The stark bifurcations of racial politics—and the identities of the
major parties as "black" and "white"—will inevitably erode in the
emerging "Global South." The question is whether Democrats can
(or will) develop a message that appeals to the three groups of
newcomers reshaping the political landscape of Dixie—remigrating
blacks, non-native whites and, most of all, Hispanic immigrants.

The reverse exodus of blacks, which began with Southern integration and the decline of Rust Belt manufacturing jobs in the Northeast in the 1970s and accelerated in the 1990s, is a clear boon to Democratic prospects. The nation's largest outflows of African Americans are from such non-Southern cities as New York, Chicago, Los Angeles, and San Francisco; the fastest-growing black populations are in such Southern metropolises as Orlando, Dallas, Charlotte, and Atlanta. While some of the remigration has been explained as a generational phenomenon (children, like Jewel McDonald in Mississippi, coming home to care for elderly parents) or pure economics, there has also been a significant warming trend in black Southerners' feelings toward the region.

In 1964, a survey found that only 55 percent of blacks in Dixie felt kindly toward "Southerners," as opposed to almost 90 percent of whites. By 1976, the proportion of blacks with positive attitudes about Southerners had risen to 80 percent, almost the same as among whites. In the earlier study, concluded Southern sociologist John Shelton Reed and political scientist Merle Black, "many Southern blacks may have been unclear about whether the category [Southerners] was meant to include them and their black friends and neighbors." After all, the word "Southerner," both inside and outside the region, had always been used to refer to whites (and all too often still is). But "by the 1970s, it appears, many Southern blacks did understand themselves to be Southerners, and they were not unhappy about it." By the start of this decade the percentage of blacks in the South who identified themselves culturally as "Southern" was actually higher than that of whites.

Joining the incoming blacks have been greater numbers of white "relocated Yankees" moving south for better jobs, lower taxes, and tree-strewn subdivisions. Georgia, Florida, and North Carolina had the nation's highest rates of domestic in-migration in the 1990s—a sea change in a region that historically attracted the fewest out-of-staters. Unlike the black remigrants, most of the white transplants are either Republicans or independents, and they have helped bolster GOP performance in the suburbs and cities. But they are also, by and large, a different breed of Republican. Uncomfortable both with the remaining vestiges of race-baiting and with the right-wing excesses of the evangelicals who control county and state Republican parties in much of the South, "They're people who are more willing in federal elections to vote for a Democrat," said North Carolina state chairman Jerry Meek. In 2000, an exit poll in his state showed that among people who had moved there in the previous decade, a plurality were Republicans—but 56 percent had voted for Al Gore. "Maybe it's because they didn't have exposure to the Southern strategy, or that they didn't grow up in a climate of states' rights and the federal government trying to impinge on our rights," Meek said. "It's also a fact that they tend to be more moderate on social and cultural issues." The upshot so far is that, while Southern Republicans have seen their registration numbers inch upward, they are also heading toward an internal culture war.

While they are a minority, the white Democrats who have moved South in recent decades are also a different species. "You look at the out-of-state voters and notice that only 20 percent of them register Democratic," said Paul Luebke, a longtime progressive firebrand in the North Carolina state legislature. "Let's say for purposes of discussion that 50 percent register independent and 30 percent register Republican. But the 20 percent of immigrants are hard-line national Democrats like me. A lot of these people run around with Dennis Kucinich bumper stickers on their car. And they get into politics. The hell-raisers in the general assembly now, most of us are out-of-staters. We have pulled the agenda of the state house to the left." To illustrate the point, the legislature was voting, the day after I spoke with Luebke in March 2007, on whether to ban smoking in restaurants and bars. (The ban was narrowly defeated.) "This is North Carolina—tobacco country!" Luebke exclaimed. To have such a vote, and to be steering toward a death-penalty moratorium and state-funded elections as well, signaled the kind of progressive energy boost that the new Yankee Democrats—white and black— have brought to North Carolina and other Southern states.

The incoming population with the greatest potential to revolutionize Southern politics is also the largest and most politically unformed. Starting in the early 1990s, an exponentially multiplying number of Hispanic immigrants (mostly Mexican, Guatemalan, and Salvadoran) gravitated to the South, filling jobs in the region's booming construction industry as well as on farms, in textile and apparel factories, and in chicken- and hog-processing plants. By the late 1990s, six of the nation's seven fastest-growing Hispanic populations were Southern—and the initially small numbers were beginning to build into a decisive political force. In Florida alone, there are more than 560,000 Hispanic voters unregistered but eligible to vote. In Georgia, a 300-percent rise in the 1990s pushed the state's official Latino population to 423,000 by the 2000 census—with demographers saying the real number was closer to 1 million. By 2005, Georgia was officially 9 percent Latino; as of 2004, Hispanic babies were accounting for 12.6 percent of all births in the Peach State. (Between 2000 and 2003, the number of Hispanic births grew at least 40 percent in five other Southern states—Kentucky, South Carolina, Alabama, Tennessee, and Arkansas.)

The political fallout from this demographic Big Bang—a region so long characterized by its black-white "color line" rapidly turning multiracial—will be immense, of course. Democrats have long expected the Hispanic population surge, all across the country, to help them build a new national majority. But Southern Hispanics— many of whom are as deeply religious and socially conservative as both white and black Southerners tend to be—will take some serious cultivating. In 2004, the majority voted for George W. Bush, who had long wooed Latino voters as governor of Texas; in 2006, with the Republican National Committee airing anti-immigration ads in several Southern states and most leading Democrats favoring (however tepidly) "comprehensive" immigration reform, 57 percent voted Democratic in the midterm congressional elections. Southern Hispanics are truly up for grabs. But neither party, for different reasons, has gotten a grip.

Up to 2006, Republican voter outreach with Hispanics, particularly in Florida and Texas, had been more expansive and effective than that of the Democrats. But the GOP has been hampered by its noisy ranks of anti-immigration activists—another source of cultural tension within the party. Democrats clearly have a historic opening with the South's emerging swing vote. But they will blow it if they keep pursuing a non-Southern strategy. "If the Democrats were to write off the South," asked Chris Kromm of the Institute for Southern Studies, "what would be the impact on the next generation of Latino voters if the party wasn't a presence in the region? For Democrats to ignore the Southern Latino voter now, with a vague plan to sweep in later and court them when they become a dominant political presence in the future, would seem like . . . an example of short-sighted thinking having long-term consequences."

The consequences would not be merely political. Hispanic immigration has spawned a growing backlash that could imperil the region's multicultural future by setting blacks against the newcomers and by rallying, one last time, the South's shrinking white majority against another perceived threat. Just as Democrats and progressives had an opportunity to help heal the South in post-civil-rights years, they can now help build a peacefully "globalized" Dixie. Or they can stand on the sidelines, as has been the party's wont, and tut-tut disapprovingly about the ugliness that might ensue.

★

"When I tell you that the area where I grew up now resembles Tijuana more than the U.S.—well, hang on, you're about to see what I mean." Theresa Harmon, Tennessee's most vociferous anti-immigration organizer, had just picked me up on a sweltering August afternoon in 2006, straight from work at a local construction firm, in her red '86 Mercury Cougar—a "kicker," she called it fondly, apologizing for the lack of air-conditioning. "Bless your heart—I'm used to the heat," she said, talking a mile a minute as she puffed a Misty long and nosed into rush-hour traffic, headed for the south Nashville neighborhood where she grew up. "I mean, who would ever have thought Nashville would be an illegal alien magnet?" she said in a booming drawl. "Nashville!"

In fact, the country-music capital has—"practically overnight," in the eyes of natives like Harmon—morphed into what one reporter dubbed "a new Ellis Island," the unlikely symbol of America's biggest refugee and immigrant resettlement since the Industrial Revolution. Music City has ranked first among U.S. metropolises in the number of foreign newcomers since 1990. Many immigrate legally, including the largest cluster of Kurdish refugees in the country. But like the rest of Tennessee, Nashville also ranks high as a destination for undocumented Hispanics—and that's what has turned it into a symbol of something else: the new nativism gathering force across the South and threatening to spawn a whole new, highly emotional, strain of racial politics.

"The Kurds are the nicest people you'd ever want to meet," Harmon said. "A lot like the Hispanic folks we've had here for a long time. Real good people. They came here legally, they respect the law, and they want to fit in, to be Americans." Not the new ones. "Sadly, I've gotten to where I can look at a row of houses now and say, 'They're legal—they're illegal.' Simply because the ones that are legal tend to take that pride of place. The illegals? They don't give a rat's hind end about being a U.S. citizen. They're here because they want money, and that's it. They brought their chickens-in-the-yard culture over here with them. You see ten cars parked in the front yard, where you used to see flower beds."

Harmon had known some of those flower beds for decades. "My neighborhood is gone," Harmon sighed, steering down a winding hill through her old haunts. "I can't read the signs because I don't speak Spanish—*in my native country*!" As she turned onto the heavily trafficked business artery of Murfreesboro Road, Harmon pointed out the evidence right and left: "Just look: Everything for blocks is either a check-cashing place, a payday loan, or something Mexican. I don't know what the deal is with *that* one," she said, pointing a burgundy fingernail at a Dry Cleaners USA sign, festooned in stars and stripes, that had been hung upside-down by its new owners. "I can tell you what was in every one of these buildings until about five years ago. Some of them have been here since I was a child. Right there was my dentist office," she said, indicating a Western Union sign. "Now if it's not for rent, it's got a Mexican sign on it."

Like the anti-immigration hysteria that erupted in 1980s California, the new Southern nativism is fueled by deeply personal emotions—including, but far from limited to, a reaction against another diminution of white privilege. Many of the new nativists simply can't stand to see their hometowns transformed "overnight," especially when so many of the new immigrant destinations are places that had always been black and white, and had generally come to a wary peace about that. In northern Virginia's Prince William County, the Hispanic population doubled between 2000 and 2006, to nearly seventy thousand, with whites suddenly no longer the majority. The rapidity of change, in places so long largely static, led many folks (mostly, but not exclusively, white) to band together with other worried and overwhelmed natives, sometimes joining a state or local group like the one Harmon formed in 2001: Tennesseans for Responsible Immigration Policy (TnRIP), now her state's biggest anti-immigration group. In northern Virginia, attempts to build (and fund) day-labor centers for undocumented immigrants have been flash points for nasty spats that spill over into local politics. Controversies over drivers' licenses and crowded schools and hospitals became hot campaign issues in Florida, Georgia, North Carolina, and post-Katrina New Orleans.

For Harmon, and for many Southerners overwhelmed by the changes wrought by immigration, it was culture shock that led to political action. But like many nativist leaders in the South, she is hardly a walking, talking backlash cliché—nor a hardcore racist. Harmon, who as a teenager cruised south Nashville with a big gold marijuana leaf decal on the back of her Camaro ("it matched"), has always had a rebellious streak as wide as Tennessee. She fell in love with activism in 1999 in a successful challenge to a new uniform policy at two of her (three) children's public schools. "I saw uniforms and I immediately thought about little Nazi kids in Hitler's Germany," she said. She staunchly opposed the Iraq War. ("How many kids did we have killed today for no good reason? Get. Them. Home.") She believed George W. Bush's presidency had "done more damage than Bill Clinton and every president before him could have even *thought* about doing. It's all about corporations. They run this country, and they run the world." In her view, opposition to illegal immigration was perfectly consistent with these liberal beliefs. "This immigration is driven by corporations who want more workers to exploit," she said. "It's killing working-class people, especially black folks. You can't *tell* me there's not a problem that needs solving here."

With Congress unable to pass meaningful immigration reform, it's been left to states like Tennessee to try—often clumsily—to deal with the practical and social impacts. The most onerous restrictions have been passed in Georgia, where the legislature voted in 2006 to prevent almost all undocumented people from receiving a wide range of social services. Most Southerners in states with high levels of immigration, however, have seen the issue become a political football—but not one that either party wants to kick too hard, in either direction. Ultimately, most Republicans as well as Democrats recognize that Hispanics will soon become less of a political piñata and more of a prized political constituency. So while Harmon had shepherded TnRIP to more than three thousand members by 2006, with initial organizing help from FAIR, the Federation for American Immigration Reform, she found that the Tennessee legislature, campaign-season pandering aside, was not willing to embrace staunch anti-immigration politics.

Though a minority of Southerners—46 percent—say that illegal immigrants are "a burden on our country," most of them say that immigrants "threaten traditional American customs and values." Harmon noted with alarm the mounting level of frustration among her fellow activists as Congress continued to fumble the issue. "I'm starting to hear things that I wasn't hearing before, from people I always considered reasonable. The most popular formula is, 'soapbox, ballot box, ammo box.' They'll X out the first two, like those options are gone now and all you can do is arm yourself and get ready. I'm looking at that going, 'Phew! It's going to get ugly.'"

It already has. There has been relatively little anti-immigrant violence documented thus far—with some ignoble exceptions, like the Ozark factory town of Rogers, Arkansas, where police officers and unaccountable locals terrorized immigrants for much of the 1990s. But there have been outbreaks of anti-Hispanic hate crimes in Georgia, Tennessee, and Arkansas, and troubling incidents of black-Hispanic violence in urban areas like Jacksonville, Florida, and Durham, North Carolina. Meanwhile, a whole new rhetoric of hate was being imported from the old Western outposts of anti-immigrant organizing. In April 2006, in an old factory complex converted into swank suburban shopping digs in the Nashville suburb of Franklin, more than a thousand Tennesseans came out to cheer their hero, 99.7 FM drive-time host Phil Valentine. The son of a former Democratic congressman in North Carolina, Valentine is the king of Nashville talk and the leading voice—and instigator—of the nativist blowback spreading across Tennessee. "Everywhere you go in this state," said Stephen Fotopulos, policy director for the Tennesseans for Immigrant and Refugee Rights Coalition (TIRRC), "you run into people with their Phil Valentine talking points." Day after day on his three-hour call-in show, Valentine beats the drums of nativism—hard. "Wake up and smell the tacos," he likes to say, flaunting his political incorrectness for thousands of delighted loyalists. On *The Phil Valentine Show*'s Web site, an even more stunningly offensive image materialized in 2006: a full-color image of the Statue of Liberty, sporting a festive sombrero, with a huge black mustache, a jar of salsa instead of a flame, and a bottle of Patrón cradled in her lower hand. Liberty tottered on a foundation of Chiclets, Tostitos, and a Taco Bell sign.

All in all, it was a lot like the "joke" that slipped out of Valentine's mouth at the "town hall meeting" in Franklin, where three Republican state legislators joined him on stage. Susan Tully, FAIR's field director, was talking about the border patrol's "catch-and-release" policy, saying that illegal immigrants were returned the first time they were caught, the second time, the third time . . . all the way to seven times. And what, Tully asked rhetorically, do we do the eighth time?

"Shoot 'em!" Valentine interjected. The white suburbanites roared their approval.

Two months later, in his nondescript studio on Nashville's Music City Circle (not quite Music Row, but getting there), Valentine didn't miss a beat when asked about his incendiary comment. "I just said that as an icebreaker and as a joke," he said. "I'm not advocating seriously that we shoot anybody. It's just the frustration level."

That frustration level had reached fever pitch in the spring of '06. First, more than ten thousand Hispanics marched in the largest demonstration in Nashville history—with smaller but impressive marches in several other towns and cities across the state—protesting draconian immigration-reform proposals in Congress. Then came the "Day Without Immigrants" boycott on May 1, when more than twenty thousand Hispanics in Tennessee stayed home from work.

"I've talked to people who said that before the protests they were just sitting on the sidelines," Valentine said, "but now they are incensed. They see that these people are carrying Mexican flags, they don't speak English—they are in your face. And people think, 'You are in my country and if you don't want to be here, get out.' People are more attuned to what the problem is." And more of them tune into your show? I asked. Valentine pleaded innocence. "If I try to get away from it, because we've just been beating it to death, I can't, because the listeners still want to talk about it," Valentine said. "The switchboard just lights up and there we go."

Like most of his fellow nativists, Valentine professed to be rankled at being considered a neo white supremacist. "The nastiest stuff I get is from the other side, with people just infuriated because they think I'm a racist," he said with mock surprise. "Nothing could be further from the truth. I have no problem with Hispanics in general. My problem is with illegal immigration." But Valentine's show was serving up the whole unsavory menu of nativist arguments, conspiracy theories, and new urban myths—many of them borrowed from Lou Dobbs's popular nightly festival of immigration horrors on CNN. As Valentine wrote in a Web column, "I've talked until I was blue in the face about the spread of TB and other diseases; about criminal elements of illegal immigration like the terrorist gang MS-13; about the immense costs associated with illegal immigration; the decay of large swaths of America." Did he believe there is an organized effort here—that there's a *reconquista* afoot? "Oh, absolutely," he told me. "Not with all of them, but with many of them. I think there's a plan to move Hispanics into the Southwest and vote it back to Mexico. I think there's a big plan to do that. They are nuts. This is the United States of America. We can't change that!"

Nor should we have to, Valentine insisted. "A lot of these people who are illegal want to come and plant their culture inside of ours," he said. "They're going to continue to speak Spanish, they're going to continue all the things they did back in a third-world country. I'll give you one example: In many parts of Mexico, it is customary when you go to the bathroom not to put your toilet paper down the toilet, because of the septic system. You either throw it on the floor, or throw it in the trash. So if you go into places and see a piece of used toilet paper—well, you know that's somebody who that was their culture. Well, we don't do that in America. We're not a third-world country, and I would think that's why you're thrilled to be here."

Then again, Valentine didn't put much stock in the adaptability of white Southerners, either. "We're having to, now, speak Spanish, and try to understand them," he complained. "We've never had to understand anybody."

★

When Democratic governor Phil Bredesen grumbled, during his successful reelection campaign of 2006, that Tennesseans were being whipped into a "frenzy" over immigration, some took issue with the culprits he cited—opportunistic Republican candidates—but not a soul could challenge the accuracy of his description. From formerly homogeneous factory towns in the big green hills of eastern Tennessee to formerly biracial Memphis in the west, the topic of the day—often the only topic—is what to do about Tennessee becoming what Theresa Harmon calls a "magnet" for illegal immigrants. The transformation began in the 1990s, when a small immigrant population multiplied 278 percent, and the pace hasn't slackened as the numbers have grown.

With large-scale immigration no more familiar to most Tennesseans than to most Kentuckians or Arkansans, there was bound to be serious friction. It broke out politically in 2001, when Tennessee became the first state to grant driver's licenses to undocumented residents. The legislative battle over licenses stoked increasing fears among many natives that the already-brisk migration into Tennessee, which had accelerated toward the end of the '90s, would just keep picking up steam. "If you make yourself a welcome wagon for immigrants, you'll get plenty," said Donna Locke, a former liberal "child of the '60s" who heads Tennesseans for Immigration Control and Reform. "That's certainly what Tennessee did."

The driver's license issue, which has also fueled anti-immigration organizing in Georgia and Virginia, became the focal point for Tennessee's immigration debates. Anti-immigrant sentiment started to crest after the license bill was signed into law. And then came 9/11. "That's when it all changed here," said David Lubell, the director of TIRRC, a statewide coalition of immigrant rights groups. "They started to talk about 'driver's licenses for terrorists.' Nativist sentiments really began to harden and, unfortunately, spread." (Bredesen changed the licenses to certificates in 2004, bowing to popular pressure, and suspended the program altogether early in 2006 after federal investigators found that busloads of immigrants from other states were getting Tennessee certificates.)

Activist groups on both sides have grown in size and sophistication since that first eruption. But in the state legislature, the upper hand has usually gone to the immigration rights folks, backed by chambers of commerce and a reasonably united Democratic state house majority. TIRRC's Stephen Fotopulos said that pro-immigrant groups fended off twenty-two of twenty-three "reform" bills in 2006. Still, that tally alone showed how much supporters of immigrant rights were on the defensive. (Nationally, more than 1,562 immigration-related bills were filed in state legislatures in 2007 alone.) Fotopulos admitted that "some bills we beat because both Republican and Democratic legislators are jockeying to commandeer the issue and don't want to give each other the political victory."

Above the level of state legislative races, nobody has yet won a Southern election by running against immigrants. With many evangelicals sympathetic to the newcomers, and with big business Republicans generally content with the inflow of cheap, unorganized labor, immigrant bashing is not even a guaranteed winner in

Republican primaries. But that didn't stop Tennessee Republicans, in 2006, from trying mightily to turn their races into referenda on immigration reform. In the hottest race statewide, to replace retiring GOP senator Bill Frist, the three Republican contenders spent much of the primary campaign honing their Wyatt Earp imitations. One of them, former state representative Ed Bryant, got so carried away that he lit out for the border at one point, local TV news crew in tow, to spend time helping the Minuteman Civil Defense Corps splice together a border fence. Frequent use of the term "illegals" became, in classic Southern political code, a new shorthand for a "one of us" Republican.

But the Democrat in the Tennessee Senate race, Congressman Harold Ford Jr., was not going to be "out-illegaled," any more than that old-time Democrat, George Wallace, would let himself be "out-niggered" in the '60s. Ford, whose once-moderate voting record on immigration had hardened into pure border-warriorhood during his run-up to the election, began the effort with a series of radio ads in the summer, targeted to right-wing and black stations alike, making it clear that he would not concede the anti-immigration vote. "Every day over fifty-seven hundred miles of border stands unsecured," Ford intoned gravely. "Every day almost two thousand people enter America illegally. Every day hundreds of employers look the other way, handing out jobs that keep illegals coming. And every day the rest of us pay the price."

With Democrats throughout the country either defensive or chiming in with the anti-immigration chorus, the hard job of defending immigrants' rights—and easing racial resentments—has fallen mostly to groups like TIRRC, staffed (and supported through volunteer work) primarily by white and Hispanic activists. "For me, it's personal," said Rick Casares, TIRRC's outreach coordinator. "My parents were illegal immigrants from Mexico." His father eventually became mayor pro tem in the predominantly white town of Rosemead, California.

While it was ugly at times, Casares said, what his parents experienced "pales to what immigrants face today in this climate of poisonous rhetoric."

Casares's job was to "detoxify"—and the messages he and other activists have cooked up should offer clues to how the Democratic Party can ultimately help reconcile Southern natives to their new neighbors. "We're trying to highlight what we have in common, and get past the stereotypes and myths that diminish immigrants' worth," said Casares. TIRRC's myth-busting has been spread around the state by regionally-based volunteers trained to address civil and community groups, churches, and minority and business groups, through a "Welcoming Tennessee" initiative. Casares helped to create pro-immigrant billboards espousing traditional Tennessee values. The first showed two grinning children and quoted the book of Matthew: "I was a stranger, then you welcomed me." The second was a collage of images of immigrants throughout U.S. history, with the message, "Welcome the Immigrant You Once Were."

TIRRC's work to explain the economic benefits of immigration was a tougher task. "The way people get their news now," said Fotopulos, "there's no way to counter the image of a white, native-born Tennessee family killed by an illegal immigrant"—referring to a locally famous case making headlines in the summer of 2006. "It is so much harder to quantify, to get your mind around, all the benefits that would go away if these same people weren't here."

That's especially true given the gut-level nature of much anti-immigration sentiment. "It's not just about immigrants and immigration," said Devin Burghart of the Center for New Community, a national nonprofit that helped TIRRC get started. "It's about something greater—the nexus of race, national identity, who we are and who we want to be."

Carol Swain, a black conservative who studies white nationalism and teaches at Vanderbilt University in Nashville, told me that "by not thinking deeply about our immigration policies, we have created the conditions for long-term racial unrest." As the day when whites constitute a minority of the population grows nearer, she said, "white people will increasingly see themselves under attack"—particularly in the South, where folks are so accustomed to such thinking. "If I were white," said Swain, "I would be feeling a lot of fear and uncertainty. I'd want to talk about it openly, too. But you can't talk about it without being labeled a racist. That's a big reason the lure of white nationalism is so strong right now. As we dance around the real issues, ordinary people will find answers where they can." And in the multiracial South, those "ordinary people" have been hearing a new application of some age-old rhetoric. "To get a few chickens plucked," asked former Klan leader David Duke at a North Carolina anti-immigration rally in 2000, "is it worth losing your heritage?"

★

Over the Blue Ridge Mountains in Georgia, the massive Hispanic immigration began a few years earlier than it did in Tennessee, setting off nativist alarm bells with a strikingly similar clangor. At first, the resistance was scattered, mostly taking the form of police crackdowns—arresting day laborers for loitering—and scattered racial slurs and threats. Some natives were less hospitable than others. In the formerly homogeneous Atlanta suburb of Chamblee, whites began complaining as early as 1992 about the "terrible, filthy people" littering their street corners. At a town council meeting, one official suggested that residents set bear traps in their yards to keep the Hispanics at bay. Another councilman wondered aloud whether Chamblee whites should form a vigilante group to scare off the intruders. Nine years later, attitudes hadn't exactly become more neighborly. Defending a mass sweep of day laborers in 2001, Police Commissioner Wayne Kennedy explained that he was simply responding to residents' complaints of trash and urine in their yards. "I guess it's a cultural thing," said the commissioner. "Probably in Mexico urinating on the sidewalk is perfectly normal."

The Phil Valentine of Georgia is D. A. King, an ex-Marine from Marietta, a white-flight suburb just outside Atlanta. A retiree from an insurance agency, King launched the radical group American Resistance after a stint working with a state branch of FAIR in the 1990s. In 2005, King founded a new project: the Dustin Inman Society, named for a marine from Marietta who was murdered by an illegal immigrant in 2000. His "coalition of immigration crime fighters" encouraged folks to take immigration enforcement into their own hands. King became known for such stunts as turning in three undocumented immigrants, pictured on the front page of the Marietta newspaper, to U.S. Immigration and Customs Enforcement (ICE). Two months later, he was apoplectic to discover two of them still free on the streets of Marietta, "walking symbols of the anarchy that is destroying the American nation." After witnessing upwards of two thousand Hispanics marching through nearby Doraville during the 2003 Freedom Ride for Immigrant Workers, King wrote on VDARE.com, an anti-immigration hate site named for the first white child born in America, "I got the sense that I had left the country of my birth and been transported to some Mexican village, completely taken over by an angry, barely restrained mob. My first act on a safe return home was to take a shower."

María de los Remedios Gómez Arnau, Mexico's former consul general in Atlanta, said the clash was hardly surprising, especially considering that the new immigrants were as unprepared for the new realities as the natives. "We're talking about a very new immigration wave into Georgia and the South," she told me. "These are mostly people who have not been involved in traditional migrant work in the past. They're from the poorest, most rural and impoverished places in Mexico and Guatemala. And they are coming to a place where people are not familiar with migrant laborers or Hispanics." A place where, said Republican state representative Chip Rogers, a leading sponsor of the state's bills to cut "illegals" off of social services,

"Everybody had a Southern accent when I was growing up. We were part of the Old South, for better or worse. We were all the same."

Now, in the hundred-mile swath of suburbs and exurbs stretching north from Atlanta, the hills are abuzz with the sound of Hispanic construction workers building McMansion developments while—in their off-time—they're moving into the older houses of traditional small towns. Beneath the radar, a new kind of "spatial segregation" is taking hold in the South—one particularly glaring in factory towns like Dalton, an old Klan stronghold.

For anti-immigrant Republicans like Rogers, the trick is to make anti-immigration legislation sound like a matter of bottom-line common sense rather than racial ideology—much like the slow-pitching Democratic leaders who tried to push race as far away from the Confederate flag fights as possible. When it comes to immigration, however, the tactic has been working in Georgia, primarily because voters don't want to believe they are adopting a racist line. So as Rogers put it, "I don't think these folks are coming to America so they can make use of our social services, our schools, and hospitals. They're coming for work. But we can't fail to recognize what it's doing to our health-care system, our prisons, and our schools. One study showed that the state of Georgia spent $260 million to educate illegal immigrants last year."

Indeed, for most of the South's anti-immigration rabble-rousers, like Republican town council member Tom Lowe of Morristown, Tennessee, any rhetoric smacking of racism is anathema. Lowe, a wise-cracking pharmacist who has organized protests against the immigrants who have flooded his old industrial town (and once sent a fake bill for what illegal immigrants supposedly cost Morristown to the U.S. Congress), can occasionally slip up. But he insisted it's not a matter of racial animus. "There ain't no colors involved here," he told me. "No color but green, that's all. People are greedy, and they take advantage of these people. They live in squalor, fifteen to twenty to an apartment, with one bedroom between them. Meanwhile, we don't know what's coming into this country. I say we're two or three illegal aliens away from an epidemic. Kids are going to pick it up at school, take it home to their dads and moms, and you're going to have a mess. Now I wish people would think about that. My God. Nothing racist, nothing hateful, just pure a hundred percent American thinking."

With Republicans kindling such cultural, "colorblind," anti-immigrant resentments—and with Democrats doing precious little to counter them—supporters of immigration rights expect to be fighting an uphill battle for a while in Dixie. "In fifteen years," said TIRRC's David Lubell optimistically, "white and black Southerners will know Hispanics personally. The stigma will be gone."

That timeline seems awfully distant, particularly to someone like Sam Zamarripa, a former Georgia state senator who has been one of the most outspoken foes of anti-immigration legislation. People's problems with immigrants in the South are not pragmatic, he told me; they're ethnic. "The issue is that they don't want America to have any more color." Zamarripa has paid a price for such blunt talk, and for proposing driver's licenses for immigrants. "I'm watched and I'm tracked," said the senator, who inspired "Zamarripa Watch" on yet another popular anti-immigrant site, American Border Patrol. The site branded him a "Mexican agent" and "reconquista." Before he gave up politics in 2006, he received reams of threatening calls and e-mail—"love letters," he called them—from anti-immigration zealots. He read me his favorite: "My hope is that when the next terrorist attack takes place in the United States, your children will be the recipients of that terror. Yes, your children. I want you to suffer."

The peril of groups like TnRIP and the Dustin Inman Society, in Zamarripa's view, stems from the fact that "they might not be traditional hate groups like the Klan, but that's part of the appeal. They provide a safe, so-called respectable haven for hatred and bigotry"—much like the old "uptown Klan," the White Citizens councils. The "respectable" nature of anti-immigration fervor—"we don't hate anybody; we just want the law enforced"—gives it the potential to infect Southern politics with new cultural divides and codes over the next twenty years. The racial elements of the Republicans' Southern strategy have always worked best when, like "states' rights," they could be couched in such a way that voters don't have to see the white supremacy in them at all. Of course, racial appeals also work best when Democrats and liberals don't make it their business to expose the racist rot beneath the "common sense."

★

In the 2008 presidential primaries, the political emergence of a *nuevo* Dixie finally became too obvious for the Democrats to ignore—especially with key contests taking place in the rapidly "browning" states of Florida, Texas, South Carolina, Virginia, and North Carolina. The party's presidential contenders first nodded to the new reality by debating in Miami on Spanish-language television in September 2007 (though the candidates were, rather oddly, forbidden to speak Spanish). Republican-bashing was the main order of business—and important business it was, given the GOP's edge in reaching out to Hispanic voters. Senator Hillary Clinton, the early "default" choice of Hispanics, accused the GOP, along with right-wing media hate-mongers, of doing a "great disservice to our country" with their eagerness to "bash immigrants." John Edwards, reading off the old black-white script, went further by putting the blame where it patently did not belong—on President Bush, who he said "uses absolutely every tool available to him politically to divide the country," though the Hispanics listening knew full well that wasn't the case with them.

It was Senator Obama, who was just beginning to make himself known to Hispanic voters, who came up with the night's most promising rhetorical flourish, recalling a telegram once sent to Martin Luther King by César Chávez that said, in part, "Our separate struggles are one." Obama would later turn that quote into a catchphrase on his Spanish-language Web site—amigosdeobama.com—and in his worker-centered organizing efforts in Texas and Nevada. Beyond the sloganeering, Obama suggested the outlines of a political framework that could spawn a multiracial, class-based politics in the South. "That's what's been missing from presidential leadership—explaining to the American people from all walks of life that our separate struggles are one. A president has to not only speak up forcefully against anti-immigrant sentiment and racist sentiment, but also make sure that all workers are being tended to."

Unfortunately, Obama had voted—along with most Democrats—in favor of a super-expensive "fence" between Mexico and the U.S. (He deflected a question in Miami about whether the Canadian border also needed one.) The Democrats were also hamstrung, in most cases, by their nervous support for trade agreements like NAFTA and CAFTA—deals that Hispanic immigrants tend to view favorably, while their black and white working-class counterparts vociferously disagree. Even so, the debate—and Republican candidates' refusal to engage in a similar one—sent a long-overdue signal that Democrats intended to take these new voters seriously. It didn't hurt that one of the faces on stage in Miami was that of New Mexico Governor Bill Richardson, himself Hispanic, who spoke with pragmatic frankness about the "border-security" boondoggle: "If you're going to build a twelve-foot wall," he said, "you know what's going to happen? A lot of thirteen-foot ladders."

When the primaries finally commenced, there were signs that the Democrats' fledgling outreach—and the Republicans' self-inflicted nativist wounds—were starting to have an effect. Latino participation shot up, with an estimated 75 percent casting their votes in the Democratic race. The Washington-based think tank New Democrat Network, which has researched the Democratic potential of the Hispanic vote, reported the rather startling news that more Hispanics voted in the Virginia Democratic contest than in New Mexico's. Clinton, who started the campaign with a favorable reputation based on her husband's NAFTA days and garnered several endorsements from national Hispanic leaders, won most of their votes. But in Texas, where Latinos made up more than one-third of the Democratic primary turnout, Obama carried the new demographic in urban centers around Houston, Dallas, and Austin.

The attention was inevitable, of course, with four hundred thousand American-born Latinos turning eighteen and becoming eligible to vote each year. According to the Pew Center, Hispanic voters overall skew "much younger than white or black voters," reflecting the relative youth of the Hispanic population overall—and underlining the opportunity Democrats have to speak to new voters whose political loyalties are anything but set in stone. Young Hispanics were an outsized force in the immigrant marches of 2006, which made it clear that they are not reluctant to plunge into political activism. So did the Hispanic youth-fueled resurgence of labor organizing in the South, symbolized by the heated, ongoing struggles to unionize the Case Farms Poultry Plant and Smithfield Foods' meat-processing behemoth in North Carolina (efforts that have led company officials, adapting time-honored tactics, to pit black and Hispanic workers against each other).

It all sounds fairly rosy for the Democrats. But the road to a multicultural majority in the South is pocked with potholes. In the 2008 general election, the Democrats will be tangling with John McCain, another Republican presidential candidate with a claim on the Hispanic vote—courtesy of his outspoken, and politically perilous, support for "comprehensive immigration reform." Longer term, the Democrats will have to bear in mind that Hispanics represent an emerging swing vote, not an emerging bloc—particularly in Dixie.

As Republican anti-immigration rhetoric cools down by necessity, giving way to a more sophisticated and insidious use of racial code, the Democrats' best hope for wooing Southern Hispanics lies in a new political formula that could—conveniently enough—win over more white working- and middle-class voters as well. Democrats will have to take a deep breath and speak truth to the South about both the economic benefits and the moral imperatives that have accompanied the region's first massive wave of foreign immigrants. They'll need to put a contemporary spin on Tom Watson's observation that race was being used as a wedge to separate working people—black, white, and now Hispanic—from the rightful fruits of their labor. And Democrats will have to be willing, as they were not during or after Jim Crow, to confront racist sentiment in the South without a hint of superiority or paternalism—and to stake out a strong moral argument against its newest incarnation in the nativist movement.

7

GETTING RELIGION

"Every good Christian ought to kick [Jerry]
Falwell right in the ass."

—SENATOR BARRY GOLDWATER, 1981

YOU CAN USUALLY gauge the mood of a revival from the first
hymn the preacher calls. At the 2005 Reclaiming America for Christ
conference in Fort Lauderdale, where nine hundred fundamentalist
activists from forty states gathered in the mega–worship center of
Coral Ridge Presbyterian, you might have expected a praise song.
Here, after all, were the hardest of the hardcore folks behind the
nation's most feared political machine.

Just three months earlier, they—and thousands like them—had
lured, cajoled, fear-mongered, and bodily carried some 6 million
new voters to the polls. Now they were credited with returning
George W. Bush to the White House, catapulting thirty-two new pro-
lifers to Congress, glomming "marriage protection" amendments
onto eleven more state constitutions, and turning "values" into the
most pressing issue for a plurality of American voters. On a weekly
basis, their leaders—not the moderates, but fire-breathing hell-shakers
like the Reverend Richard Land of the Southern Baptist Convention—
were conference-calling with top White House officials. Their judges

were being appointed (and approved!). Their youngsters—graduates from right-wing institutions like Pat Robertson's Regent University—were the hottest hires in Washington, D.C. And in return for their electoral devotion to the GOP, they were pulling in some one hundred million dollars a year in faith-based government funds.

Long marginalized as a stock Southern stereotype, right-wing evangelicals finally held the balance of power in the nation's dominant political party. Their three-decade campaign to "Christianize" the U.S. government had succeeded in replacing racial phobias with traditionalist "values" as the prime motivator of conservative voters. Increasingly, they were not just helping to elect regular old-fashioned, pro-business Republicans, they were putting real, live "Bible-believers" into some of the highest elective offices in America. Including *the* highest.

So what did they sing? Three stadium-sized video screens flashed the old battle hymn "Soldiers of the Cross, Arise," and the overwhelmingly white, overwhelmingly fifty-plus crusaders gazed up at the words, with semi-psychedelic pinks and purples swirling behind them, and dutifully belted out: "Seize your armor, gird it on / Now the battle will be won / Soon, your enemies all slain / Crowns of glory shall you gain." Despite their unprecedented power, these fundamentalist stalwarts still saw themselves as a persecuted minority, waging a holy war "for the soul of America." They didn't know how to see it any other way.

★

For more than a quarter century, after Coral Ridge televangelist and Reclaiming America godfather D. James Kennedy helped the Reverend Jerry Falwell kick-start the Moral Majority, a constant state of siege both inflamed the rhetoric of religious right politics and lent it the urgency needed to keep the most disciplined troops in American politics on perpetual high alert. Two weeks after the movement's first major triumph, helping to elect Ronald Reagan and defeat several Washington Democrats in 1980, *Time* magazine breathlessly reported that religious right leaders were already "preparing for another assault on the liberals in 1982," drawing up a "hit list" of potentially vulnerable Democrats and riding their momentum to raise millions for negative-advertising blitzes.

The frantic, 24/7 organizing that came to characterize the movement flagged at times. In the late 1980s, the evangelical right weathered a backlash over Kennedy's, Falwell's, and other pastors' crude attacks on gay people with AIDS. At other times, particularly after Republicans nominated the relatively moderate and insufficiently pious Bob Dole in 1996, the religious right's political crusade was nearly given up for lost by the faithful. But the grassfire kept being rekindled—by Pat Robertson's stunning second-place finish in the 1988 Iowa Republican caucuses, by the Christian Coalition that rose from that campaign, by the 1994 GOP takeover of Congress. The movement reached a crescendo in 2004 during the Republicans' "seventy-two-hour campaign," which mobilized an unprecedented number of volunteers, mostly evangelical Christians, to bring out fellow believers to boost the GOP and outlaw gay marriage.

The majority of evangelicals might have been satisfied with the fruits of their efforts in 2004, but their leaders entertained higher ambitions. "Our job is to reclaim America for Christ, whatever the cost," was how Kennedy put it, in materials handed out to conference-goers. "As the vice regents of God, we are to exercise godly dominion and influence over our neighborhoods, our schools, our government, our literature and arts, our sports arenas, our entertainment media, our news media, our scientific endeavors—in short, over every aspect and institution of human society." Clearly, there was still a bit of work to do.

Like his fellow right-wing Christian activists Jerry Falwell, James Dobson, Pat Robertson, and Tim LaHaye, D. James Kennedy (who died, like Falwell, in 2007) was a Christian Dominionist, a biblical literalist who believed God had called his kind to take over the U.S. government. These Christian Reconstructionists were hardly content to turn back gay marriage and see abortion rights slowly but steadily eroded by "strict constructionist" judges. Instead, they pushed an agenda that made Newt Gingrich's Contract for America look like *The Communist Manifesto*: rewrite schoolbooks and curricula to reflect a history of America as a "Christian nation"; pack the courts with judges who follow Old Testament law; post the Ten Commandments in every courthouse; and make it a felony for gay men to have sex and women to have abortions under any circumstances. Their ultimate goal was a "faith-based" government that would endure far longer than Bush's judicial appointments—all the way till the sinners are left behind and Jesus materializes to take the reins from His regents.

"Most people hear them talk about a 'Christian nation,' and think, 'Well, that sounds like a good, moral thing,'" said the Reverend Mel White, who made films and ghostwrote books for the Reverends Billy Graham, Falwell, and Robertson before coming out as gay in the early 1990s. "What they don't know—what even most conservative Christians who voted for Bush don't know—is that 'Christian nation' means something else entirely to these Dominionist leaders. This movement is no more about following the example of Christ than Bush's Clean Water Act is about clean water."

Until Kennedy's death in 2007, the movement's infantry has received its marching orders at conferences like Reclaiming America, which attracted former vice president Dan Quayle to its 1994 inaugural. "I was afraid you would think the election settled everything," Reclaiming America executive director Gary Cass told the faithful on opening day in 2005. "We're going to turn you into an army of one." A burly ex-marine with a bushy mustache and a hawkish intensity, Cass himself rose from these pews—he was an anti-abortion activist who got fired up about running for office after a Reclaiming America experience and ended up leading an evangelical takeover of the San Diego school board. "We used to be a minority," Cass said, "and now we've got to learn to lead." Also, of course, to follow. When a military honor guard, bearing both U.S. and Christian flags, paraded solemnly into the hall, the activists stood reverently, hands over hearts, and recited the pledge of their true alliance: "To the Christian flag and to the Savior for whose Kingdom it stands. One Savior, crucified, risen, and coming again, with life and liberty for all who believe."

In between inspirational speeches by evangelical luminaries— including Congresswoman Katherine Harris of Florida, who in her whispery voice urged the Reclaimers to "win back America for God"—the activists were treated to brass-tacks training sessions on "Practical Steps to Impact Your Community with America's Historical Judeo-Christian Heritage" and "The Facts of Stem-Cell Research," the newest attempt at a "pro-life" political wedge. But as long as Bush, one of their own, held the White House, the most important marching order was to remake the federal courts in God's image.

In the Dominionist view, the Founding Fathers never intended to erect a barrier between government and religion. "The First Amendment does not say there should be a separation of church and state," declared Alan Sears, president and CEO of the Alliance Defense Fund, a team of more than one thousand attorneys trained to fight abortion, gay marriage, and "secularism" in public schools. Sears, who worked on Reagan attorney general Edwin Meese's infamous Commission on Pornography, argued that the constitutional guarantee against state-sponsored religion was actually designed to "shield" the church from federal interference—allowing Christians to take their rightful place at the head of the government.

"We have a right, indeed an obligation, to govern," agreed David Limbaugh, brother of Rush and author of *Persecution: How Liberals Are Waging War Against Christianity.* And that meant, first of all, making sure there were plenty of sitting judges who also saw it that way. "Activist judges have systematically deconstructed the Constitution," roared Rick Scarborough, Texas evangelist and author of a booklet called *In Defense of Mixing Church and State*. "A God-free society is their goal!"

Activist judges are, of course, precisely what the Dominionists want. Their model is Roy Moore, the former chief justice of Alabama who, in the summer of 2001, installed a 5,300-pound granite monument to the Ten Commandments in his state's judicial building. Moore had it wheeled into the rotunda of the venerable building, under cover of night, with a camera crew from Kennedy's *Coral Ridge Hour* TV show as his only witnesses (besides the heavy-laden workmen hauling it). A former professional kickboxer and admirer of George Wallace, Moore had been a frequent guest on the show since 1994. That's when he nailed a crude Ten Commandments plaque on the wall of his district courtroom in Gadsden, Alabama, and landed in a highly publicized spat with that all-purpose bugaboo of the evangelical right, the American Civil Liberties Union. He had run for chief justice, with financial backing from Coral Ridge, James Dobson's Focus on the Family, and Pat Robertson's Christian Coalition, promising to bring the Ten Commandments to the state Supreme Court—but he hadn't said just how.

As soon as the news got out about "Roy's Rock," busloads of church groups and Christian schools were streaming through the judicial building, many of them kneeling to pray in front of the slab (with its injunction against worshipping graven images). A federal court soon ordered Moore to remove it. When he refused, claiming Christian persecution and "judicial tyranny," thousands of Dominionists (joined by neo-Confederate activists from the League of the South and Sons of Confederate Veterans) protested around the clock, vowing to give their lives to save the monument. At last, it was hauled back out—and so was Moore, deposed by his fellow Republicans on the Alabama Supreme Court.

In his brief spell as chief justice of Alabama, Moore offered a lively demonstration of what Dominionist justice might look like. Agreeing with a majority opinion to deny a lesbian mother custody of her children, Moore penned a fiery "special concurrence" denouncing homosexuality as "an act so heinous that it defies one's ability to describe it," and declaring that the state "must" stop gay sex by using "physical penalties, such as confinement and even execution." While human-rights groups were outraged at his Taliban-like pronouncement, right-wing evangelicals hailed Moore as a hero for such principled "biblical" stands. Thrown off the bench, he toured the nation's religious right hot spots and shared his story for ten thousand dollars a pop. Roy's Rock had arrived at Reclaiming America fresh from a tour of twenty-one states, and activists at the conference circulated a petition urging President Bush to appoint Moore to the U.S. Supreme Court.

Now that they'd re-elected Bush and damned gay marriage to a constitutional hell, the Reclaimers aimed to tip the scales toward Old Testament justice for generations to come. "They've bashed the judiciary for years," said Rob Boston, author of *Close Encounters with the Religious Right: Journeys into the Twilight Zone of Religion and Politics.* "Now they want to take it over." The plan was to blitz the media, pressure the White House, and charm and twist the arms of powerful senators who owed the movement. Meanwhile, folks at the grassroots level were urged to consider their Christian duty to run for office, particularly to stack school boards with Dominionists.

"The most humble Christian is more qualified for office than the best-educated pagan," Cass assured them. Humble Christians were called to stir things up for Christ in other ways, too. Cass pointed to Gary Beeler, a small-town Baptist minister from Tennessee who had gotten permission for thousands of students in the public schools to skip class and attend weeklong "old-time revivals, with preaching and singing and soul saving and the whole nine yards." With some monetary support from Coral Ridge, Beeler told me, he had sold his house and bought a mobile home to spread his crusade nationwide. "It's not exactly what I planned to do with my retirement," Beeler confessed.

"But it's what God told me to do." Cass also spotlighted small-town activist Kevin McCoy, who had led a successful campaign to shut down an anti-bullying program in West Virginia. McCoy, a soft-spoken, prematurely gray postal worker, objected to the program because it counseled tolerance for gay people—and thus, in his view, amounted to a "thinly disguised effort to promote the homosexual agenda."

"What America needs," Cass said, "is more Kevin McCoys."

The Dominionists' efforts had been backed by some of America's richest entrepreneurs. Amway founder Rich DeVos, a Kennedy ally, had tossed more than five million dollars in the collection plate by 2005. Jean Case, wife of former AOL chief Steve Case—who made his riches largely from sex–chat rooms—had donated more than eight million dollars. Tom Monaghan, founder of Domino's Pizza, has been an even larger source of cash for Dobson's Focus on the Family. The one-two punch of militant activists and big money ensured that Washington Republicans had to pay attention to the Kennedys and Dobsons of the movement. Kennedy had launched the D.C.-based Center for Christian Statesmanship, which trained elected officials to "more effectively share their faith in the public arena." Among the alumni is former House majority whip Tom "The Hammer" DeLay, a winner of Kennedy's Distinguished Christian Statesman Award.

Highlighting the Dominionists' political pull, the keynote address at Reclaiming America came courtesy of Walter Jones, a lanky, mop-headed Republican congressman from North Carolina. Jones, who had ironically won kudos from liberal magazines like *Mother Jones* over his opposition to the invasion of Iraq, had come to champion the Houses of Worship Free Speech Restoration Act of 2005, designed to "restore" the freedom of ministers to endorse political candidates from the pulpit without putting their churches' tax-exempt status at risk. "You are my brothers and sisters in Christ," Jones said, his eyes flashing the sincerity of someone about to uncork a big secret. "And America is under assault. Everyone in America has the right to speak freely today, except for those standing in the pulpits of our churches!" The amen chorus rose. Hands flew heavenward. It was one thing to hear such talk from Cass or Kennedy, after all—but to the Reclaiming America crowd, there was nothing more thrilling, more indicative of their intoxicating power, than getting the gospel straight from a member of Congress. "You cannot have a strong nation that does not follow God," Jones preached, working up to a passionate plea for a biblical republic. "God, please—God, please—God, please—save America!"

Little did the cheering Reclaimers suspect that, by the 2006 midterm elections, it would be Christian Dominionism that needed saving.

★

In 1965, as the Voting Rights Act moved through Congress and threatened to burst through the cracked foundations of Jim Crow, the Reverend Jerry Falwell, an ambitious young fundamentalist preacher in Lynchburg, Virginia, gave a sermon called "Ministers and Marches" at his fast-growing Thomas Road Baptist Church. Voicing the resentments of many white Southern evangelicals, the pudgy pastor grudgingly allowed that "there are, no doubt, many very sincere Christians who have felt a compulsion to join in civil rights efforts across the nation." But, he said, "at the same time, I must personally say that I do question the sincerity and nonviolent intentions of some civil rights leaders such as Dr. Martin Luther King Jr. and Mr. James Farmer and others, who are known to have left-wing associations. It is very obvious that the communists, as they do in all parts of the world, are taking advantage of a tense situation in our land, and are exploiting every incident to bring about violence and bloodshed. . . . I must say that I believe these demonstrations and marches have done more to damage race relations and to gender hate than to help!"

While Falwell was accusing the liberals of being communist pat-
sies, his larger point was one equally familiar to Southern fundamentalists: Christians had no calling to participate in politics. Since the
humiliation stemming from their anti-evolution campaign and the
1925 Scopes "monkey trial," white Southern fundamentalists had
long steered clear of the moral contaminations of the political system. They believed the Lord did not want them to soil their souls in
politics, citing verses like the one from 2 Corinthians that Falwell
quoted on that Sunday night: "For though we walk in the flesh, we
do not war after the flesh."

Fourteen years later, thousands of Southern evangelicals received
a fund-raising letter, postmarked Lynchburg and signed by the same
Jerry Falwell, containing a "Declaration of War."

"Be it known to all that *The Old Time Gospel Hour*"—Falwell's
weekly TV show—"hereby declares war against the evils threatening
America during the 1980s," the letter began. "This shall be a Holy
War, not a war with guns and bullets, but a war fought with the
Bible, prayer and Christian involvement." The bullet-point catalog
of the evils to be combatted by Falwell's new Moral Majority highlighted the remarkable ideological consistency of the movement during its twenty-five-year boom: legalized abortion, pornography,
homosexuality, socialism, and—last but not least—"the deteriora-
tion of home and family."

What had changed Falwell's mind about warring after the flesh?
A combination of cultural, racial, and religious grievances he shared
with millions of born-again and unreconstructed Southerners, who
were "extremely unhappy with the 'rights' movements that had
sprung up in the 1950s and '60s," said historian Didi Herman, author
of *The Antigay Agenda: Orthodox Vision and the Christian Right.*
"For black people, then women, now *gay* people? The frustration had
been mounting. Now their actions were catching up with their views."

Falwell uncovered biblical invocations of a "Christian duty" to
take the field, but the roots of his "new right" politics were hardly

theological. Falwell had been frank about his preference for segregation. In 1964, he'd told a local newspaper that the Civil Rights Act had been misnamed: "It should be considered civil wrongs rather than civil rights," he said. His *Old Time Gospel Hour* had hosted such white-supremacist superstars as George Wallace and Governor Lester Maddox of Georgia. In "Ministers and Marches," Falwell aimed his moralisms squarely at Wallace's put-upon white Southerners. "While the church leaders are so obsessed with the alleged discrimination against negroes in the South," he noted, "very little is said about the same situation in the North."

Falwell's political approach was heavily influenced by Dr. Francis Schaeffer, a rebellious fundamentalist who had spread the word about "Dominion theology" and whom many saw as the father of the anti-abortion movement. Dubbed the "Guru of Fundamentalism" by *Newsweek* in 1980, Schaeffer taught that Christians were meant to rule—and, given the sorry state of post-'60s America, they had better get about it. With the unholy obstacles presented by a democracy, that meant first winning elections—which, in turn, necessitated temporary political alliances with people outside the faith to achieve those "moral majorities."

"Dr. Schaeffer convinced Jerry," said the Reverend Mel White, his onetime collaborator, that "there was no biblical mandate against joining with nonbelievers"—Wall Street Republicans, most notably—"in a political cause."

The role of Southern evangelicals in the Republican rise has certainly not gone unnoticed (or unlamented). The religious right's political crusade coincided quite neatly with Republican efforts to de-emphasize economic issues and turn elections into referenda on traditionalist wedge issues. From the start, the evangelical right concentrated on building "an army of Christian soldiers" to both undergird and overwhelm the GOP. While Moral Majority co-founders Richard Viguerie and Paul Weyrich perfected the arts of direct-mail fund-raising and grassroots organizing, Falwell (along with Robertson, Kennedy, and others) adapted the right-wing rhetoric of Christian anticommunism and white supremacy to attack a new set of enemies: feminists and other evil spawn of the 1960s and '70s.

"The homosexuals are on the march in this country," Falwell warned in an August 13, 1981, appeal for Moral Majority cash. "I believe that a massive homosexual revolution is always a symptom of a nation coming under the judgment of God." Thirty years before, Oklahoma preacher Billy James Hargis's Christian Anticommunist Crusade had loudly made identical claims about the Reds among us. "The rhetoric is highly adaptable," said Randall Balmer, author of *Thy Kingdom Come: How the Religious Right Distorts the Faith and Threatens America*. So is the enemy.

By putting a religious seal of approval on the Republicans' politics of scapegoating, the evangelical right was instrumental in reassembling white Southerners into a voting bloc. "Even though the emphasis is not on race," said Southern historian Dan T. Carter, "it's the same kind of appeal to people who feel under siege. . . . Traditionalist Americans *do* feel under siege. A lot of it comes from popular culture, which they're immersed in but disgusted by— people hopping into bed every time you turn on the TV and all that. Rather than thinking, 'The real problem is this corporate consumer culture we're being fed through the mass media,' they've been taught to say it's the liberals' fault." And thus, by extension, the Democrats' fault.

Evangelicals haven't always been an organized force in Southern politics, but what's preached in Southern pulpits has always had an outsized influence on the way both blacks and whites vote in Dixie. That's not simply because there are more churchgoers and "Bible believers" in the South; it's also because of the unique social role that churches have traditionally played in what were often, essentially, still frontier communities well into the twentieth century. People's communal lives have to center around something, and in the poverty-soaked post–Civil War South, through the 1950s, churches and schools were the only options. Not every church preached politics, but, even so, the parishioners usually knew which way their shepherd leaned—and if the church was white it was a near certainty that he leaned toward the Democrats and the maintenance of Jim Crow.

As the South became more prosperous, the booming Sunbelt suburbs spawned a whole new, lavish kind of community center with the megachurch. These churches, growing up at the same time that the Republican Party was reaching out to white suburbanites and putting a new emphasis on grassroots organizing, have often served as de facto Republican Party headquarters. People vote there. Their kids go to school there. They meet their friends for coffee there. They get political literature there. In many of the churches, if not most, they also get sermonized on politics there. For people who believe, as evangelicals do, that faith is more important than any worldly concern, the content of those sermons is almost always going to outweigh any practical or ideological thoughts to the contrary. The preachers once said, "Vote Democratic," and lo! the white South did. Since the 1970s they've been saying, "Vote for Jesus' values" and "Vote for family values," and the parishioners have known just what that meant, too.

From the beginning, the union between the evangelical right and the Republican Party's historically dominant business wing was marked by mutual distrust. Long before John McCain—infuriated by the evangelicals' slanderous attacks on his family during the pivotal South Carolina primary against George W. Bush in 2000—labeled Falwell and Robertson "agents of intolerance," George H. W. Bush had responded angrily to a warning from Weyrich that he needed to take a harder line on abortion and get more enthused about school prayer. "I am not intimidated by those who suggest I

better hew the line," the senior Bush said in 1980. "Hell with them."
By 1992, however, this same Bush was turning over the first prime-
time speaking slot of his presidential nominating convention to Pat
Buchanan, who memorably thundered the quintessential Falwell
line: "There is a culture war going on in our country for the soul of
America."

There was a pragmatic reason (beyond fund-raising) for these perpetual declarations of war: the rising political clout of evangelical
Christians did not stem from a growth in their numbers so much as
their increasing cohesion under the Republican tent. (Now, as then,
evangelicals made up about one-quarter of the U.S. population.) And
nothing made Southern whites of Falwell's generation cohere quite like
a perceived threat to their "way of life." As late as 1987, white evangelical Protestants were divided in their partisan attachments, with 34
percent identifying as Republicans and 29 percent as Democrats. But
by 2004, evangelical Republicans outnumbered evangelical Democrats
within this group by more than two to one, at 48 to 23 percent. A mere
19 percent of Southern evangelicals (and 21 percent nationally) voted
for John Kerry for president. The mobilization of evangelicals in such
Dominionist hotbeds as Colorado and Ohio, turned the election in
Bush's favor just as surely as the record turnout of evangelical
Southerners did.

But evangelicals' doubts about politics had not disappeared in the
clouds of new political glory. As recently as 1998, during President
Bill Clinton's second term, the evangelical right had been deeply
divided over whether to continue emphasizing partisan politics. Cal
Thomas, a widely syndicated right-wing columnist and FOX News
commentator, counseled his fellow evangelicals to get back to saving
souls and helping the poor and leave the politics to the secularists.
Evangelicals seemed to be drifting back toward their traditional
ambivalence about politics. Weyrich even suggested that the evangelical right build its own separate-but-equal subculture and forget
about taking over the rest of America.

That was not surprising, really, given the fact that most evangelicals are "premillennialists," who believe that the world has to go plumb off the rails, Book of Revelation–style, before Christ will return to save it; a smaller number, the "postmillennialists," believe that Christians must rule the earth for a thousand years to pave the way for the Savior. "The pendulum swings back and forth," Rob Boston, who watches the religious right for the liberal group Americans United for Separation of Church and State, told me in 2005. "They're in a political phase now, but who knows how long that will last." For most evangelical conservatives, end-time beliefs do not compel them to make politics a top priority; they have to be motivated—frightened, threatened, prodded. And there are only so many ways to manufacture the requisite terror among largely middle-class suburbanites who pay low taxes and send their kids to improving schools in the prosperous Sunbelt South.

The fracturing movement got an unexpected, unifying boost in 2003 when the Massachusetts Supreme Court ruled four to three that gay and lesbian couples had the right to marry. In the *Washington Dispatch,* Weyrich expressed the sentiments of many religious right warriors, declaring gay marriage "The Final Frontier for Civilization as We Know It." A few months earlier, that well-known coven of judicial activism, the U.S. Supreme Court, provoked outrage with its ruling in *Lawrence v. Texas,* which overturned state sodomy statutes while finding that gay people were entitled to "an autonomy of self that includes freedom of thought, belief, expression, and certain intimate conduct." Justice Antonin Scalia, speaking directly to the religious right in his bitter dissent, complained that "the court has largely signed on to the so-called homosexual agenda."

Meanwhile, President Bush cynically pandered to evangelical voters by announcing his support for a Federal Marriage Amendment in February 2004, shortly after San Francisco officials set off a media frenzy by issuing marriage licenses to gay couples. By election day, eleven states—including prized swing state Ohio—had placed anti–gay marriage initiatives on their ballots. Dobson's Focus on the Family Action organized huge "Mayday for Marriage" rallies in six major cities, drawing an estimated 150,000 to Washington, D.C., where his high-pitched voice shouted, "Everything we care about is on the line. It's now or never."

In Ohio, fundamentalist Phil Burress's antigay group gathered 575,000 signatures in fewer than ninety days to put their constitutional amendment on the ballot. "It's a forest fire with a hundred-mile-per-hour wind behind it," Burress said.

But once the great surge of 2004 was over, evangelicals' doubts about their churches' political activism were quickly resurrected. Their leaders, unaccustomed to exercising power rather than challenging it, perhaps predictably pushed too far—especially in the infamous case of Terri Schiavo. When the courts ordered the Florida woman's feeding tube removed, Dominionist groups like Reclaiming America for Christ howled about "state-sponsored murder," organized twenty-four-hour vigils, and pressured Governor Jeb Bush to defy the law and take Schiavo into state custody. Between President Bush's unprecedented alacrity in responding to the "crisis"—flying back to Washington in the midst of a Crawford Ranch vacation—and Senate majority leader Dr. Bill Frist's politically convenient diagnosis of Schiavo based on watching twenty minutes of video, there was a widespread sense of "real overreach," according to Clyde Wilcox, a longtime religious right scholar at Georgetown University. "I heard evangelicals asking, 'Why won't they let that poor woman go to heaven?'" The public strongly opposed the extraordinary interventions of the Bushes and Congress into what almost everyone, evangelical and secular, saw as a private family issue being ruthlessly exploited by right-wing Republicans.

The fallout was swift. Frist morphed from a presidential contender into a political has-been. Bush's popularity sank further, as did that of congressional Republicans and the pro-life movement. Hardcore Dominionist groups like Reclaiming America saw their memberships dip, their political influence in Washington plummet, their golden touch tarnish. The myth of ruthless savvy that the evangelical right had earned with its performance in the 2004 elections was punctured. Meanwhile, the un-Christian compromises of earthly politics were about to become matters of pressing concern for the faithful—especially in the South.

★

Ralph Reed was ready to own this room. Granted, it was merely a standard-issue campus auditorium at Emory University, half-filled at best for the political speaking portion of the annual Georgia College Republicans convention. But to the former boy wonder of evangelical politics, it looked like heavenly shelter on a drizzly Saturday morning in February 2006. The Christian Coalition cofounder's first campaign for public office—lieutenant governor of his home state, the kind of position Reed and his fans had always envisioned as a stepping stone toward greater things—had turned into a waking nightmare. Every week brought a new revelation about the millions in dirty money Reed had earned by duping his fellow Southern evangelicals into putting their political muscle behind super-lobbyist Jack Abramoff's gambling clients. Reed's huge leads in both popularity polls and fund-raising had almost disappeared. Instead of making his triumphant political debut, the man *Time* magazine once called "The Right Hand of God" was fast becoming the poster boy for Christian right corruption—and for the post-2004 breakdown of the evangelical machine.

"Ralph Reed symbolizes the rise of the Christian right to political power," said Frederick Clarkson, author of *Eternal Hostility: The Struggle Between Theocracy and Democracy*. "He became the story of the movement—the face and voice for those millions of conservative Christians in the mainstream press. Now he's becoming a symbol of what's gone awry."

Among the Georgia College Republicans, though, he still expected a hero's welcome. As an undergraduate dynamo at the University of Georgia in the late 1970s and early '80s, Reed turned the Georgia CRs into a political force that helped elect the state's first Republican U.S. senator since Reconstruction. "Tricky Ralph," as he was known on campus, went on to make a similar splash with the national CRs, teaming with Abramoff, who was national CR chairman in the early 1980s, and Grover Norquist, the well-connected right-winger whose Americans for Tax Reform was also caught up in the casino-lobbying scandals. Those associations went unmentioned in the introductory roll call of achievements before Reed bounded up to the podium and spread his Howdy Doody grin. "It's great to be back home," he chirped, fondly recalling how he ran a mock campus election in 1980 in which Ronald Reagan surprisingly beat President Jimmy Carter, Georgia's native son—and how he timed the results perfectly for maximum impact. "Right before Ronald Reagan walked out on stage for his one and only debate against President Carter," he remembered, "they distributed a news release announcing Reagan's victory in Georgia!"

Here was vintage Reed, the incorrigibly boastful, shamelessly self-aggrandizing operator who so long dazzled—and blinded—evangelical Christians, big-money Republicans, and mainstream journalists alike. At forty-four, he still looked like a million bucks, his elfin face perma-tanned a brick red, his pencil-thin body, always electric with nervous energy, subtly bulked out by a well-tailored suit. Only one thing was missing: applause. Maybe some of the CRs knew the real history of that 1980 mock election from Nina Easton's book *Gang of Five: Leaders at the Center of the Conservative Crusade,* in which it was revealed that Reed's first big political victory had been rigged—his first notable act of mass deception. Maybe they were just waiting for Reed to finally offer a satisfying explanation for his star turn in the Abramoff scandal. But when it came, his mea culpa smacked more of false piety than genuine gut spilling.

"I was approached in 1999 by a friend that I met in the College

Republicans. He said, 'There's an effort to bring five new casino-style operations to Alabama. Would you be willing to help us stop them?' And I said, 'Yes, I would. I'm opposed to casino gambling expansion, but I can only do it if I won't be paid with revenue from other casinos.'" Before the kids got a chance to chew on that, Reed quickly offered a Nixonian apology. "If I had known then what I know now, I would have turned that work down. But I will tell you that the work that I did either prevented from opening, or closed, eight gambling casinos, and we will never know how many marriages and lives were saved by the work that I did."

A few awkward minutes later, Reed was heading for the exit, wearing an iron-willed grin. It was another low moment in a campaign that was supposed to be a practice run for higher office (and greater glory)—but it was not the worst. Just a month earlier, Reed's campaign had been reduced to offering twenty dollars and a free hotel stay to supporters who would attend the Georgia Christian Coalition's annual convention and cheer for the man who had largely *invented* the group.

While other evangelical leaders and political allies were taking their hits in the Abramoff affair—former House Speaker Tom DeLay and antigay crusader Lou Sheldon of the Traditional Values Coalition among them—Reed's involvement ran the deepest and broadest. And the particulars of his cloak-and-dagger activities particularly galled the evangelical movement. "His M.O. is to tell evangelical Christians that his cause of the moment, for which he has been hired, is their religious duty," wrote Georgia's former GOP house minority leader, Bob Irvin, in an *Atlanta Journal-Constitution* op-ed. "As an evangelical myself, I resent Christianity being used simply to help Reed's business."

That sense of being used—more than a sneaking suspicion from the early days of the Moral Majority's red-alert fund-raising bulletins—was rubbing some raw evangelical nerves by 2006. The Abramoff and Schiavo shenanigans were bad enough. But Washington Republicans had also harbored a potential pedophile, Florida congressman Mark Foley, until suggestive e-mail messages he sent to a teenage page finally got out, while movement leaders such as Ted Haggard, the charismatic president of the National Association of Evangelicals, were having their own hypocrisies flushed out into the open. Meanwhile, many working- and middle-class evangelicals were struggling financially and beginning to wonder aloud whether Republicans weren't using "morality" as cover for a corporate, free-trade, cheap labor agenda.

The Reed scandal tied it all together in one squalid package. Reed, who had been executive director of the Christian Coalition from its founding in 1989, had left the group in 1997 to lay the groundwork for his political future while "humping" some serious cash, as he told Abramoff in an infamous plea for work, at his Georgia-based consulting firm, Century Strategies. From 1999 to 2002, Abramoff's Indian casino clients paid Reed some $5.3 million to set up "antigambling" coalitions in Alabama, Louisiana, and Texas to oppose proposed new competitors (and in one case to shut down an existing casino). Reed convinced dozens of influential pastors in those states, along with some of the biggest names on the evangelical right, including James Dobson, Jerry Falwell, Pat Robertson, and Donald Wildmon, president of the Mississippi-based American Family Association, to mobilize their flocks. The front groups Reed established in the states, with upright names like Citizens Against Legalized Gambling, organized religious rallies, sent out mass mailings decrying the evils of wagering, and flooded legislators and state officials with thousands of calls from concerned Christians.

From the start, Reed denied that he knew Abramoff was paying him gambling money. But their e-mail exchanges, made public by the Senate Indian Affairs Committee, showed that Reed knew where his bread was being buttered. In a 1999 message, Abramoff asked him to "get me invoices as soon as possible so I can get Choctaw to get us checks ASAP. The firm has held back all payments pending receipt of a check from the Choctaw." The correspondence also showed that Reed played an active role in diverting tribal money through faux Christian groups like the U.S. Family Network. Rather than receive his payments directly from Abramoff or from the tribes, Reed made sure his checks came from pure-sounding sources. "That's sometimes called laundering," Senator Byron Dorgan said during congressional hearings.

Reed's lucrative manipulation of the Christian right had not been limited to the gambling scandal. The *Atlanta Journal-Constitution* uncovered a pattern of similar instances in which Reed "tapped into his vast network of conservative religious activists" to do the bidding of big-money clients on false pretenses. In one example from 1998, Reed had invented the Alliance of Christian Ministries in China, a group of missionary organizations supporting favorable trade status for China as a way of benefiting efforts to spread the gospel there. The alliance turned out to be an empty shell, serving only the interests of Reed clients such as Boeing, which hoped to sell $120 billion worth of airplanes to China.

Like his efforts on behalf of the Indian casinos, Reed's pro-China lobbying was not just dishonest but hypocritical to boot. Just as he had often warned against the "nationwide scourge" of gambling, Reed had spoken out consistently against favorable trade status for China. "We believe that human and civil rights and religious freedom and liberty should be at the center of our foreign policy," he had declared at a 1997 Christian Coalition press conference. "We believe that if the United States makes the center of its foreign policy profits rather than people, and money rather than human rights, then we will have lost our soul as a nation."

Among movement leaders, the Reed revelations were mostly greeted with "an embarrassing silence," to quote Ken Connor, former head of Dobson's Family Research Council. One notable exception was Marvin Olasky, President Bush's longtime Texas adviser who literally wrote the book on compassionate conservatism. Olasky, now editor of the popular evangelical news magazine, *World,* was outspoken in his opinion that Reed had "damaged Christian political work by confirming for some the stereotype that evangelicals are easily manipulated and that evangelical leaders use moral issues to line their pockets."

But that had been Reed's modus operandi all along. His Christian Coalition stewardship had embodied—and promoted—that odd alchemy of godliness and big-bucks politics. His slick style and winning ways had offered living, breathing assurance that Christians could play power politics as effectively as the secularists. But from the get-go there had been a dark undercurrent that troubled many in the movement. The coalition had made an immediate impact in several local and statewide elections in 1990 and 1992, but it had done so partly by means of deception—among other things, allegedly using churches as political headquarters and spending tax-exempt funds for political purposes. Candidates were advised to hide their social views in an attempt to sneak into office and promote their agenda. The coalition's famous voter guides distorted some Democratic candidates' records to make them look "antifamily."

"It's like guerrilla warfare," Reed told a reporter in 1992. "If you reveal your location, all it does is allow your opponent to improve his artillery bearings. It's better to move quietly, with stealth, under cover of night." It was widely suspected that Reed grossly exaggerated both the coalition's membership numbers (apparently closer to 600,000 at its peak, rather than the 1.7 million he claimed) and the distribution of its supposed 40 million voter guides, which were often found discarded in great, fat bundles after elections. When Reed made his hasty exit in 1997, the coalition was foundering under a cloud of lawsuits from disgruntled employees, federal investigations into illegal ties with the Republican Party, and sagging membership.

For most of his unlikely career, evangelicals had given Reed "a pretty easy pass on any questions of hypocrisy," said Clyde Wilcox of Georgetown University. As with other shady Christian leaders and congressional allies like DeLay, there was "a tendency to say, 'I worry that he might be fudging the corners, but I'm not gonna look. He's doing too much good for our cause.'" Now evangelicals could hardly avert their eyes. And what they saw went straight to the heart of their longstanding ambivalence about mixing it up in politics. "Historically, many Christian conservatives were not involved in politics because they saw it as inherently corrupt," said John Green, senior fellow with the Pew Forum on Religion and Public Life. The convergence of faith-shaking scandals, disappointments, and the deaths of Dominionist leaders like Falwell and Kennedy may not have "risen to a level where it would deactivate the religious right," Green told me in 2006. "But for the first time in a long time, when I'm talking to my evangelical friends, I keep hearing, 'My preacher used to say when I was growing up that we ought to stay out of politics because it was dirty. You know, he was right.'"

The potential for a demobilization of the Republicans' evangelical base in 2006 was as nagging a worry for GOP strategists—and candidates—as the historically low levels of support for President Bush and his war. "What will happen on Election Day when 2 to 3 percent of the previously most passionate Republicans stay home?" wondered Joseph Farah, editor and publisher of the Dominionist news Web site *World Net Daily*. "Think of what it will mean when 20 to 30 percent of the grassroots activists Republicans have counted on don't show up to work for them." They didn't have to imagine it for long.

★

"You can feel the surge!" exclaimed Senator Jim Talent, his nerdy visage beaming over a makeshift podium in an airless, jam-packed conference room way in back of Springfield, Missouri's old Lamplighter Inn. Late on the afternoon before election day 2006, more than a hundred GOP volunteers had temporarily abandoned their posts at phone banks and in neighborhoods across Missouri's most "Southern" city to cheer their man. And their campaign. "If we can finish and execute this plan in the next twenty-seven hours," Talent assured them, "I'm convinced you're going to reelect yourself a United States senator."

The troops—an all-white mix of mostly evangelical senior citizens and students, including a gaggle of fraternity brothers shipped down from Brigham Young University for the final push—let out a ceiling-panel-shaking roar. Like thousands of religious right activists across the country, they had managed to look past the scandals in Washington and Colorado and Florida and Georgia. "Yes, what Mark Foley did was wrong," Focus on the Family's James Dobson had said on his radio show, leaving out a few other names, "but it is still important to go to the polls and let our voices be heard. . . . It would be a sin not to." With Talent locked in a skintight race with Democratic state auditor Claire McCaskill, the faithful had knocked on forty-five thousand Springfield doors and placed eighty thousand calls to registered Republicans and independents locally. They had not gotten the usual warm reception.

"I am still shocked by the things some folks said to my face," said Steve Helms, who had been knocking on doors since December in his Republican campaign for the state house. Some had vented their displeasure over Iraq, but others had railed about the evangelical scandals. "The national mood's kind of harsh on us," said Helms, shaking his head.

The previous spring, it had become clear that 2006 was going to be a major comedown for evangelical Republicans. Reed had been thumped in the Georgia primary, losing to his previously obscure, underfunded opponent by twelve points. "It is time for Christians to confront and rebuke Ralph Reed," Christian lobbyist Clint Austin, a former Reed adviser, had written in an open letter to Georgia Republicans in the final days of the campaign. They certainly had—especially younger evangelicals, who, said Randall

Balmer, "really see the lack of ethical standards among their elders as a problem."

In Alabama, "Ten Commandment Judge" Roy Moore's upstart crusade against incumbent governor Bob Riley, a Republican whose popularity had plummeted when he backed a statewide referendum to raise taxes for education, had failed by an even more emphatic two-to-one vote. It was a stunning rejection of Moore, who had been admired by 72 percent of the state's Republicans when he began his gubernatorial run. Outside the South, practically every leading light of Christian Dominionism up for major office—Ohio's Ken Blackwell, Pennsylvania senator Rick Santorum, Indiana congressman John Hostetler—was bracing for what President Bush would later call "a thumping." But evangelicals in the Show-Me State seemed poised to demonstrate how potent the GOP's "seventy-two-hour campaign" could still be. Instead, Missouri ended up exemplifying why the Republicans lost the midterms—and why evangelicals are less and less likely to fall in lockstep in the future.

All the ingredients for a massive, 2004-style turnout appeared in place in the evangelical stronghold of southwest Missouri and the Christian right suburbs of St. Louis and Kansas City. There was Talent, the devout (and scandal-free) candidate with impeccable "family values" credentials and a bottomless ad budget to make McCaskill look like Hillary Clinton's (even more) evil twin. There was also the requisite moral wedge issue to drive out the evangelical right: Amendment 2, a constitutional referendum to enshrine the right to federally approved stem-cell research and therapies into the Missouri constitution. For folks like Mike Bacheleder, a Springfield volunteer who was steering BYU students around the city on their door-knocking errands, stem-cell opposition had overwhelmed concerns about misdeeds in Washington, not to mention the Iraq War. "I'm personally embarrassed by all that," he told me at Talent headquarters. "But I haven't heard much talk about Foley or Abramoff or the war in my church."

That wasn't true in every church. Dee Wampler, a longtime evangelical right activist and Republican stalwart, told me that conservative misdeeds had repulsed plenty of his counterparts in the Bible Belt of the state's southwest. "We're the worker bees of the party," he said. "A lot of us are disgusted—about the Foley scandal, among other things. We elected them to stand guard and not let this kind of thing happen. I'm hearing a lot of dissension coming out into the open now."

While the stem-cell controversy did come to dominate the campaign, it proved to be anything but a magic wedge. Opposition to stem-cell research remains an extreme extension of the pro-life position—an extension too far in the view of many Christian voters. As popular former senator John Danforth, an early Christian-right vote getter and Episcopal priest in Missouri, wrote in the spring of 2006, "It is not evident to many of us that cells in a petri dish are equivalent to identifiable people suffering from terrible diseases"—people who might benefit from the research. In his book *Faith and Politics: How the "Moral Values" Debate Divides America and How to Move Forward Together,* Danforth also blasted the religious right as a dangerously divisive force with goals too radical for the average evangelical Christian.

As if bent on proving Danforth right, stem-cell opponents waged a hate-filled campaign that ended up alienating many moderate and conservative Missourians—and turning them away from Talent, who strongly opposed the stem-cell amendment on biblical grounds. "God hates you," Republican activist Alan Keyes reportedly informed stem-cell backers at a rally of seven hundred Springfield Christians in late September 2006. Then radio screamer Rush Limbaugh mocked actor Michael J. Fox, who, quaking from the effects of Parkinson's disease, filmed an emotional TV ad supporting stem-cell research and McCaskill's Senate bid. The attacks stopped the anti-stem-cell tide and made voters question where the real morality lay.

"To me, the stem-cell thing is just silly," Springfield's Tom Rollings told me on election night, holding the hands of his wife, Donna, and their toddler son. A committed evangelical, Rollings said that he and Donna "usually vote Republican, but not this time." To them, a far less publicized ballot initiative, one ignored by the Christian right, was the more legitimate "values" issue. "People's wages—*that* is a moral issue," Rollings said. "Especially when you're trying to feed your family."

Most Missourians agreed, as the initiative to raise the state's minimum wage to $6.50 passed with 75 percent. Both McCaskill and the stem-cell measure carried the day, too—partly because the evangelical opposition to both was far less intense in southwest Missouri than expected. Contrary to dire predications, evangelical voters came out in Missouri—and elsewhere in the country—in numbers comparable to 2004. (Whether they volunteered for the GOP at the usual clip is impossible to accurately measure.) The big difference was in how they voted: both in the South and elsewhere, evangelicals were 8 percent more likely to punch their ballots for congressional Democrats than they had been in 2004. Even in a lousy year for Republicans, it looked like a sign that evangelicals, in Missouri and across the country, were opening their minds to a broader political gospel.

Evangelical voters had expressed frustration not only with the scandals swirling around Reed, DeLay, Foley, and Haggard, Olasky wrote in *World,* but with "Republicans' inability, despite congressional majorities, to move ahead a compassionate conservative agenda." Evangelicals had organized politically to elect leaders who would govern differently—morally, by their lights. But Republicans had "once again become the party of corporate suits," Olasky lamented, and their defeats were well-deserved. "It's right that some Republicans lost after they betrayed the principles that brought the GOP to congressional power in 1994 and elected George W. Bush."

While the Dominionist catastrophes of 2005 and 2006 were

discrediting the old-style politics of the evangelical right, a more expansive Christianity was spreading across the megachurch universe—with revolutionary implications. At the same time, Democrats were trying to figure out how to take advantage of their new opening with moderate evangelicals—one that could reshape partisan politics in Dixie—without selling out their own base of social progressives. "It will be fascinating to watch Democrats try to make their tent bigger without alienating their Christophobic base," said Olasky. "I hope they succeed, because America could use two parties that respect biblical belief, so that evangelicals aren't captive to one."

★

On the January Sunday before the 2008 Florida Republican presidential primaries, former Arkansas governor Mike Huckabee got praised and blessed and prayed over during two morning services at one of the biggest conservative megachurches in the political swing region of central Florida, Orlando's fourteen-thousand-member First Baptist. In a year when the evangelical political machine was unmistakably flying apart, the church had engineered a momentary return to the old order. Pastor David Uth was doing just what an evangelical megaminister was supposed to do in the run-up to an election—anointing the nearest thing to a theocratic candidate as the more-or-less official choice of his church and urging his "Christian soldiers" to take up arms and get out votes.

But while Uth was reinforcing that well-worn commandment, his encomium for Huckabee had something fresh about it. Rather than emphasize the governor's Dark Age convictions on culture war issues, or his wild-eyed pledge to amend the Constitution in the Lord's image, the megaminister told a story dating from the civil rights era, when Uth's father had tried to integrate his Baptist flock in Pine Bluff, Arkansas. The Uths got chased out of town by the Klan, but the elder pastor Uth was succeeded in the pulpit by a young Mike Huckabee, who "successfully broke the race barrier."

His admiration for the candidate, Uth said, stemmed from their common conviction that when the church "isn't for everybody, it isn't for anybody." If this wasn't exactly revolutionary talk (and if Huckabee had hardly run the kind of inclusive campaign Uth's anecdote implied), the change in tone was characteristic of evangelicals' turn away from the "wrath of a warrior God" approach that peaked in 2004 with James Dobson's furious screeds. It seemed that even if you were endorsing Huckabee, these days you were duty-bound to try and sound like you were doing it for broad-minded reasons.

Twenty miles up the road, deep in the suburbs of Seminole County, a more thoroughgoing departure from Moral Majority–style politics was on display at Northland, central Florida's "cutting-edge" megachurch. More than twelve thousand folks—mostly middle-class, mostly (but not exclusively) white—worship there at four elaborately choreographed services each weekend. They are drawn not only by the rock-concert atmospherics and full-service approach (day school, child care, coffee bar), but also by the genial magnetism and post–religious right message of the Reverend Joel C. Hunter.

But what, pray tell, does "post–religious right" mean? In Northland's case, it meant that, on this critical political Sunday, there was almost nothing said about politics at all. During his opening announcements, assistant pastor Sean Williams, a lanky thirty-two-year-old in slim-fitting, prewashed jeans, made a casual reference to Tuesday's elections, encouraging first-time voters to "believe in the process that God has called this country to." That was about as political as it got. The service segued into a performance by the four-piece house band, which ably strummed its way through two trippy tunes of U2-inspired praise rock, both tied to Hunter's equally trippy theme for the day: "Beautiful Collision." The concept came from the theologian N. T. Wright, who observed that the purpose of Jesus's work was to bring Heaven to Earth, resulting in inevitable "explosions." Materializing onstage, as the swirling pink, purple, and blue lights calmed down, Hunter kicked off his message by proclaiming: "They say at the birth of the universe, there was a big bang. I can believe it!"

It's impossible to imagine Jerry Falwell having opened an election week sermon quite like that—and with an implicit embrace of a scientific fundamental, for goodness' sake. But Hunter's chief aim is to crack open the closed minds of his fellow conservatives. "He's the only evangelical pastor I've ever heard call on his congregation to donate during an NPR pledge drive," said Mark Pinsky, the *Orlando Sentinel*'s religion writer, who has followed Hunter's ascendancy for more than a decade. "Certainly the only one who references *Foreign Affairs* in his sermons—I mean, *I* don't read *Foreign Affairs*."

Hunter clearly relishes kicking against his parishioners' intellectual, spiritual, and political limits. His sermon was chock-full of reminders, explicit and implicit, that this was not your grandfather's evangelicalism. He made a playful break from hidebound literalism: "There were twelve apostles," he said at one point, interrupting himself to add, "maybe a few more than that. Maybe a hundred." He distanced himself from the feel-good Christianity of prosperity preachers: "A lot of times life doesn't get better" when a person accepts Christ, he said. "Things become not clearer but more complicated." And he embraced mainstream culture, informing the folks that he'd agreed to be interviewed on *The Colbert Report*. "This guy is really hilarious," he explained, making an exaggerated sour face to mimic people who had said to him, "Why would you want to do *that*? Why?" he asked rhetorically. "Because anybody can be on a religion channel. But when Christians are on the news channel, on the comedy channel, we're out there where God is. . . . What we're interested in is taking the Bible out of these rooms. It's not about religion. It's about changing the world into what Christ wants."

Like *The Purpose-Driven Life* author and Saddleback Church pastor Rick Warren and the Reverend Bill Hybels, who heads up the twelve-thousand-church Willow Creek network, the fifty-nine-year-old Hunter had vaulted to national prominence as a front man for the new wave of evangelicalism.

"You've gotta go back to the reengagement of Christian activism in the '70s," Hunter told me, in order to understand how the movement took the incongruous form it did through 2004. "All of these new things had started happening with the cultural shift and the free sex, and abortion, and taking prayer out of the schools, all these really shocks to the system. There arose some real reaction, and it was really negative, very protectionistic: 'Hey, our society's gone down the tubes because now we're killing babies, and we're taking prayer out of the schools, and we've gotta rise up and fight this.'" That, he said, was "the origin of the movement—which wasn't bad. But I think what happened was there was just kind of a fixation on a very narrow agenda, a very self-centered agenda, because what you heard over and over again was, 'They bash Christians, this is all about going after faith in this country.' So it was a very kind of paranoid language and still is to this day, partly because that's the easiest way to mobilize people and raise money."

But that's not the end of the story, Hunter said. "In the first level of maturity, most movements are started out in a negative cause," he said. But "then you mature, then you start tilting toward, 'Wait a minute. Are we just against stuff, or are we actually *for* something? Can we really build something good instead of just being against something bad?'" What this "something good" might add up to, particularly when it comes to politics, is anybody's guess at this point. At Northland on Primary Sunday, the clues were decidedly mixed. Hunter was almost done prowling the church's broad stage, enthusing his way toward the benediction, when he finally touched on politics. First, he asked folks to consider signing a petition for a statewide referendum banning gay marriage—something old. Then he encouraged people to vote but not to expect the pastor to tell them how—something new. "I don't care who you vote for,"

Hunter said, shrugging theatrically. "Vote your values. Vote what you think Jesus's values would be." He laughed. "As close as you can get!"

★

In the grim days after the 2004 elections, I asked the Reverend Mel White, who founded the Christian GLBT rights group Soulforce, what progressives and Democrats could do to reach out to evangelical voters. White made it clear that their message would have to emphasize what the two sides have in common. "We forget that Jesus was intent on liberating us from materialism—while fundamentalists are all about materialism," he said. "Jesus's message was, 'Sell everything you have; give your money to the poor; take up your cross and follow me.' The real Jesus calls us to justice and mercy."

That sort of moral appeal was made in the 2008 Democratic presidential primaries by Barack Obama and John Edwards, who both spoke freely and often about the profound influence their personal faith had in shaping their social politics and who both criticized liberal Democrats for their reluctance to court evangelical voters. But, as White had cautioned me, there is only so much that the Democrats can do about changing most evangelicals' minds and hearts. "Only people of faith can take on people of faith who've gone nuts," White said. "Jesus had no problem going against these same sorts of people, the Pharisees."

None of the rising generation of evangelical leaders has been more outspoken against the contemporary Pharisees, for longer, than Joel Hunter. In 1988, when Northland was still meeting in a skating rink, he became alarmed by Pat Robertson's campaign for president and penned a warning tract called *Right Wing, Wrong Bird,* observing that "Christians have this image of just being raving lunatics; and in some respects, it is well-deserved." Hunter exhorted evangelicals to think for themselves, to look past the culture war issues that had come to define Christian politics. He told me he was especially disturbed by "people's kind of shallow thinking about Christian political involvement—i.e., if we just elect a religious-enough person, then everything's gonna go okay. It's magic-bullet thinking."

At the time, Hunter's dissenting voice was drowned out by the media-amplified cacophony of the Falwells, Dobsons, and Robertsons. But by 2006, when Hunter mounted his most audacious challenge to the religious right hierarchy, new voices were being heard. There was Jim Wallis, whose book tour for *God's Politics: Why the Right Gets It Wrong and the Left Doesn't Get It* turned into a Christian left minirevival, declaring, "The religious right is being replaced by Jesus." There was the Reverend Gregory Boyd, losing a thousand congregants in his St. Paul megachurch after delivering a series of six "Cross and the Sword" sermons decrying Christian right imperialism: "Never in history have we had a Christian theocracy where it wasn't bloody and barbaric," Boyd said. "I am sorry to tell you that America is not the light of the world and the hope of the world. The light of the world and hope of the world is Jesus Christ." There was former rock guitarist Rob Bell, the "revolutionary" leader of Mars Hill Bible Church in Grandville, Michigan, preaching an unorthodox, scripture-centered social gospel for young evangelicals while poking the Christian right in its tenderest spot: "[R]eligious people killed Jesus because He threatened their system. So what they say is faith is actually fear, no matter what it masquerades as and no matter what high and lofty language they employ—it is fear that is rooted in ignorance and, actually, a lack of faith."

Hunter took a long leap of faith in October 2006, when he signed on to the unlikely challenge of reviving the debt-plagued, internally divided Christian Coalition. The episode made headlines when Hunter resigned under duress before officially assuming the post. Though he had, in the interest of full disclosure, given coalition leaders a copy of *Right Wing, Wrong Bird* and told them he intended to change the focus to "compassion issues," it was a doomed match from the start. Once rank-and-file stalwarts got wind of Hunter's opinions on religious-right excesses, his opposition to the death penalty, and his support for a two-state solution in Israel and Palestine, his backing withered. Hunter admitted to me that he now wonders, "Man, what was I thinking?" But, he said, "I was curious as to whether or not any of the traditional hard-right organizations could really expand the agenda."

He got his answer. But the story made great copy, and it turned Hunter into a symbol of the generational clash in evangelical politics. In 2007, the National Association of Evangelicals asked him to star in a thirty-second "creation care" commercial. "Did you know that evangelical leaders are telling us that global warming must be stopped because it will bring more devastating floods, droughts, and disease?" Hunter said in the spot. "As Christians, our faith in Jesus Christ compels us to love our neighbors and to be stewards of God's creation."

It sounded meek enough, but it set off a major fuss among traditionalists like Dobson and Paul Weyrich, who refused to sign on, and warned their followers that ignominious retreat had begun toward the liberal social gospel of mainline Protestantism. Hunter, who had endured death threats after he announced his views in favor of an independent Palestine, was still surprised at the blowback against creation care. "It was, 'You're un-American. You hate America because you believe America ought to do things.'"

Which is precisely the point of the new politics, he told me the week before the Florida primaries: doing things. Redeem the Vote, an evangelical and ostensibly nonpartisan effort to register young voters, had come to Seminole County in the form of a bus full of registration forms, Cokes, and doughnuts, and Hunter greeted folks in the breezy chill outside with some college-aged kids from Northland. "This whole younger generation of evangelicals say, 'You know? I'm not so sure that I'm mad at anybody. But I care about the earth. I care about poor people. I care about those who have been exploited by the system. So I don't care what's conservative or liberal; I care about getting stuff done.'"

Jeremiah Shaw, a twenty-year-old student at Rollins College in Winter Park, Florida, comes as near as anybody to exemplifying that generation. Registered independent, he said he was equally open to Democrats and Republicans and still undecided about a candidate after sitting through Hunter's recent seminar on the presidential candidates. (The main topic, he said, was Barack Obama.) As an international affairs major because of his passion for missionary work, Shaw said he's "heavily involved in Africa, working with villages with orphaned children." He pshawed at the to-do raised when pro-choice Barack Obama spoke at Rick Warren's conference on global AIDS in 2007. "I don't find that controversial, actually. The more people are educated about the pandemic, the better off we are. I think that people are entitled to make decisions themselves," Shaw said of abortion, "but at the same time knowing what the consequences are."

Under-thirty evangelicals like Shaw hold the keys to a new political kingdom. They are less likely to be weekly churchgoers, less likely to adhere to biblical literalism, and more likely to support strong environmental reforms. Even on the core culture war issue of gay marriage, they increasingly stray from the fold, with more than 60 percent supporting either marriage or civil unions. While they remain overwhelmingly anti-abortion, a large majority would like to see some kind of civil cease-fire in the abortion wars. And they are all too vividly aware of the unflattering reputation given to the very name "Christian" by many of their evangelical elders. When I asked Shaw if people ever assume that he's going to be narrow-minded and hateful when they find out he's a Christian, he laughed. "All the time, man. And I always find myself kind of saying, 'I'm a Christian, but . . .'" It gets wearisome, Shaw admitted, because he is so not one of *those* Christians. "I just look at the life that Jesus lived, and I don't think he came to establish the kind of Christianity that a lot of people see. I try to model my life on Jesus's life, not on that other kind of Christianity. And I'm going to try and vote the same way."

All of which would have made his pastor proud. Except that Hunter was busy at the moment, casting his early vote for Mike Huckabee at the local elections office across the street.

★

For students at Birmingham's Samford University, there was no missing the Redeem the Vote bus on the brisk Friday morning before Super Tuesday '08. Pumping Christian rock out of its exterior speakers, the long bus had parked smack-dab in front of the Christian school's campus union. All morning, students passed by in clusters of threes and fours, eyeing the spectacle somewhat suspiciously as local TV cameras and a print reporter from Sweden milled around on the sidewalk, shivering and chatting with Redeem the Vote's three-person crew. When they ventured close enough, or stopped to wonder what the fuss was about, the students were immediately seized upon by a lanky, balding, high-octane fellow asking rapid-fire questions: "Are you registered? Are you planning to vote? Good. Absentee? Well, look, you're going to need to know what the law is for absentee voting in the state where you're from. We have all kinds of information inside the bus."

With his wife, Pam, Dr. Randy Brinson, a successful gastroenterologist in Montgomery, founded Redeem the Vote in 2003. This vigorous, fly-by-the-seat-of-its-pants effort to register young voters became an unlikely smash in 2004, with estimates of Redeemed voters ranging from 78,000 to nearly 100,000. The effort was boosted by public service announcements featuring *Passion of the Christ* star Jim Caviezel, which aired for free on some 2,500 Christian radio stations and was flashed on JumboTron screens at Christian concerts and festivals. "*USA Today* called us the most influential group in the 2004 elections," Brinson boasted.

In 2008, the bus—a new twist—had already pulled into twenty college campuses and countless church parking lots, with stops in Iowa, South Carolina, Florida, and Alabama. In Iowa, Redeem the Vote had set up tables at rallies for both Democratic and Republican candidates, and the Brinsons had offered their e-mail database—which they claimed was the largest in the country—to candidates of both parties. The only one to make extensive use of the database, which *US News & World Report* called "God's black book," was Mike Huckabee, the Republican winner in Iowa. The only candidate besides the Arkansan to accept Redeem the Vote's invitation to pray with them was Barack Obama, the Democratic victor. The group was credited with helping multiply voter turnout among both "faith voters" and under-thirties.

But who was Redeem the Vote turning out? Jeff Sharlet, *Rolling Stone* contributor and religious right scholar, had called it a "thinly veiled GOP vote machine" in 2004. After all, with the focus on Christian colleges and concerts, the youngsters being reached were naturally going to be mostly the products of Republican homes. But Brinson insisted that there was nothing partisan in Redeem the Vote's pitch. "Just because we're from the faith community, we're not antagonistic toward the Democratic Party," he said. "And just because we're interested in issues like health care and poverty, we're also not hostile to the Republican Party."

This even-handedness sounded like a bit of a stretch to some, especially given that Brinson was president of the Alabama Christian Coalition, hardly a nonpartisan entity. Sharlet also noted that the effort had been heavily staffed in 2004 by graduates of the religious right Patrick Henry College and that its board—including Huckabee, who was briefly the group's chairman before he announced his run for president—was overwhelmingly Republican, despite the inclusion of some evangelical Democrats. Redeem the Vote's "partners" included FOX News and Robertson's Christian Broadcasting Network. Plus, two of the Brinsons' sons, Christopher and Phillip, appeared on the 2008 Alabama primary ballot, running to be delegates for Huckabee.

But the point of Redeem the Vote, Brinson said, was not to breed Republicanism but to disperse evangelicals' political power across the spectrum. "Evangelicals in their voting blocs were supposed to be like sheep," he told me. No more. And whatever the short-term partisan effect of this effort might be, there was no question that young evangelicals were looking at politics from very different angles. When the most popular magazine for young evangelicals, *Relevant,* asked its readers to characterize their "political views on social issues (health care, poverty)," the largest portion—44 percent—called themselves "liberal" on that score. Asked, "Who do you think was a better president?" 55 percent picked Bill Clinton over George W. Bush. Asked the most crucial question of all, "Who would Jesus vote for?" the most popular answer was a Democrat, Obama.

"Obama holds the youth card," said Samford senior Caroline Bell. She had friends on campus working on his campaign, and that was fine with her, though she was working for John McCain and the local Republican Party. "I like McCain, because I think what the country needs right now is a middle man." But not, she said, a religious right man. "Huckabee will win Alabama, of course," Bell said. "But that's the past. I'm not one to play the Christian card. We want to move away from that, to no longer be thinking, 'Is this the Christian view? Is this the Christian candidate?' It's a whole lot more about policies now."

"It's almost shocking," said Rob Howell, Samford's student government president, "that abortion and gay marriage were so important before, and now those issues have disappeared." Instead, Howell said, "People are talking about health care and social reform. The economy is talked about more than anything. There's a lot of focus on the war and on the morality of our foreign policy. One of the main objections I hear is our insistence on being an occupying force in a foreign country." It was all cutting the Democrats' way, he said, except that the perception of the party as "antireligion" lingered. "It's not as prevalent as it used to be," Howell said, "but it's still there beneath the surface." (Pew polls found evangelicals' perceptions that the Democratic Party is unfriendly to religion rising from 20 percent in 2003 to 34 percent in 2006.)

By the time the bus pulled out of Birmingham, headed for Tuscaloosa, about one hundred Samford students had registered and solemnly promised to vote. (The day before, the Redeemers had made successful stops at two public universities, signing up about two hundred new voters at traditionally black Alabama State in Montgomery and one hundred while tailgating before an Auburn University basketball game.) What clearly interested Brinson more than the numbers was what happened when he could lure an audience into the bus. Around 11 a.m., he was perched in the middle of its comfy lounge area, surrounded by half a Samford journalism class (the others waited outside), doing his darnedest to make them think. "You've grown up in sheltered environments," he informed them. "As Christians we have to caution ourselves not to be cloistered, holing ourselves up in our own comfortable bunker."

In the course of ten minutes, Brinson plunged into all sorts of uncomfortable territory: gay "lifestyles" ("Everybody is a unique creation of God"), abortion ("If a woman has ended up in a situation where she feels compelled to make that decision, we're not going to condemn her for that"), and finally—eyeing his mostly female audience—something that really woke them up. "There is a strong connection between domestic abuse and the traditional idea of male supremacy and wifely submission to husbands in the church," he said, launching into a frank discourse on the church's role in the subjugation and abuse of women. "The gay community puts more resources into this issue, into fighting domestic abuse and violence, than anybody!" he bellowed at one juncture.

The students seemed a bit dumbstruck by it all. Eventually Brinson dialed back his voice to "Can I pray with you?" The students nodded yes, yes, a little nervously. "Lord," he said rather tenderly, "I just pray that you light them up."

8

CORNBREAD AND ROSES

"I never intend to accommodate myself to the tragic inequalities of an economic system which takes necessities from the many in order to give luxuries to the few."

—REVEREND MARTIN LUTHER KING JR., 1957

"I THOUGHT WE'D ride right down through North Wilkesboro and show you," said Dick Sloop, the newly elected chairman of the Wilkes County Democrats. Show me, that is, what has become of a place that was once a typical post–World War II Southern boom town. Much like hundreds of others, the small North Carolina city had brimmed with manufacturing jobs in furniture, textiles, and glass, then gradually added more white-collar service-sector jobs, boosting the townspeople's sense of optimism about an ever-expanding middle class. Compared to what folks made in the Manufacturing Belt for similar jobs, Southerners in union-unfriendly places like North Wilkesboro were hardly making out like bandits; even today, per capita income in Dixie lags at just 92 percent of the U.S. average. But the cost of living was low. And considering where the South had started—as practically a second-world economy, with wages at less than 60 percent of average Americans' in 1940—things were looking up, steadily, for a long time. They had kept on looking up right through the 1990s, helping Republicans as well as "New Democrat"

Bill Clinton sell their laissez-faire economics in these parts. But that was then.

Sloop took a quick left and a right, and pointed ahead of him to a vast slab of horizontal concrete, empty except for a couple of scattered, and perhaps abandoned, cars. "This used to be a street," he said. "It used to be a merchant street, called A Street. They tore all the commercial buildings down and put in that parking deck. Nobody ever used it. It was grant money that built it. Killed the street." It was about two o'clock on a balmy spring Saturday, and there was not a soul in sight, except a couple of young women who appeared to be simply out for a walk, in what once was downtown. "Saturday used to be a big day," Sloop said, wheeling us slowly up toward Main Street. "With the advent of Wal-Mart, big commercial enterprises—they killed Saturdays. Now everybody goes out to the mall. See here," he said, gesturing at the old storefronts, "this used to be a Rose's building. They've turned it into a little emporium for little shops. People are trying. All these buildings used to be mercantile. Most of it has turned into storefronts for CPAs, attorneys, investment firms. And then you have just flat-out empty buildings. Look at it: these streets are empty!"

If North Wilkesboro is an archetypal small Southern city—one more place where Democrats have continued to lose votes even as economic insecurities have spiked—Dick Sloop seems a lot like an archetypal old Southern boy. He graduated from high school in the last class before Wilkes County integrated, in 1966. A witty, churchgoing freethinker with the kind of ultra-neat white hair you would expect from a career army retiree, Sloop has a blocky face that easily and often reddens with merriment. Sloop retired from the National Guard in 1999 and got a nice job as a buyer for the county's largest employer, the Lowe's home-improvement chain. The company's leadership has always been staunchly Republican, and there was concern before Sloop was elected Democratic chairman in the county whether it might cause trouble at the workplace. "People asked, 'Do you think if you get elected it would have an impact on your job at Lowe's? And I said, 'I don't know. We'll find out.'"

Sloop, for all his military training, was irritated enough about America—and North Wilkesboro—and the Republican Party—that he was ready to break some rules and take some risks to wake people up. "This nation's in bad shape," he told me. "We're losing jobs right and left. The administration said, 'Oh, well, we're up a hundred thousand jobs this month.' And yeah, but at eight bucks an hour, that's not a living. You're right to call it a job, technically, but you can't make a living out of it. And, of course, all those jobs have no benefits now.

"We've lost sight of what we're all about," he continued. "I keep hearing all that crap about the middle class, and I'm gonna tell you something: I don't *see* a middle class anymore. There's haves and have-nots, you know? I've been fortunate, for a man that lacked a college education. I've always been able to have a job where I could make a living. I just can't make a lot of money. I've had a job where I could have a car every six or seven years, but never been out of debt—and that's OK. That's part of the American dream. And, of course, like any good American, I have access to more money than I could ever spend. I've got more credit than I've got sense."

Hard economic realities have settled in as the dreams have shriveled up. Aging Southern baby boomers like Sloop lived through the civil rights movement, the rise of the religious right, and the Sunbelt boom that helped make both movements possible—and today feel, all the more keenly, the loss of hope and security that has set in as manufacturing and white-collar service-sector jobs, the backbones of the Southern middle class, have swiftly disappeared. Since the early 1990s, North Wilkesboro has been hit hard—along with hundreds of similar Southern small cities—by what Lou Dobbs long ago took to calling, on his CNN show, "the outsourcing of America." The world's largest mirror plant, Carolina Mirror, was here; that's gone. La-Z-Boy and a bunch of other furniture plants were here; they're gone. Lowe's Companies Inc., which has grown into a Fortune 50 company, was "headquartered here for some fifty years," Sloop noted; it's just about gone, too. Earlier this decade, the company moved most of its operations to neighboring Iredell County, taking some two thousand jobs with generous benefits and retirement plans with it.

The defection of Lowe's was a particular sore spot. "The Republican commissioners, the powers at Lowe's made a deal with them," Sloop sighed. "We want to stay in Wilkes, but you're going to have to build us new high schools. Build us the schools, and we will keep them modernized technologically. We'll provide you with computers and everything. The commissioners initially said yes, but then when it came down to an actual vote, they said, 'Hey, wait, we can't raise taxes! We're gonna have to put this to a general referendum.' It was a full Republican board, all five members. Baptists. I called them the Zeroes. They got nothing done. They just couldn't make this decision, even though they knew there were thousands of jobs and all those tax dollars at stake."

Wilkes County voters, steeped in the antitax, antigovernment gospel of the GOP, voted down the "subsidies" to Lowe's—which had, indeed, asked for its share of favors through the years. But the Republicans' backlash mentality, Sloop said, didn't consider what towns like North Wilkesboro stood to lose because of "no new taxes." Over the previous two decades, the town's ruling Republicans had largely failed to build the kind of "capital"—good schools, appealing public spaces, thriving downtowns—that attracted "new economy" service and professional jobs. Elected on low-tax, government-is-not-the-answer platforms, local Republicans—and those in state legislatures and governors' mansions as well—faced a predictably tricky time governing effectively in the South. They were hamstrung by their own ideology. And their towns, as a result, became hamstrung as well. For folks like Sloop, North Wilkesboro was a symbol of the transformation taking place across America in the "ownership society"—meaning, "no-governance society"—of the Bush years. It was enough to turn a mid-fifties middle manager into something of a radical.

"Right up here on this corner, every Saturday, we stand here with our 'End the War' signs," Sloop said, pointing. "It's led by a lady who's a Quaker. We have a varying group of folks who show up. The Marine Corps League is our counterprotest. Now, I've yet to see anything that they stand for except that they support the troops. I have a banner"—a big teal one in the backseat—"that says, 'Support the Troops.' It's amazing. You learn a lot, standing on a street corner and standing up for something. I've been number one," he said, holding up his stubby middle finger, "a whole lot." Sloop's wife, Sheri, lost some of her business at a local beauty shop when the local newspaper printed a photo of the couple and others who traveled to Washington for the big antiwar rally in 2006. "Sure enough, she probably lost eight or ten customers over it. One guy came in there and yelled, 'Don't you ever let your name be associated with Cindy Sheehan again!' She was pretty embarrassed." But she didn't stop protesting.

The Sloops' tree-lined subdivision is a rolling stretch of Junior McMansions, mostly occupied by the remaining local Lowe's executives—the only people, according to Sloop, who can afford such digs in North Wilkesboro. "Our house was one of the first built out here, fourteen years ago. We got by under the covenants just by the hair of our chinny-chin-chins. I've always considered ourselves the trailer trash of Beacon Ridge." Sloop laughed and then quickly got serious again. "They say now that you've got to make a combined income of about $120,000 to be considered middle class. I'm gonna tell you right now: this is one of the few neighborhoods in this whole damn county where anybody makes that kind of money. Most people here are making in the mid to high twenties, I'd say."

Many of the town's residents work in the nearby Tyson Foods chicken plant, across the river in Wilkesboro. Otherwise, said Sloop, "there aren't really any living-wage jobs here. I work in a building with a thousand people, Monday through Friday, and most of them are women whose husbands are in some kind of self-employed-type situation, carpenters and whatnot. Most of these women are just there to pay for child care and to get health benefits. They're not trying to accumulate wealth. Everything goes to raise a family. It's tough. It takes every damn dime you got."

In the South's small, declining manufacturing towns, another economic trend has become all too obvious over the past few decades—the multiplying wealth of the wealthy. "When you start making millions of dollars a year," Sloop said, looking around his tidy neighborhood, "your idea about keeping all that becomes more and more acute. You want to protect it. And of course, even if you've got two or three million already, you don't have enough. The president of our company, Robert Niblock: nice guy. But oh my gosh," he said mockingly, "he took a two-million-dollar pay cut this year because we didn't meet expectations. But still made six. Well, bless your heart, I'm glad you could pull off such a sacrifice."

How is he managing to get by? I asked.

"It makes you wonder," Sloop said, chuckling.

Considering the perilous economic times in Wilkes County and so many communities like it in the postmanufacturing South, Sloop sees big opportunities for Democrats to make gains—if they can find their populist voice. "The Republicans, no matter how good they think they've got it, in the end they always wind up beating themselves," he said. "You're seeing it now. But this time, I think you're seeing a *huge* unraveling. Because they didn't deliver for the religious right." But Democrats have not, so far, found a way to take advantage. "They've been gutless," Sloop said with a disgusted frown. "Gutless."

During all those years of running Republican Lite campaigns, Southern Democrats never learned how to combat the reductive political thinking that Republicans have so long nurtured. "The thing I have the most trouble with Republicans with—and they're good people, don't get me wrong—is the single-issue voter," Sloop said. "They cannot see beyond guns. They cannot see beyond abortion. They cannot see beyond flag burning. And then they talk about immigration. They say, 'What would you liberals do about this?' I say, 'I'd make them raise their hands, swear 'em in, say, "You're all Americans. Start paying taxes." That's easy, a no-brainer. Instead, y'all want to make some sort of ordeal out of it.'" Sloop observed that more than half of the workers at the Tyson Foods plant are Hispanic. "People talk about getting rid of them. I say, 'Who's going to feed us? They grow and harvest most of our food. Are you gonna go out there and pick artichokes all day for six bucks an hour? I don't think you are.'"

He wound up his tour on a traffic-choked, plug-ugly business highway. "This is the strip," he said. "This is America. It's all homogenized now. All your local flavor has been reduced to Applebee's." He passed the time at red lights by perusing the bumper stickers on the neighboring cars. "Let's see: 'I love my wife.' Uh-huh. 'Evolution is a lie.' Well, we know where *he* stands. You have to love these people." And you have to wish, if you're Sloop, for a Democratic Party that will finally help rouse them and make them "see there's only one way—until we get a real third party, maybe—that we can bring any kind of forward-thinking government and any kind of hope for a new middle class back. I'm finally seeing some Democrats getting some cojones on 'em. That's what has to happen. Speak out some truth. And stop pandering—*stop your damn pandering!* Lay it out in a way that people can hear, and stand back and watch what's going to happen."

★

When even Bill Clinton's relative popularity in the South couldn't stop the Democratic Party's slide in the 1990s—partly because he didn't try to organize the party's grassroots to compete with the GOP—the strategists who didn't want to write off Dixie began recommending drastic measures to cut into the Republicans' edge with white, male, rural, "NASCAR" voters like Sloop. Most prominent among them was Dave "Mudcat" Saunders, who helped "countrify" the modernizing, high-tech entrepreneur Mark Warner into the Virginia governorship in 2001.

"Get though the culture with true tolerance, give Bubba a cause, and he *will* pull the 'D' lever," Saunders said. "Stick up your nose at Bubba, give him no causes, and he'll vote for the Republican for cultural and social reasons alone. For a long time now, he's been told by everybody from Rush Limbaugh to Charlton Heston that Dems are nothing but a bunch of antigun, anti-God, tax-and-spend wimps."

The Bubba focus seemed to work, especially in such economically battered spots as the southwest Virginia hamlet of Chilhowie. Between 1988 and 2002, Chilhowie had lost 1,430 factory jobs; the town's total population in 2001 was just a few hundred more people than that, 1,827. The cultural unity shtick alone could not win those votes. But, unlike Harold Ford Jr. in his "Republican squared" 2006 campaign in Tennessee, Warner had a bold agenda for affordable health care and job creation—and once he had the ears of rural white Virginians, those were the issues that Warner hammered home. In spite of a last-ditch spate of race-baiting—leaflets and radio ads blanketed conservative Virginia, painting Warner as an anti-gun, death-penalty opponent with a jones for gay marriage—the first Democrat in decades won the state's southwest. Some leaflets featured a photograph of Warner with the Democrats' candidate for attorney general, Donald McEachin, an African American. But most of the folks who saw them apparently decided that jobs and medicine outflanked the liberal menace.

The bluegrass bands and Sportsmen for Warner clubs might have helped inoculate Warner against those clichéd attacks. He had signaled to folks that he was "all right"—*hell, if sportsmen are for him, he must be.* But a little bit of Bubba goes a long way. It helps less and less in the populous suburbs, and hardly at all in the new-economy metropolises; if a Democrat's stab at cultural populism becomes an end rather than a means, as Ford's did, it's just another spin on the old Republican rhetoric, and that dog won't hunt in the emerging South. Without a tremendously appealing economic message, one that recognized the hard realities of the present while pointing forward to smart-sounding solutions, all the cultural pandering in the world wouldn't have won Virginia for Warner—or for Governor Tim Kaine and Senator Jim Webb after him.

Democratic candidates—both national and Southern—could do much worse than to study how those three economic populists broke through. Goodness knows they could use some fresh models. Right around the moment when the South's rising economic tide began to subside, especially in manufacturing counties like Wilkes, the Democratic Party had ditched economic populism—derided as "Old Democratic" thinking by the Clintonites—in favor of a Wall Street–friendly, free-trade agenda. Between 1993 and 2000, the South lost almost 250,000 manufacturing jobs that were attributable to NAFTA. In this decade, the bottom started to fall out— to a total of almost 920,000 factory jobs gone from 1990 to 2006. Meanwhile, the corporatization of farms brought deep cuts in agricultural employment across the region, from 20 percent of the workforce in 1981 to 15 percent in 2002. By the end of the 1990s, even some Republicans were renouncing free trade. But Democrats were slow to press the issue to their advantage. They continued to write off the region with the country's highest poverty rate (more than 14 percent, against a national average of 12 percent), lowest median income (in 2004, about $41,000 to the nation's $47,000), and highest percentage of people without health insurance (more than 18 percent to the country's 14 percent). They failed to sell a good-government, invest-in-the-future message in a region that badly needs it: according to one study, six of the ten states in the nation least prepared to adjust to the idea-driven information economy are Southern.

But there had also been a new economic South rising while the industrial South fell to decay. In North Carolina and Virginia, among others, the state governments invested heavily in "idea economy" meccas in Research Triangle Park and the D.C. suburbs; new financial hubs popped up in the big cities of Dallas, Charlotte, Nashville, Houston, and Atlanta. Much of the South's population—which was 79 percent urban by 2006—clustered around these "postindustrial metropolises," where city, suburb, exurb, and office park flow together in a seemingly endless (and all too often barren) landscape of tasteful newness. The white-collar, nonnative professionals who settled with their families in these places generally conformed to a political profile that offers Democrats yet another opportunity to sharpen an economic message that can remake the South's political map. As journalists like Jacob Hacker and Rick Perlstein have noticed, these folks tend to be independent-minded, not traditional liberals. But they are also, despite relative prosperity, experiencing what Perlstein calls "proletarianization" in the workplace, a trend that portends "more solidarity and economic populism."

The "new economy" has had a less than sweeping political impact on the South so far—partly because the national Democratic party has not bothered to craft an economic message that speaks to both the struggling working class and the insecure white-collar folks in the ideapolises. What is needed, in the post-NAFTA South, is a populist Democratic pitch that can be heard by white working-class voters and embraced by the newly emerging office populists—one that reestablishes Democrats as the people's party by capturing not only the economic but the moral tenor of the emerging South.

Rather than harking back to the demagogic populism of old, this new populism should aim to unite folks against corporate excesses (including the outsized tax breaks and similar perks that Southern states have used to lure car plants and other big manufacturers) and remind them of the value of good government at the same time. The long-term key to building a durable progressive base in the South is not cultural pandering; it's crafting a Democratic (and democratic) economic populism, a morally-based, multiracial vision of fairness and progress that marginalizes Republican populism. Just as the Republicans succeeded in claiming some centrist Southerners in the 1960s and '70s with suburban Christian populism, the Democrats now have an opportunity to take the populist mantle. And in the wake of the surprising successes of populist Democrats nationwide in 2006, one presidential contender banked his campaign on it.

★

Shawn Dixon had to blink back tears. The twenty-four-year-old son of factory workers in rural western Kentucky, Dixon had already cemented his status as the pride of Columbus—population 229—by graduating from the University of Kentucky and matriculating at the prestigious New York University Law School. Now he was back home, on a steamy Thursday afternoon in the fall of 2007, to introduce presidential candidate John Edwards at the most improbable rally of the campaign.

"I've never seen a candidate close to my house at all," Dixon told me later. "And there I was, standing next to Senator Edwards with a microphone in my hand, looking out at this unbelievable crowd"— upward of two thousand people, nearly ten times the size of the town. For weeks, volunteers had worked to spruce up the Columbus-Belmont State Park. "Everybody in town had mowed their yard. Schools had sent kids in buses. Folks took vacation days from work. But still, right up till Edwards got there, a lot of them still didn't believe it was happening. People were saying, 'Will he actually come? He's not really going to come *here*.'" A presidential candidate was actually materializing—it didn't really matter which one—with Columbus looking as shiny and proud as it had in decades. "It was completely overwhelming," Dixon recalled, "just such a powerful demonstration of how hungry people are for attention in the rural South and rural America."

They are particularly hungry for some Democratic love. A couple of months earlier, Dixon had read on the Web site Eventful.com that the Edwards campaign had agreed to send the candidate to whichever town in America had the most folks go online to "demand" his presence. Edwards promised to answer at least ten questions wherever he went. "I'm sure they were hoping it would be somewhere in Iowa or New Hampshire," Dixon said, "or at least some good-sized place with a lot of media." Instead, thanks to a campaign Dixon stirred up on Facebook, MySpace, and DailyKos, by far the most "demands"—more than 1,800—were for Edwards to speak in a town with no stoplights, three hours from the nearest airport, and fifty minutes from a McDonald's, where his appearance would be, in the words of one ballcap-wearing local fellow, "the biggest thing that's happened here since the Civil War."

During the "late unpleasantness," Columbus had been a key Confederate fortress, used to block the passage of Union gunboats and supply vessels to the Deep South and western theaters of the war. Since Dixie fell, it had not been key to much of anything— unless you were looking for a symbol of what's eaten away at small-town America in recent decades. "Like many rural communities across the South," Dixon wrote on Eventful, "job loss in the face of rising health-care costs and education costs have crippled the economy" of Columbus, such as it was. A friend of Dixon's dad had recently been forced to sell his house and move into a trailer.

"Most people in this area live paycheck to paycheck at eight dollars an hour," local postal worker Bruce Cunningham said before the rally. "It's really tough."

The town of Columbus, a native calling herself "harleymoma"

wrote on Eventful, "definitely is rural America. Why, we are as country as a turnip green." As in so many rural towns, the mostly white population has been aging and declining and struggling to afford even turnips. It has also, despite a six-to-one Democratic edge in voter registration countywide, increasingly been voting Republican: George W. Bush won 57 percent of Hickman County's votes in 2004. Which, as Dixon stood among the throng at the Columbus-Belmont State Park, where the Civil War glories are enshrined, was making him a little fretful. Dixon had planned to talk about ending the war in Iraq, about the crying need for broadband access in Hickman County, about the pressing need for universal health care. "I was nervous because I wasn't sure how the crowd was going to react to the progressive ideas I wanted to talk about. I wrote my speech with applause lines that I knew would appeal to liberals—but I thought, maybe this will fall flat. It's been untested because people in places like Hickman County haven't been hearing this message."

But after Dixon collected himself and began to hold forth, "people were going crazy, yelling, for every issue I brought up. And it was the same with Edwards." After reminding the folks of his own humble roots in Carolina factory towns, the candidate told them what they already knew: "The system in Washington is rigged. It is rigged against you. You will never have a voice unless and until the Democrats have a candidate who understands your lives, who won't give up on your part of America and places like this all across the country."

When it came time to ask the candidate some questions, the folks showed they were more than ready to have a voice. "This one man with a full beard and overalls, heavyset, stood up," Dixon said, "and I remember thinking, 'Huh-oh, what's *this* going to be?' Then he asked this very well-informed question about the erosion of civil liberties under the Bush administration, the executive orders authorizing wiretaps and incarcerations." A few minutes later, a young man from Hickman High raised his hand and challenged Edwards: "You talk about redeeming our reputation in the world. How will the world see us as a force for good when we reflexively support everything Israel does?" An older man rose to ask a question on health care on behalf of his daughter, a diabetic who had dearly wanted to come but was home suffering from a rotator cuff injury they couldn't afford to get treated without insurance. "If we had the kind of health-care system you're talking about," he said, "she would have already had it took care of."

Edwards responded with a story he'd picked up while campaigning in rural southwest Virginia. James Lowe, age fifty-one, "told me he had been born with a severe cleft palate. Because he had that, he could not speak. It was completely fixable; he just had no health-care coverage, so he couldn't fix it." The only sound in the park, as Edwards told the tale, was the distant rush of the Mississippi. "But here's the problem: they fixed it when he was fifty years old. James Lowe lived in America for fifty years without being able to speak." In most places on the campaign trail where Edwards told that story, folks were aghast; in Columbus, folks just nodded solemnly. They could all give him a story to match it.

"A big country guy came up to me afterward and said, 'That really touched my heart,'" Dixon said. "People here don't parade their emotions; if somebody said that, they really mean it." The people in Columbus might or might not have been converts to the principle or morality or business sense of universal health care; they all knew damn well how desperately they and other folks needed it.

But ever since Bill Clinton had won Kentucky in 1996, they had barely seen a Democratic candidate in the state. So they had no reason to think the politicians knew a whit about their lives, let alone that one would work to get them the thing they most needed to get their economic lives in order. "We've really let Republicans create this monopoly in rural America that is totally unnecessary," Dixon said. "It's less 'D' and 'R' than, Who's going to pay attention to us?

When you talk to voters in western Kentucky about the issues, they are largely progressive people. But you have to make the race about those issues. I can't tell you how many people Edwards converted that day, folks with Bush stickers on their trucks. They hadn't heard a Democrat say, 'I know who you are. I have sat around a kitchen table trying to figure out how in the world to pay the bills'"—something Edwards recalled his blue-collar parents doing when he was growing up. "You have to engage the Republicans on what people are *really* worried about."

More to the point, you have to do it in a way that people can relate and respond to—one of the Democrats' greatest weaknesses in recent years. One of Edwards's biggest applause lines in Columbus came when he was asked about No Child Left Behind. Where Al Gore or John Kerry would almost surely have answered by talking about policies and proposals, Edwards had a plainer way of explaining why he wanted to ditch the test-heavy federal mandate: "No kid ever got smarter from filling in bubbles. Or, as a friend of mine said, you don't make a hog fatter by weighing it."

Edwards was the first Democratic candidate to recognize the importance of rural Southern votes since Jesse Jackson tried to woo struggling white farmers and laid-off factory workers into his Rainbow Coalition in 1988. Like his fellow South Carolina native, Edwards was out to reinvent populism—and give the Democratic Party a renewed sense of purpose. But the limitations as well as the promise of Edwards's formula were obvious from the moment his second run for president kicked off.

In 2004, Edwards's wing-and-a-prayer candidacy had been propelled by much the same happy populism that won Bill Clinton the White House in 1992 (and was not too far afield from Ronald Reagan's morning-in-America vision of giddily content milk-truck drivers, postal workers, and nursing home attendants). The one-term senator from North Carolina constantly invoked his inspiring rise from his humble roots as a mill-worker's son—to the point of near self-parody—but he also developed a compelling diagnosis of the "two Americas" created by growing economic inequities, an economic problem more pronounced in the South than elsewhere.

His prescriptions for healing the rift, however, sometimes sounded as threadbare as his foreign-policy expertise. Edwards later admitted to me that he hadn't given much thought to what he would do as president before he ran. But after an often-bitter experience as John Kerry's running mate, Edwards came away disgusted by the safe, poll-tested politics he had embraced—and determined to build the "two Americas" message into a full-blown reinvention of Democratic populism. "In our effort to be reelected," he told me during his 2005 "poverty tour" of the country, "we've become minimalists, tinkering around the edges—our tax cut is better than yours, we'll have smaller class sizes. That's not what the country wants. There's a hunger to be about a big moral cause—a moral cause that's bigger than our own self-interest."

After a disastrous Republican presidency, during which Americans were asked—at wartime—not to sacrifice or unify, but instead to continue shopping and pretend that everything was dandy-fine, it seemed like high time for Edwards's sense of nobler purpose. "We need to ask Americans to be patriotic about something beyond war," was how he put it. Challenging the country to conquer poverty was a timely message, too, after Hurricane Katrina's grim aftermath forced Americans' eyes to fix, at least for a few unforgettable moments, on the vivid evidence of how their fellow citizens were living, and dying. The reminders of the still-strict correlation between race and economic well-being—all those thousands of black New Orleanians, right there on our televisions, with whites sprinkled only sparsely among them—served as bracing slaps to the national consciousness. Edwards also caught the drift of the "purpose-driven" evangelicalism being preached by the next generation of Christian leaders. "I can go into any megachurch in the South or

Midwest or West," Edwards said, "and talk to people about poverty, and they will respond."

But Edwards, in the end, did not reach enough of them. That's partly because his message was hard to hear beneath the media-hyped clamor of the Clinton-Obama prizefight. It's also because the noble Democratic crusade came to be led by Obama instead. And, of course, it didn't help when Edwards, the champion of moral populism, got caught paying four hundred dollars for a haircut, building—while publicly fronting an anti-poverty center at the University of North Carolina—a lavish new home best described as a "compound," and drawing a half-million-dollar consulting fee from a Wall Street investment firm that turned out to be connected with dozens of home foreclosures in Iowa, of all inconvenient places.

One of the perils of moral politics, whether it be the socially conservative brand offered by Republicans or the economically moral brand offered by Democrats, is the way it brings hypocrisy so naggingly into the mix—and makes the slightest perception of it potentially crippling. There is, of course, no logical connection between candidates' personal wealth—or their use of it—and the sincerity or validity of their plans to help the poor. The president whose portrait has graced more Southern drawing rooms (and bathrooms, to be honest) through the years, Franklin D. Roosevelt, was pretty persuasive proof of that. But Edwards was seen as perhaps a bit too smooth, too starched and smiley and perfect to be a regular guy. The haircuts and foreclosures did not help that image.

In the early states where Edwards did get a hearing—Iowa, South Carolina, and Nevada—another flaw was exposed: his support was almost exclusively rural and white. That was partly because his campaign, especially in Iowa, focused intently on small, rural caucus sites where just a few dedicated voters could carry the day. But it is also because, while his emphasis on lifting people out of poverty helped mark him as a "values" candidate in a way he wasn't in 2004, this message also played into what William Greider, former *Washington Post* and *Rolling Stone* national reporter and author of *The Soul of Capitalism: Opening Paths to a Moral Economy*, called "a liberal fallacy that has injured Democratic prospects for thirty-five years. American prosperity is going along okay, they seem to assume, but we just left out the poor." Middle-class voters know that's false—and so do those who are struggling to climb up into the middle.

That's the economic reality that Edwards's populism emphasized too little. He talked about "the middle class" a lot, as politicians are practically sworn to do, and his policies would certainly have bene-fited them. But as with most progressive economic policy since the 1960s, Edwards's proposals—including mandated universal health care and affordable college for everyone, along with an ambitious public-works program to rebuild the nation's infrastructure—would have done more to help folks on the lower rungs than those in the slipping middle.

"It's the right thing to do, of course," Greider said. "But people don't find it convincing. How exactly do you push the bottom up in any substantial way when the middle is falling?" However morally oriented the Democrats' economic message may be, it also has to speak to the troubles and aspirations of the huge population making between $30,000 and $75,000 a year. Nationally, these voters went for Bush in 2004 by a narrow margin, but in the South Bush won them by more than 20 percent. A new Democratic populism that wins in states like Kentucky has to bring these folks—many of them in white-collar, service-sector jobs, in debt up to their ears from overbuying oversized houses in the exurbs of Atlanta or Dallas—into the fold with the low-wage and out-of-work folks at the bottom.

That means recognizing and offering creative solutions to what Greider called "the long, gradual slide in middle-class well-being during the last generation." He noted, "The structure of wages and jobs has been deeply damaged by globalization, and the protective mantle of government was withdrawn by deregulation." The South was the last region to feel the psychological wallop of this, in part because things had been looking up for so long that middle-class aspirations still burned bright. But as mortgage and housing crises spread like viruses across the Sunbelt in 2007 and 2008, along with job losses and spiraling gas prices and health-care costs, the old optimism became a precious commodity.

Edwards's populism was sometimes a downer. In his genuine dedication to waking up Americans to the destitution in their midst, Edwards felt compelled to spend a lot of time laundry-listing just how bad things had gotten for so many folks. Despite his naturally upbeat demeanor, this educational effort—and the sometimes strained anger he flashed at those big corporations—took some of the air out of Edwards's message. While the Republicans could be fairly characterized as having spread false economic hope in their campaigns, Democrats (other than Bill Clinton) had long showed a tendency to sound the trumpet of doom.

"What does it mean today when Dave McCune, a steelworker I met in Canton, Ohio, saw his job sent overseas and the equipment in his factory literally unbolted, crated up, and shipped thousands of miles away with that job?" John Kerry asked in his 2004 acceptance speech. Recognizing the economic struggles and worries of "regular people" is essential for Democrats—it's the primary way to draw a flattering contrast with the out-of-touch, corporate-controlled Republicans. But it is one thing to feel people's pain; another thing to dwell on it with the morbid obsessiveness of the Book of Job.

The Democratic message that has worked best in the postwar South, for moderately progressive governors from Terry Sanford in North Carolina in the early '60s to Mike Beebe today in Arkansas, focuses not so much on the economic woes of the present as on opening brighter vistas for the future. Sanford had the "crazy" idea to buy a huge swath of pine forest in the undeveloped center of North Carolina and turn it into an office park for the high-tech future; the payoff was Research Triangle Park, which now employs about 40,000 white-collar workers. In that spirit, Virginia governor Tim Kaine spent heavily on ambitious highway and public-transit projects in booming northern Virginia, just as his predecessor, Mark Warner, dedicated millions to improving the "capital" of struggling southwest Virginia. The emphasis of successful Southern Democrats has been on tackling problems and overcoming them—not just on articulating the troubles and pointing out how wrong they are. Where the old Democratic populists spent a lot of time wagging their fingers at working people's enemies, while squinting sympathetically at their struggles, the new Democratic populists will win by pointing the way ahead.

The rising evangelical social movement, conveniently enough for those new Democratic populists, is not about taking moral stances on issues—it's about working, both with other religious groups and with secularists as well, toward solutions to moral catastrophes. "We just want to get things done," said Northland's Joel Hunter. That is also, just as conveniently, the attitude of younger Southerners, both evangelical and otherwise. In Shawn Dixon's generation—a generation happily removed from the post–civil rights backlash, sick of the narrowness and hatefulness of the religious right's old-style politics, and rejecting anti-government Republicanism—the South's political future lies.

It is a future where Democrats and progressives will still face considerable challenges, some due to the cultural friction caused by unprecedented immigration. As the Republican Party loses its grip on white voters in Dixie, there is every reason to expect that race-baiting and culture-warring will be resurrected with increasing desperation. But that doesn't mean it will work any better than the GOP's anti-immigration campaigns in 2006. The rising generation shows few signs of being susceptible to the old lures of the Southern strategy—and many signs of offering real hope for a postracial, post–religious right, postbacklash South that will view progressive politics not as culturally alien but as an increasingly snug fit.

★

Growing up poor in Neshoba County, in the postintegration South, Donna Ladd always knew one thing about her future: it wouldn't unfold in Mississippi. After graduating from Mississippi State ("I wanted to go somewhere else but didn't have the money"), she deejayed in New York and Washington, D.C., clubs and broke into alternative journalism. In 2001, she completed a master's project at Columbia about Neshoba County's unsolved civil rights–era cases. "All of a sudden," she said, "I had this urge to report about Mississippi."

A year later, Ladd and her partner had abandoned their Manhattan sublet for the capital city of Jackson, where they decided to launch an alternative weekly of their own. "I got here and found that it was the most interesting place," Ladd said. "There were all these progressive people who didn't want to admit it—at least not in mixed groups. I'm not sure what Republicans were supposed to do to you if you admitted it. I remember sitting at Hal and Mal's," the liberal hangout in Jackson, "with this woman I'd met who was a business owner and clearly a progressive. Well, I dissed Bush very loudly. And the poor woman said, 'You're not a Republican?' It was bizarre, because obviously no one at that table was a Republican. I just looked at her like, 'No! Why would I be? *Please.*' It was one of those moments where I realized people just aren't speaking up in the South! That's been our problem. Progressive people weren't finding each other." From the time Ladd kicked off the *Jackson Free Press* in 2002, she said, "a big part of our role has been to make young people feel like they don't have to leave" just because they're not down with the Republicans.

The *Free Press,* named after a multiracial Mississippi civil rights–era paper, makes a powerful case, as Ladd said, "that you can stay right here and do it." Starting the paper was "a gamble," Ladd acknowledged, understating the case considerably. Its viability would depend on local advertisers, and "initially they were reticent. A lot of small-business owners who were more progressive-minded were afraid to advertise with us at first—afraid they'd lose their business." Most came around—though it often took some personal, and very Southern, persuasion.

A few months after its launch, the *Free Press* ran its first feature story about a gay person. "So the people in this black beauty shop who just loved the paper said, 'We're not so sure about this gay thing.' I just looked at them and said, 'Well, you know, there were a lot of people who weren't so sure about equal rights for black people, either. You don't have to agree with this. But I sure appreciate your having the paper here.' And to my knowledge there's never been another problem," though the paper doesn't shy away from controversy by any stretch.

"The day we went to war in Iraq, it was a very nervous time for us. We pulled a cover story and ran some Alternet stories about the myths of the war, which turned out to be correct. We were up all night. This was just the February after we'd started it. We didn't sleep. We ran an antiwar cover. We lost three distribution spots. One was a white beauty shop down south: 'We'll drop a lawsuit on you if you bring your paper over here.' There was a CD Exchange place up north that didn't like it. Another place was 'just scared'—but they're now advertising with us." The week after the antiwar cover, the *Free Press* set a new advertising record.

When I visited the *Free Press* in April 2007, Ladd and her staff were still ticking off "milestone" advertisers who had finally signed up. A year later, the paper's business had become a matter of trying to turn a profit rather than just staying afloat. The paper circulates seventeen thousand copies a week, with an estimated fifty thousand readers—and twice that number online, where the *Free Press* has a buzzing Web site. Ladd's investigations into unsolved racist murders have garnered awards and helped lead to convictions, marking the paper as one of the feisty weeklies that have helped fire up progressive communities in Little Rock (*Arkansas Times*), Raleigh-Durham (the *Independent*), Nashville (*Scene*), and Texas (the hard-hitting *Observer*). But it's not only progressives who appreciate having a fresh, bracing blast of liberal media in places where the decline of crusading, locally owned newspapers has left a void filled mostly by Rush Limbaugh and Bill O'Reilly.

"You wouldn't believe the calls we get," Ladd said. "In the beginning I'd get this kind of phone call, and I'd hear the voice and think, 'Oh, hell, here it comes.' You think back to Howard Dean's comment and you think, 'This is that guy driving the truck.' Then he'll start launching into how much he loves the paper and what we're doing." At the same time, the paper's readership is between 50 and 60 percent African American—far higher than most alternative papers in major urban centers.

"Now we have church ads coming to us. We haven't sought them out," Ladd reported. "Recently we got an ad from a conservative church in the suburbs that is doing this purpose-driven stuff, trying to find volunteers. And we have discovered that Mississippi is filled with religious progressives. We're respectful of religion, so they feel comfortable with us—even if we do challenge them plenty. We're very pluralistic about it. I'll use a Bible verse in my editor's note, but I'll also quote Buddha. People like that, because they don't feel like they're being beaten up for being religious." There's a lesson in this for the Democrats. "There's a potential for using religious language to move people on the fence to be more progressive. The culture here speaks in that language. We're starting to get back in touch with it."

Southern Democrats are also getting back in touch with the fighting spirit of a working people's populism—a far cry from Clintonian compromise. "Tear into their tail on economic issues and don't let up" is the war cry of Jamie Franks, a thirty-four-year-old who grew up in rural poverty, became the youngest legislator in Mississippi history, and ran a plucky but losing race for lieutenant governor in 2007. "Knock 'em down. Hit 'em right between the eyes. That's what you got to do," Franks said, leaning forward over his desk while whapping a balled-up fist into his open left hand. "Talk about the issues. Talk about the people that matter. If you can get your message across, you can kick their tail every time."

The trouble has always been how to define "your message" as a Southern Democrat. Not quite young enough to belong to the under-thirty generation of Southerners who tend to see culture war issues as a distraction from the real substance of politics, Franks belongs to the Mudcat Saunders school. "The challenge for a Democrat is, number one, to get past those social issues," he said. "I think you've got to have a candidate who can say, *I'm* not for abortion. I'm not for same-sex marriage. And I've got the voting record to prove it. Then the Republicans can't cloud the real issues of whether or not someone's going to get their health-care needs taken care of, or whether someone's going to have a job. We have seen that, under Republicans, anything big business wants, from tort reform to how Katrina relief contracts were given out, it gets. What happens if a ninety-year-old woman gets injured in a nursing home? Or even killed? You can do anything you want to her, and her life's worth fifty thousand dollars now. That's wrong. In 2004, Governor Barbour kicked sixty-five thousand elderly and disabled Missis-sippians off Medicaid. That's wrong. He thought they were all, let's face it, black folks that didn't vote for him anyway."

Ladd likes Franks's pugilistic populism, but believes that the Democrats' need to play up their social conservatism to open Southerners' minds to progressive economic messages is dwindling. "Democrats do need to deflect the wedge issues," she said, "but not by not talking about them. Democrats keep losing in part because they run from debates over things like abortion. One thing

Southerners like in a politician is courage. I don't mean that you have to be stupid about it," she said, laughing. "But if you're pro-choice, make your argument. Argue that the legislature should just stay out of it if that's what you think. The point is, you don't win by running away from tough issues, like so many Democrats have done for so long. Once you start running, you're on your way to losing the debate."

Even with the Democrats' nonexistent Southern campaign in 2004, the under-thirty vote in almost every Southern state rose considerably—and swung considerably left of the older vote. John Kerry won the youth vote in most Southern states, but nowhere more convincingly than in Mississippi. What that portends, Ladd argued, is the end of good-hearted Southerners' long habit—lamented by Martin Luther King Jr. in his "Letter from Birmingham Jail"—of being too quiet and polite to fight back against the extremists in their midst, whether segregationists or religious right zealots. If national Democrats finally start to listen—especially to the portents of a progressive groundswell that began to announce themselves even more loudly in the 2008 presidential campaign—Southern voters have the potential to reshape the partisan landscape of America.

★

When history's most symbolically charged Democratic presidential campaign steamed southward in mid-January 2008, with Hillary Clinton and Barack Obama headed for their showdown in South Carolina, the blue state bloggers and pundits immediately began to fear the worst. If racism and religious bigotry had not previously infected the campaign, they warned, it was surely now about to take over. *New York Times* columnist Bob Herbert flew down to the Palmetto State—brave soul!—and hammered out a scathing column about how "South Carolina, where the Confederate Flag still flies on the grounds of the State Capitol, is a disturbing example of how difficult it is for people of good will to dispose of the toxic layers of bigotry that have accumulated over several long centuries." Despite his palpable revulsion against the very idea of South Carolina, Herbert said something quite wise: "In South Carolina the Confederate flag is flying right out there in the open and Pitchfork Ben is on display for all to see. But in most other places, the hostility to blacks remains on the down-low. No one wants to deal with it."

When the returns came in from South Carolina, and the Southern primaries that followed, there was clear evidence that more and more white Southerners *were* dealing with those layers of bigotry— and longing to shrug them aside. The "race issue" did indeed slither to the surface in South Carolina, courtesy of an apparently concerted effort by Clinton's campaign to undercut her opponent's "postracial" appeal. Her top adviser in New Hampshire had gotten the race-baiting under way by telling a reporter that past cocaine use—which the candidate had discussed openly in his book, *Dreams from My Father: A Story of Race and Inheritance*—might come back to haunt the party if he won the nomination. Stumping for Clinton in South Carolina, Black Entertainment Television founder Bob Johnson made an even cruder reference to "what Obama was doing back there in Chicago." Former president Bill Clinton, who spent more time in South Carolina than his wife in the month leading up to the primary, told Charlie Rose on PBS that nominating Obama would be a chancy "roll of the dice" for Democrats. In a South Carolina debate, Hillary Clinton tried to undercut Obama's community work in black Chicago neighborhoods by pointing out his relationship with notorious slumlord Tony Rezco. The Clinton campaign also hoped to convince black voters—often stereotyped as "go-along" types—that the Illinois senator would be "unelectable."

All in all, it was a low-down effort to "racialize" the campaign in the part of the country where folks are supposed to respond to racial fears and resentments. But it did not have all the intended effects. After having trailed in the state for most of 2007, Obama won a sweeping, two-to-one victory in South Carolina over Clinton (with John Edwards in third). The attempt to package Obama as some kind of coke-dealing, slumlord-pimping, possibly Muslim cousin of Al Sharpton no doubt helped Clinton carry some older white voters, but a much larger number of black South Carolinians rejected Clinton's message in the profoundest way—after first supporting her. A sound majority of whites also rejected Clinton; they split their votes between Obama and Edwards. Among younger white voters, age eighteen to twenty-nine, Obama won a majority. It was a majority that mattered, too, with under-thirty turnout nearly triple the level of 2004.

Given every opportunity to live up to their stereotypes, South Carolina voters demonstrated that there was less truth to them than ever. On Super Tuesday, the pattern was repeated in Georgia, Alabama, and the border state of Missouri—groundswells of young voters, and even stronger white support for Obama. Overall, the multiracial candidate won majorities in the South on Super Tuesday from every population segment except white women, Hispanics, and whites over forty-five. In Georgia, 58 percent of young voters went for Obama—and those between thirty and forty-four went for him as well. In Virginia, Obama won 72 percent of whites under thirty and 58 percent of those between thirty and forty-four.

Baptist preacher Mike Huckabee's own successes in Dixie—he finished a close second to John McCain in South Carolina, then swept six Southern states on Super Tuesday—bore further testimony to the new winds blowing through Southern politics. Running a shoestring campaign—he had spent just $7 million by the end of Super Tuesday, winning more votes than Massachusetts governor Mitt Romney could muster with $134 million—Huckabee had relied on both his considerable wit and charm and on a novel message combining hardcore cultural conservatism with an economic message that bore more comparison with the "Louisiana socialist" Huey Long than with supply-side Ronald Reagan.

In South Carolina, Georgia, and Alabama, Huckabee enthusiastically gunned for the NASCAR vote, stumping with wrestling legend Ric "Nature Boy" Flair in barbecue joints, holding meet-and-greet-and-shoots at local gun clubs, and dishing out regular-guy populism, like his quip in Columbia that "in many ways, I'm like a lot of people in the United States. I'm a guy over fifty looking for a job." It was a class-based twist on the good-old-boy populism that had worked so well for George W. Bush. But Huckabee was, in other ways, the anti-Bush—and, for some, the very antithesis of a "real" Republican. His economic populism was a leap beyond where the GOP had traditionally dared to go, with its focus on people "who are living from one paycheck to the next, who are literally one paycheck from not being able to pay the rents, one paycheck from not being able to pay for their kid who falls in the playground and breaks his arm, one paycheck from not being able to put gas in the truck."

Huckabee's solutions to the struggles of the working and middle classes were not worked out particularly well. (His central economic plank was the "fair tax," a quacky scheme that would abolish the income tax and replace it with sales and luxury taxes.) But his rhetoric unsettled Republican traditionalists, especially given Huckabee's reputation during his tenure as governor of Arkansas for being willing to raise taxes to improve education and build better roads. When he proposed a major new public-works project to build a superhighway through Middle America in 2008, the cries of the right-wing punditry that he was, in Tennessean and GOP candidate Fred Thompson's terms, a "pro-life liberal" were loud and wild. A bemused *Christian Science Monitor* columnist wondered if the ultimate effect of the former Baptist pastor's run might be to "convince evangelicals to vote Democratic in November."

Not only had Huckabee talked about economic suffering and good government, he had articulated the "compassion" issues of the new purpose-driven church, calling on folks to "be conservationists and good stewards of the earth," adding that, "we have to deal with issues like poverty and AIDS. If we don't do that, we're not even being true to our own Christian beliefs." In Iowa, he had elaborated: "If I really know what it means to follow Jesus, it means no kid goes hungry tonight. It means no wife gets the daylights beat out of her by some abusive alcoholic husband. . . . It means not one single elderly person has to make the choice between food and medicine."

While Huckabee was unsettling the corporate-Christian alliance that fueled the GOP's Southern dominance since the 1970s, Obama's ease with matters of race and faith—challenged surely by the Reverend Jeremiah Wright controversies—and his emphasis on building grass-roots networks in the South and elsewhere showed glimmers of changing the very image of the Democratic Party in Dixie. During the primary season, his economic message lacked detail and bite, and so it was not clear whether Obama stood as the first transformational fig-ure in twenty-first-century Southern populism—or whether his suc-cess was largely the product of the generational changes bubbling up. But there was no question that Democrats throughout the South were energized in ways unthinkable in the four decades since LBJ signed the Voting Rights Act: in every Southern primary, even the early ones when the Republican race was every bit as competitive as the Democrats', more Democrats voted in the primaries than their counterparts. In South Carolina, where the GOP contest proved decisive nationally, 220,000 more votes were cast on the Democratic side, with Barack Obama winning more than twice as many as Republican victor John McCain.

It also happened in some of the strangest places. While Obama racked up huge margins—often three to one—in the swelling "postindustrial metropolises" of Dixie, he was also besting his white opponents on some of the most conservative white terrain remaining in the region. In rural Edgefield County, South Carolina, a neo-Confederate stronghold that boasts a 57 percent white population and produced both Pitchfork Ben and twentieth-century segre-gationist senator Strom Thurmond, Obama won 65 percent to

Clinton's 26 percent. In picturesque Abbeville, where South Carolina legislators met to vote on secession in 1861 and the white supremacist League of the South has its headquarters, the population is 68 percent white today; Obama won 56 percent to Clinton's 23 percent.

In Georgia on Super Tuesday, a little-noticed result emerged from scrubby northeastern McDuffie County, which is 61 percent white: Obama carried it two to one. It was in McDuffie County, in the early 1890s, where the first—and only—multiracial populist movement in Southern history flared up most notably and was defeated most spectacularly. Tom Watson, a fiery local attorney who had become a national hero to the burgeoning People's Party movement of black and white "agrarian populists," was headed to victory against the local establishmentarian Democratic congressman. Watson insisted on holding fully integrated campaign rallies, and his biracial class-warfare rhetoric further shocked the system: "You are kept apart that you may be separately fleeced of your earnings," he told an integrated audience during that fateful campaign. "You are made to hate each other because upon that hatred is rested the keystone of the arch of financial despotism which enslaves you both. You are deceived and blinded that you may not see how this race antagonism perpetuates a monetary system which beggars both."

Watson's challenge to the pro-business, white-separatist Democrats attracted constant death threats and heaps of denunciation from white newspapers across America. His surrogate campaigners, black and white, put themselves at just as much risk. H. S. Doyle, a young black preacher, made sixty-three speeches on Watson's behalf during the 1892 campaign. As C. Vann Woodward recalls in *Tom Watson: Agrarian Rebel*, Doyle was threatened with lynching at one late campaign stop, and he "fled to Watson for protection. Watson installed him on his private grounds and sent out riders on horseback for assistance. All night armed farmers roared into the village. The next morning the streets were 'lined with buggies and horses foaming and tired with travel.' All that day and the next night they continued to pour in until 'fully two thousand' Populists crowded the village— arms stacked on Watson's veranda. Prominent among them was the Populist sheriff of McDuffie County." As Woodward puts it, in his understated manner, "The spectacle of white farmers riding all night to save a Negro from lynchers was rather rare in Georgia."

The populist movement that inspired the spectacle turned out to be tragically short-lived. In one of the most fraudulent elections in American history, Watson was defeated by ballot-box stuffing, bribery, voting of minors, violent intimidation at the polls, and by "Negro plantation hands and laborers . . . [who were] hauled to town in wagon loads, marched to the polls in squads, and voted repeatedly" against Watson. Though he was later elected a U.S. congressman and senator, Watson eventually became an ardent white supremacist himself, bowing much the way George Wallace later would to the racial deformities that so long ruled Southern politics, by force if not always by popular demand.

There have been other false dawns since the 1890s. The New Deal infused Southern Democrats with a progressive sense of purpose, and a small-but-welcome measure of class consciousness in their voting, but the pull was not so strong that it could transcend, or break, the chains of racial apartheid. The civil rights movement finally broke those chains, but a new form of white political solidarity evolved. Now the post-'60s backlash generation is dying, both literally and figuratively. A multiracial, post–religious right generation of Southerners has begun to emerge, with precious little patience for the politics of the past. This new generation is joined by millions of middle- and working-class boomers who have lived through too many false economic dawns to keep believing the same old lines and by millions of laid-off and forgotten industrial workers. Together, these Southerners are rebelling against the religious right's narrow definition of what "values" mean in politics. They are questioning the Republican Party's ethics and its Wall Street agenda. They are impatient with Southern Democrats' timidity and national Democrats' Dixiephobia. And they are swelling up into a force that, with proper care and tending, will turn Dixie blue.

NOTES

★

This book is probably best described as a mix of journalism and polemic; it is not a work of scholarly history, as you might have noticed, any more than it's a work of so-called political "science." Most of my observations, insights, and quotations were drawn from firsthand reporting, stretching from 1972 through the 2008 presidential primaries. Below, I've noted primary sources as economically as possible; any source without an initial full citation is listed in the bibliography.

When I refer to "the South" in this book, I mean the eleven former Confederate states plus Kentucky, Oklahoma, and West Virginia, unless otherwise specified. One frequent exception occurs when I cite statistics and projections from the U.S. Census Bureau, which adds Delaware, Maryland, and the District of Columbia.

Introduction: Mess of Trouble

2 "esoteric cult": Key, *Southern Politics,* p. 277.
2 "criminal forces": Quotes from Richard Nixon's speech at Greensboro, N.C., Nov. 4, 1972, are drawn from a transcript at *The American Presidency Project* (www.presidency.uscb.edu).

4   "What is needed": Jesse Helms, *Viewpoint*, WRAL-TV, Oct. 19, 1964, quoted in Grace Nordhoff, ed., *"A Lot of Human Beings Have Been Born Bums": 20 Years of the Words of Senator No* (Durham, N.C.: Carolina Independent Publications, 1984), p. 62.

4   "now realize they have been Republicans": Dent quoted in Egerton, *Americanization of Dixie*, p. 130.

5   "The story of the Republican Party's march": Ryan Sager, "Purple Mountains," *The Atlantic*, July/Aug. 2006.

6   By the 2032 elections: Based on U.S. Census Bureau figures and projections, Census 2000 and 2005. By 2030, New York, Ohio, and Pennsylvania are expected to lose a total of fourteen electoral votes, almost as many as the South will gain. For a handy map, see William H. Frey, "The Electoral College Moves to the Sun Belt," Research Brief (Washington, D.C.: Brookings Institution, 2005), p. 3.

1. The Solid Southern Strategy

9   "There is a party for Caesar": Tom Watson, *Life and Speeches of Thomas E. Watson* (Thomson, Ga.: Jeffersonian Publishing Co., 1916), pp. 210, 234, 238; and *New York Tribune*, Aug. 19 and Oct. 6 and 15, 1904.

10   "delivered the South": Johnson quoted in William E. Leuchtenburg, *The White House Looks South* (Baton Rouge: Louisiana State University Press, 2007), p. 325.

10–11   "The South is no longer": Thomas Schaller, "A Route for 2004 That Doesn't Go Through Dixie," *Washington Post*, Nov. 16, 2003.

11   more folks still said they were Democrats: Jeffrey M. Jones, "Democratic Edge in Partisanship in 2006 Evident at National, State Levels," Gallup News Service, Jan. 30, 2007. The South's most Democratic-leaning states were Arkansas (26 percent edge), West Virginia (24), Kentucky (13), Florida (11), North Carolina (11), and Virginia (10).

11   They . . . strongly favor progressive populist: See Pew Research Center, "Demographic Profile of Party and Ideology 2003," "December 2004 Political Typology Survey" (Washington, D.C.: Pew Research Center, 2004), and Scott Keeter, "In Search of Ideologues in America" (Washington, D.C.: Pew Research Center Publications, Apr. 11, 2006).

12   "extremism in the defense": Barry Goldwater, address to Republican National Convention, July 16, 1964.

13   "Forced integration": Goldwater quoted in Black, *Rise of Southern Republicans*, p. 152.

13   "the five-chambered, race-obsessed heart": Egerton, "Southernization," in Dunbar, ed., *Where We Stand*, p. 207.

14   "wags the dog": Lassiter, *Silent Majority*, p. 6.

14   "revolved around the incisive recognition": Ibid., p. 233.

14–15   "Let us listen now": *Nixon/Wallace 1968 Election Spots*, International Historic Films, 1985; ibid., p. 236.

15   "Republicans turned out": Lassiter, *Silent Majority*, p. 232.

15   But its impact on Southern politics: See Degler, *Other South*, pp. 21–22; and C. Vann Woodward, "Southerners Versus the Southern Establishment," *Future of the Past*, p. 285.

15 "The great popular heart": Vance quoted in Tyson, *Blood Done Sign My Name*, p. 172.

16 "The South is a big, complicated region": Nicholas Lemann, "What Is the South?" *The New Republic*, Jan. 29, 2007.

16 "even on the question of race": Key, *Southern Politics*, p. 664.

17 "Quote me as saying": See Frady, *Southerners*, p. 18.

17 "As long as the Negroes": Folsom quoted in Frady, *Wallace*, p. 105.

17 "practically a communist": Ibid., p. 101.

18 "segregation forever": George Wallace, inaugural address, Jan. 14, 1963.

18 "first-class citizenship": Sanford quoted in Drescher, *Triumph of Good Will*, p. xix.

18 "fighting words": Yardley quoted in ibid., p. xix.

18 "must be done with law and order": Hollings quoted in "The Nitty-Gritty Senator," *Washington Post*, Oct. 14, 2004.

18 "That speech": Clyburn quoted in ibid.

19 "conjures up notions": Key, *Southern Politics*, p. 664.

20 Between the midterm elections of 1966 and 1970: See "Black Power at the Dixie Polls," *Time*, June 15, 1970.

20 61 percent in 1963: *Gallup Poll: Public Opinion, 1935–1971*, p. 2248; *New York Times*, May 3, 1970; Lassiter, *Silent Majority*, p. 249.

20 21 percent in 1976: Hetherington, *Why Trust Matters*, p. 104.

20 elected 665 blacks: "New Day A'Coming in the South," *Time*, May 31, 1971.

20 "humanistic South": Askew quoted in Egerton, *Americanization of Dixie*, p. 10.

20 "future . . . shaped and shared": Bumpers quoted in Yoder, "Southern Governors," in Ayers and Naylor, eds., *You Can't Eat Magnolias*, p. 162.

21 "The era of defiance": Ibid., p. 161.

21 "Our state government": Wallace quoted in "New Language on Inauguration Day," *Time*, Feb. 1, 1971.

21 "We in the South": Jackson, "Glory Hallelujah," in Ayers and Naylor, eds., *You Can't Eat Magnolias*, p. 134.

21 some 1,800 speeches: "New Day A'Coming in the South," *Time*, May 31, 1971.

21 "The Negro belongs to": Talmadge quoted in ibid.

22 "discrimination is over": Carter, Jan. 12, 1971, quoted in *You Can't Eat Magnolias*, p. 364.

22 "the region is abandoning": "New Day A'Coming in the South," *Time*, May 31, 1971.

23 "The party abandoned": Egerton, *Where We Stand*, pp. 220–21.

23 "Today the Democratic Party stands": William Jennings Bryan quoted in Witcover, *Party of the People*, p. 275.

24 "Bona fide Democrats": Egerton, *Where We Stand*, p. 232.

24 "an officeholder who was a flagrant racist": Kazin, *A Godly Hero*, p. 149.

25 "The Dixiecrats are dead, right?": Author's interview with Julie Wham, Aug. 2003.

25 "Shit, just try being Democrats": Author's interview, Oct. 2005.

25 the pollsters at Pew, who define populists: Keeter, "In Search of Ideologues in America."

26 Nine of the nation's fastest-growing: Analysis of U.S. Census data by William Frey, Brookings Institution, 2008.

26   Hispanics swung back: Edison/Mitofsky exit polls.

27   "Why does the Democratic Party persist": Reed, "A Lost Cause," *Boston Review,* Summer 2004.

27   "The answer to the question": Hackney, "Identity Politics, Southern Style," in Dunbar, ed., *Where We Stand,* p. 196.

27   "dangerously inadequate": Henry Louis Gates Jr., "A Liberalism of Heart and Spine," *New York Times,* Mar. 27, 1994.

29   "wielding power successfully": "Under the Weather," *The Economist,* Aug. 9, 2007.

29   perhaps five cows: See Alex Koppelman, "George W. Bush, the Ticklish Cowboy from Crawford," *Salon,* Aug. 29, 2005.

2. The Lite Brigade

32   "Don't nobody get moved": Jackson quoted in Frady, *Jesse,* p. 380.

32   "the eight-hundred-pound": Egerton, *Where We Stand,* p. 216.

33   "I don't give a shit": Author's interview with Steve Jarding, Oct. 2005.

33   "as strategists, they were as blind": Judis and Teixeira, *Emerging Democratic Majority,* p. 119.

34   "an issue of social justice": Webb, *Born Fighting,* p. 293.

35   "the younger white-collar": Pat Caddell memo to Jimmy Carter, Dec. 10, 1976, quoted in Judis and Teixeira, *Emerging Democratic Majority,* p. 120.

36   "They spend 95 percent": Author's interview, Aug. 2003.

36   "That's the irony": Author's interview, Mar. 2007.

37   "Democratic Party cannot serve God and Mammon": Bryan quoted in Kazin, *A Godly Hero,* p. 52.

37   "to steer, not to row": David Osborne and Ted Gaebler, *Reinventing Government* (New York: Plume, 1993); for foundations of the DLC philosophy see also William Galston and Elaine Ciulla Kamarck, "The Politics of Evasion: Democrats and the Presidency" (Washington, D.C.: Progressive Policy Institute, 1989).

37   "they didn't try to become Democrats": Bill Bradley, "A Party Inverted," *New York Times,* Mar. 30, 2005.

39   "response to every election cycle": Reed, "A Lost Cause," *Boston Review,* Summer 2004.

39   "Bill Clinton blew an opportunity": Author's interview, Mar. 2007.

39–43   2000 Democratic National Convention: All material and quotes from Rose Marie Lowry-Townsend, Steve Jarding, Willie Legette, John Wilson, Stella Adams, Bill Clinton, and Al Gore are drawn from author's interviews, notes, and transcripts.

44–48   Oconee Democrats: All material and quotes from Charles Hamby, Barry Butler, Maxie Duke, and Don Aiesi are drawn from author's interviews, notes, and transcripts.

45   the South's 173 electoral votes: Total as of 2004 (Alabama 9, Arkansas 6, Florida 27, Georgia 15, Kentucky 8, Louisiana 9, Mississippi 6, North Carolina 15, Oklahoma 7, South Carolina 8, Tennessee 11, Texas 34, Virginia 13, West Virginia 5).

45   "It just about killed me": Author's interview, Aug. 2007.

48   "really believed what they were saying?": Author's interview, Oct. 2005.

49   "Bowing and scraping": Schaller, *Whistling Past Dixie,* p. 6.

49   "lets Democrats be Democrats": Ryan Lizza, "Forget the South," *New York Times,* Dec. 14, 2003.

49   "What are the Democrats smoking?": Author's interview with Todd Taylor, Jan. 2004.

50   "a big damn contradictory mess": Author's interview, Feb. 2006.

50   "Everybody always makes the mistake": Kerry quoted in William Saletan, "The South Carolina Debate," *Slate,* Jan. 30, 2004.

50–51 archly noted on air: Jake Tapper, *World News Tonight,* ABC News, Jan. 25, 2004.

51   "Presidential campaigns are the primary vehicle": Author's interview, Oct. 2005.

51   "see all Southerners as culturally alien": Teixeira quoted in Dick Polman, "If Democrats Look Away from Dixie, Winning White House May Be Tough," *Philadelphia Inquirer,* Nov. 27, 2003.

51   "they can't fucking count": Saunders quoted in transcript of "Mind of the South: Understanding Public Attitudes," conference on New Strategies for Southern Progress, University of North Carolina, Chapel Hill, Feb. 25, 2005.

52   227 electoral votes: Author's calculation, based on news reports and jibing with Steve Jarding and Dave "Mudcat" Saunders's calculations in *Foxes in the Henhouse,* p. 105.

53   ads in Ohio alone: "Presidential Election Inequality: The Electoral College in the 21st Century" (Takoma Park, Md.: FairVote, 2006), p. 43, http://www.fairvote.org/media/perp/presidentialinequality.pdf.

53   "bothered to talk to them": Author's interview, Oct. 2005.

3. Dixiephobia

54   "The actual history of the South": Tyson, *Blood Done Sign My Name,* p. 172.

54   "We had the money": Ickes quoted in James Carney, "What Happens to the Losing Team," *Time,* Nov. 3, 2004.

55   23 percent: Ruy Teixeira and Alan Abramovitz, "The Decline of the White Working Class and the Rise of a Mass Upper Middle Class" (Washington, D.C.: Brookings Institution, 2008), http://www.brookings.edu/~/media/Files/rc/papers/2008/04_demographics_teixeira/04_demographics_teixeira.pdf.

55   Bill Clinton had carried 510: Post-election analysis in Ronald Brownstein, "GOP Has Lock on South, and Democrats Can't Find Key," *Los Angeles Times,* Dec. 15, 2004.

55   "the altar of centrism": Thomas Frank, "What's the Matter with Liberals?" *New York Review of Books,* May 12, 2005.

55   "Fuck the South": Anonymous, "Fuck the South," Nov. 3, 2005, http://www.fuckthesouth.com.

56   "form its own nation": Beckel quoted in Joseph Curl, "Blue States Buzz Over Secession," *Washington Times,* Nov. 9, 2004. My thanks to Glen Browder, in "The Real Southern Problem and My Democratic Party's Future," special report for the University of North Carolina's Program on Southern Politics, Media & Public Life, 2005, for pointing me to many of these Dixiephobic quotes.

56   "'Oh, poor Alabama'": O'Donnell quoted in Curl, ibid.

56   "and it can go to hell": Zell Miller, "How Democrats Lost the South," *Washington Times,* Nov. 3, 2003.

56   "Blue States Buzz": "Blue States Buzz Over Secession," *Washington Times,* Nov. 9, 2004.

57   "You see your neighbors": Author's interview, Jan. 2004.

57   "deception in its eye": Zinn, *Southern Mystique,* p. 217.

58   "[T]he country and, by natural extension": Levenson, "Divining Dixie," *Columbia Journalism Review,* Mar./Apr. 2004.

58   "not quite a nation": Cash, *Mind of the South,* p. viii.

58   "Like most stereotypes": Author's interview, Mar. 2007.

59   "a separate and distinctive place": Egerton, *Americanization of Dixie,* p. xxi.

59   "There ain't no South anymore!": Fowler quoted in Ann Gerhart, "Rebel Y'all," *Washington Post,* Feb. 2, 2004.

59   "Every Arkansas likes to have": Author's interview, Apr. 2007.

59   "The South is everything its revilers have charged": Zinn, *Southern Mystique,* p. 262.

60   "Talking about race": Levenson, "Divining Dixie," *Columbia Journalism Review,* Mar./Apr. 2004.

60   "has enabled us to carry along": Wilson, *Patriotic Gore,* pp. xxxi–xxxii.

60   "the Mason and Dixon line not only divided": Woodward, "Antislavery Myth," *Future of the Past,* p. 269.

60   a revolution every twenty years: See David Saville Muzzey, *An American History* (Boston: Ginn and Company, 1911), p. 187.

60   "back into a savage state": Dwight quoted in Woodward, *Future of the Past,* p. 345.

61   "halitosis of the intellect": Ickes quoted in Frady, *Southerners,* p. 10.

61   "stunning blow": William Lloyd Garrison, *Narrative of the Life of Frederick Douglass, An American Slave* (New York: Penguin, 1982), preface.

61   "the prejudice of race": Alexis de Tocqueville, *Democracy in America* (New York: Library of America, 2004), p. 460.

61   "the Negro is free": Ibid., p. 343.

61   "they castrate you": Baldwin quoted in Zinn, *Southern Mystique,* p. 226.

61   "shoddy cities and paralyzed cerebrums": H. L. Mencken, "The Sahara of the Bozart," *New York Evening Mail,* Nov. 13, 1917.

62   "Sahara of the Electoral College": Noah, "Forget the South," *Slate,* Jan. 27, 2004.

62   "The town, I confess": Mencken, *Religious Orgy,* pp. 28–29.

62   "Nor is there any evidence": Ibid., p. 29.

62   "no bitterness on tap": Ibid., p. 36.

63   "The man felt at home": Ibid., pp. 128–29.

64   "whatever appeared retrograde": Woodward, *Future of the Past,* p. 68.

64   "look away! Dixie Land!": Ibid., p. 67.

64   "casual barbarities": Meyerson, "Wal-Mart Comes North," *The American Prospect* online, Mar. 18, 2007, http://www.prospect.org/cs/articles?article=walmart_comes_north.

65   "a good place for you": Pew Research Center, 2005.

65   "cost in blood, rightfully crushed": Meyerson, "Wal-Mart Comes North."

65–66   "The South is a place": Schaller, *Whistling Past Dixie,* pp. 272–73.

66   "[H]ow can Iowa": Clinton quoted in David Yepsen, "Iowa Presents Steepest Hill for Clinton to Scale," *Des Moines Register,* Oct. 23, 2007.

67   "You know all those white guys": Dean quoted in Timothy M. Phelps, "A Run on Road Less Traveled: Dean Speaks Mind in Race," *Newsday,* Mar. 9, 2003.

67   "I intend to talk about race": Dean quoted in Scott Shepard, "Liberal Democrat Energizes Party," *Atlanta Journal-Constitution,* Feb. 22, 2003. The quotes from Donna Brazile and Maynard Jackson are also drawn from this article.

67–68   "extremely offended": Scott Shepard, "Democrats Aim for Dean in Debate: Comment on Southerners Draws Ire," *Atlanta Journal-Constitution,* Nov. 5, 2003. The quotes from John Edwards, Al Sharpton, John Kerry, and Richard Gephardt are also drawn from this article.

68   "black voters think for themselves": Reverend Joe Darby, "Black Voters Think for Themselves, Parties Should Recall," *The State,* Nov. 12, 2003.

69   "could've found a better way": Author's interview, Oct. 2005.

69   "I was really mad": Author's interview, Mar. 2007.

69   "He wasn't condoning": William Saletan, "Confederate Flag: The New Bum Rap on Howard Dean," *Slate,* Nov. 5, 2003.

69–70   "pain that I may have caused": Howard Dean, "Opening Remarks at Cooper Union," Nov. 5, 2003.

70   "What hurts Democrats most": Gene Lyons, "A Political Dead End," *Arkansas Democrat-Gazette,* Nov. 12, 2003.

70   "The thing that impresses me": Cummings quoted in Susan Baer, "Dean Is Expected to Get Support of Cummings," *Baltimore Sun,* Nov. 21, 2003.

70–71   "Democrats know the divide": Jesse Jackson Jr., "Howard Dean Offers Democrats a New Southern Strategy," *Roll Call,* Nov. 20, 2003.

71   "Gore chose a populist": Al From, "Building a New Progressive Majority," *Blueprint Magazine,* Jan. 24, 2001.

71   "wired workers": Mark Penn, "Turning a Win into a Draw," *Blueprint Magazine,* Jan. 24, 2001.

72   "ceaseless courtship": Noah, "Forget the South," *Slate,* Jan. 27, 2004.

73   "Democratic coalition must cease": Schaller, *Whistling Past Dixie,* p. 74.

73   "running *against* the conservative South": Ibid., p. 18.

74   "Tom DeLay mode": Kevin Phillips, "All Eyes on Dixie," *The American Prospect,* Feb. 1, 2004.

74–75   "If this war had smashed": Cash, *Mind of the South,* pp. 105–6.

75   "The trick of effective politics": Cooper, "Thinking of Jackasses," *Atlantic Monthly,* Apr. 2005.

76   "persisted in all along": Watterson, "'Solid' South," *North American Review,* Jan. 1879.

76   "If you fuck the South": Neal Pollock, "Don't Fuck the South," Nov. 10, 2004, nealpollack.org.

77   "not a single, solitary problem": Biden quoted in George Will, "Front-Runners Who Can Still Be Tackled," *Washington Post,* Nov. 15, 2007.

77   "For Democrats to turn their backs": Chris Kromm, "Election Lesson: Democrats, DON'T Write Off the South," *Facing South* online, Nov. 15, 2006, http://southernstudies.org/facingsouth/2006/11/election-lesson-democrats-dont-write.asp.

4. The Donkey Bucks

78–83   2006 Jim Webb Senate campaign: Material and quotes from Jim Webb, Mac McGarvey, Mark Rozell, Brittany Brading, Jimmy Taylor, and Robert Ervin are drawn from author's interviews, notes, and transcripts.

81   "Macaca": George Allen, "Allen's Listening Tour," Friday, Aug. 11, 2006, www.youtube.com.

82   "[T]he fight over ending legal segregation": Webb, *Born Fighting*, p. 293.

84–87   "Nobody believed this guy could win": Quotes from John Yarmuth and Mark Nickolas are drawn from author's interviews, Dec. 2006.

88   "increasingly the party not of 'the South'": Kromm, "DON'T Write Off the South," *Facing South*, Dec. 5, 2006.

88   Ford NRA rating: Nancy Zuckerbrod, "NRA-Backed Candidate Lacks Hunt License," Associated Press, Sept. 15, 2006.

89   "I share your values": Ford quoted in Steven Thomma, "Democrat Courts Conservative Voters in Tennessee Senate Race," *Seattle Times*, Oct. 6, 2006.

90   "At first a lot of the real committed Democrats said": Author's interview, Apr. 2007.

90   86 percent of Southerners were in favor: Pew Research Center, 2004 Political Typology survey.

90   "The irony is that if he'd run as a Democrat": Author's interview, Aug. 2006.

92   "It's a toss-up": Author's interview, Feb. 2004.

92–95   "Welcome to red-hot Republican terrtitory": Material and quotes from Seth Chapman, Dick Sloop, Mark Hufford, Clyde Ingle, and Bob Johnston come from author's interviews, notes, and transcripts of the Wilkes County Democratic Party convention, Apr. 2007.

93   Republicans have nearly a two-to-one edge: Voter registration figures from Wilkes County Board of Elections.

96   "if we knock on their doors": Dean quoted in Bill Walsh, "Demos Split on Electoral Strategy in South," *Times-Picayune*, Feb. 20, 2005.

96   "pick their nose": Paul Begala, *The Situation Room*, CNN, May 11, 2006.

96   "They start the next campaign": Author's interview, Aug. 2007.

97   helped win . . . congressional elections: Elaine C. Kamarck, "Assessing Howard Dean's Fifty State Strategy and the 2006 Midterm Elections," *The Forum: A Journal of Applied Research in Contemporary Politics,* vol. 4, 2006.

97   "Democrats have become outsiders": Wayne Holland, "Letter from Utah State Democratic Party Chair to Paul Begala," *Democraticunderground .com,* May 12, 2006.

98   "The Republicans sat down thirty years ago": Author's interview, July 2007.

98   "If you make your living": Author's interview, Jul. 2007.

98–99   "Washington's idea of accountability": Author's interview, Mar. 2007.

100   "We were the first county in the nation": Author's interview, Apr. 2007.

100–101   "My future grandchildren": Mark Hufford memo to Democratic National Committee, Nov. 2006.

101   "finally stands for something": Ibid.

101   "walking the talk": Johnson quoted on BlueNC.com, Apr. 4, 2007.

102–5   "a variety of signs you can't even imagine": Quotes from Judy Munro-Leighton, Jim Pence, Matt Gunterman, Jonathan Miller, and Shawn Dixon are drawn from author's interviews, Aug. 2007.

102 Despite the South's reputation: Pew Research Center polls, 2002 and 2003.

103 "the radical '60s antiwar movement on steroids": McConnell quoted in "Begging for Bucks," *Louisville Courier-Journal* blog, June 20, 2007, http://www.courier-journal.com/blogs/politics/2007/06/begging-for-bucks.html.

105 On the day in August: Larry Dale Keeling, "McConnell Vulnerable," *Lexington Herald-Leader,* Jul. 29, 2007; Al Cross, "How Much Trouble Is McConnell Really In?" *Louisville Courier-Journal,* July 29, 2007.

5. Color Codes

106 "[T]here is nothing indestructible": Zinn, *Southern Mystique,* p. 37.

106 "that dang, damn Confederate flag": Steve Spurrier quoted in "Flag Should Come Down from S.C. Statehouse," Associated Press, Apr. 16, 2007.

107 Orangeburg massacre: See "S.C. College Marks 'Orangeburg Massacre' Anniversary," CNN, Feb. 8, 2001, http://archives.cnn.com/2001/US/02/08/orangeburg.masscre/index.html.

109 Polled in the summer of 2007: Adolphus Belk and Scott Huffmon, Winthrop/ETV poll of African American South Carolinians, Sept. 14, 2007.

109 devoted to stirring up socially conservative black voters: See "Black Democrats Urge Media Counteroffensive," The Black Commentator, no. 18, Nov. 28, 2002, http://www.blackcommentator.com/18_commentary_2.html.

110–11 "The first thing I wanted to hear": Author's interview, Mar. 2007.

111–16 Eight months after that first debate: Material and quotes from Kevin Alexander Gray, Josie Barton, Michelle Barton, Reverend J. W. Sanders, Harold Mitchell, Carolyn Reed-Smith, Scott Huffmon, and Amaya Smith are drawn from author's interviews, notes, and transcripts, Dec. 2007.

112 Jackson's wildly successful 1988 uprising: See Frady, *Jesse,* pp. 378–401.

112 "garbage out of their cars": Perry Bacon Jr., "Obama Reaches Out with Tough Love," *Washington Post,* May 3, 2007.

114 Early on . . . Clinton's support among African Americans: CNN poll, Oct. 2007. Polls differed: Belk and Huffmon's Winthrop/ETV poll, www.winthrop.edu, in Aug. and Sept. 2007, showed Obama taking the lead among black voters.

114 It was a familiar routine: Jason Spencer, "Black Pastors Stand Behind Clinton," *Spartanburg Herald-Journal,* Nov. 28, 2007.

115 "Every Democrat running on that ticket": Ford quoted in "Race Doesn't Give Obama Edge in S.C.," Associated Press, Feb. 15, 2007.

117–20 Later, after Obama's overwhelming black support: Material and quotes from Efia Nwangaza, Kevin Alexander Gray, and Marjorie Hammock are drawn from author's interviews, notes, and transcripts, Dec. 2007.

117 he won a majority of under-thirty whites: CNN exit polls.

117 "Race defines vote": Real Clear Politics, Mar. 12, 2008.

120 he would bring out 30 percent more black voters: Nedra Pickler, "Obama Says He Can Turn Out Black Voters," Associated Press, Aug. 20, 2007.

120 turnout rises 2 to 3 percent: Ebonya Washington, "How Black Candidates Affect Voter Turnout," Working Paper No. 11915 (Cambridge, Mass.: National Bureau of Economic Research, 2006).

122 "Some white people feel": Author's interview, Apr. 2003.

123 the sheer voting muscle: 2004 Edison/Mitofsky exit polls.

123–24 Forty-six percent of white Southerners: Findings on white and black voter attitudes in the South from Pew Research Center polls, 2006.

124 Nowhere in the country: Pew Research Center polls, 2003–2007.

125 "a wholesome social leavener": McGill, *South and the Southerner,* p. 202.

125 "The destruction of the normal party": Cash, *Mind of the South,* p. 132.

126 fewer than one-third of Southern families owned slaves: U.S. Census 1860.

126 "protect a besieged social order": Hackney, *Where We Stand,* p. 189.

126 In Mississippi, black turnout: See Danny Duncan Collum, "Flagging Racial Progress," *Sojourners,* Jul./Aug. 2001.

127 "Power over the past": James C. Cobb, "On Flag, Look Ahead, Not Back," *Atlanta Journal-Constitution,* Feb. 23, 2003.

127 "bring in more money and jobs": Author's interview, Aug. 2003.

127 "They tried to trick it": Author's interview, Mar. 2007.

127 "slimy brown mass": Heidi Beirich and Bob Moser, "Communing with the Council," *The Intelligence Report,* Fall 2004.

128 "expressed a profoundly distorted view": Barack Obama, "A More Perfect Union," speech, Philadelphia, Pa., Mar. 18, 2008.

129 cause of "states' rights": Reagan quoted in Bob Herbert, "Righting Reagan's Wrongs?" *New York Times,* Nov. 13, 2007.

129–35 "Neshoba County is the Mississippi": Material and quotes from Donna Ladd, Stanley Dearman, Jewel McDonald, Leroy Clemons, and Susan Glisson are drawn from author's interviews, notes, and transcripts in Mar. and Apr. 2007.

130 "We deeply regret": Dick Molpus, Philadelphia, Miss., June 21, 1989.

130 During his campaign for governor: Reed Branson, "Popular Fordice Survives Stall in GOP 'Revolution,'" Memphis *Commercial Appeal,* Nov. 9, 1995.

131 found in an earthen dam just outside Philadelphia: For an excellent local chronicle of the murders, see "44 Days in 1964" on the Web site of the *Neshoba Democrat,* www.neshobademocrat.com.

131 When McDonald returned: William H. Frey, "Institute View," *The Milliken Institute Review,* Second Quarter 2001, p. 92.

134–41 "Natchez is a partying town": Quotes from Casey Hughes, Donna Ladd, Rita Royals, DeMiktric Biggs, Emma Sanders, and Renee Shakespeare are drawn from author's interviews, Mar. 2007.

135 young voters who went 63 percent: Todd Staufer, "Mississippi Youth Vote 'Blue'," *Jackson Free Press,* Nov. 11, 2004.

138 largest crowd ever for a DFA training: According to DFA chairman Jim Dean.

140 But it could also portend: See Adam Nossiter, "In Mississippi, a Judge's Ruling on Crossover Voting Raises Older Issues," *New York Times,* July 18, 2007.

140 Tellingly, black turnout was low: See Charlie Mitchell, "Thousands of Democrats Stayed Home," *Biloxi Sun Herald,* Nov. 14, 2007.

6. Big Bang

142 "I'm 'overqualified' for everything": Author's interview, Aug. 2006.

142 In Georgia, the drop: U.S. Census Bureau, 2005 American Community Survey.

143   The nation's largest outflows: See "Concerning Dixiephobia," *Booker Rising*, Nov. 28, 2006, http://bookerrising.blogspot.com/2006/11/concerning-dixiephobia.html; Cliff Hocker, "African Americans Are Leaving Major Cities for Opportunities in the South," *Black Enterprise*, May 2005.

143   "many Southern blacks may have been unclear": Merle Black and John Shelton Reed, "Blacks and Southerners: A Research Note," *Journal of Politics*, vol. 44, no. 1, Feb. 1982.

144   a different breed of Republican: See Rob Christensen and David Raynor, "Growth Transforms State GOP's Identity," *News & Observer*, Nov. 5, 2006.

144   "They're people who are more willing": Author's interview, Mar. 2007.

144   "tobacco country!": Author's interview, Mar. 2007.

145   By the late 1990s, six of the nation's seven: "The New Latino South: The Context and Consequences of Rapid Population Growth," Pew Hispanic Center, July 26, 2005.

145   In Florida alone: John W. Wilhelm, "Do We Care About the Future?" *The Democratic Strategist*, May 23, 2006, http://www.thedemocraticstrategist.org/ac/2006/05/do_we_care_about_the_future.php.

145   In Georgia: U.S. Census Bureau statistics, 2000 and 2005; Michael Hoefer, Nancy Rytina, and Christopher Campbell, *Estimates of the Unauthorized Immigrant Population Residing in the United States, January 2005* (Washington, D.C.: Department of Homeland Security, Office of Immigration Statistics, 2006).

145   the number of Hispanic births: National Center for Health Statistics report, May 2006.

146   57 percent voted Democratic: CNN exit poll, 2006. The national Hispanic vote in 2006 was estimated at 69 percent Democratic. See Cornell Belcher and Donna Brazile, "The Black and Hispanic Vote," *The Democratic Strategist*, http://www.thedemocraticstrategist.org/ac/2007/03/the_black_and_hispanic_vote_in.php.

146   "If the Democrats were to write off": Chris Kromm, "Latino Voters: More Evidence the South Is Competitive," *Facing South* blog, Nov. 28, 2006, http://southernstudies.org/facingsouth/2006/11/latino-voters-more-evidence-south-is.asp.

146–53   "When I tell you that the area": Material and quotes from Theresa Harmon, Stephen Fotoulos, Rick Casares, Tom Lowe, and Phil Valentine are drawn from author's interviews, notes, and transcripts, July and Aug. 2006.

147   "a new Ellis Island": Anne Farris, "New Immigrants in New Places," *Carnegie Reporter*, Fall 2005.

148   whites suddenly no longer the majority: Stephen Ohlemacher, "Whites Now Minority in 1 in 10 Counties," Associated Press, Aug. 9, 2007.

150   "a burden on our country": Pew Research Center, 2004 Political Typology Survey.

150   "threaten American customs and values": Pew Research Center reports, 2003 and 2004.

150   incidents of black-Hispanic violence: See Paula D. McClain, et al., "Black Americans and Latino Immigrants in a Southern City: Friendly Neighbors or Economic Competitors?" *Du Bois Review*, vol. 4, no. 1, 2007.

151   "Shoot 'em!": Valentine quoted in P. J. Tobia, "The Natives Are Restless," *Nashville Scene*, Nov. 30, 2006.

153   The transformation began: "The New Latino South: The Context and Consequences of Rapid Population Growth," Pew Hispanic Center, July 26, 2005.

153–57   "If you make yourself a welcome wagon": Material and quotes from Donna Locke, David Lubell, Stephen Fotopulos, Rick Casares, Devin Burghart, and Carol Swain are drawn from author's interviews, notes, and transcripts, July and Aug. 2006.

154   Nationally, more than 1,562: "2007 Enacted State Legislation Related to Immigrants and Immigration," National Conference of State Legislators, Jan. 31, 2008, http://www.ncsl.org/print/immig/2007Immigrationfinal.pdf.

155   helping the Minuteman: See William Schneider, "The Politics of Illegal Immigration," *National Journal*, June 20, 2006.

156   "Welcome the Immigrant You Once Were": See the campaign's billboards at www.welcomingtn.org.

157   "To get a few chickens plucked": Duke quoted in Ned Glascock, "Rally Divides Siler City," *News & Observer*, Feb. 20, 2000.

157–61   Over the Blue Ridge Mountains in Georgia: Material and quotes from Remedios Gomez Arnau, Chip Rogers, Tom Lowe, and Sam Zamarripa are drawn from author's interviews, notes, and transcripts, Feb. 2004 and Aug. 2006 (in Lowe's case).

158   "coalition of immigration crime fighters": D. A. King, "Freedom Ride—Or Freedom Denied?" *VDare.com*, Oct. 1, 2003, http://www.vdare.com/king/ga_march.htm.

161   "bash immigrants": Transcript of Univision Democratic debate, Sept. 9, 2007, Federal News Service, http://media.miamiherald.com/smedia/2007/09/09/23/English_transcript.source.prod_affiliate.56.pdf. The quotes from John Edwards, Barack Obama, and Bill Richardson are also drawn from this transcript.

163   But in Texas: CNN exit polls; Marisa Treviño, "Texas Primary Part II: The Latino Vote Mattered," *Latina Lista*, Mar. 24, 2008, http://www.latinalista.net/palabrafinal/2008/03/texas_primary_part_ii_the_latino_vote_ma.html.

163   "much younger than white or black voters": "The New Latino South: The Context and Consequences of Rapid Population Growth," Pew Hispanic Center, July 26, 2005. The median age of Latino immigrants in the six fastest-growing Southern states is twenty-seven.

7. Getting Religion

165   "Every good Christian": Goldwater quoted in Ed Magnuson, "The Brethren's First Sister," *Time*, July 20, 1981.

166–73   For more than a quarter century: Material and quotes from the 2005 Reclaiming America for Christ conference are taken from the author's interviews, notes, and transcripts. See also Moser, "The Crusaders," *Rolling Stone*, Apr. 7, 2005.

167   "preparing for another assault": Edwin Warner, "New Resolve by the New Right," *Time*, Dec. 8, 1980.

168   "Most people hear them talk": Author's interview, Jan. 2005.

168   takeover of the San Diego school board: Sandi Dolbee, "On a Mission to Unite Politics with Faith," *Union-Tribune*, Oct. 10, 2004.

169 "To the Christian Flag": The Christian flag pledge; see www.allstatesflag .com.

170 Moore had it wheeled: "Magistrate Orders 'Ten Commandments' Judge to Release Papers," Associated Press, Apr. 10, 2002.

170 That's when he nailed: For Roy Moore's own account of the Ten Commandments controversies, see *So Help Me God.*

170 A federal court: Stan Bailey, "Justices Overrule Moore," *Birmingham News,* Aug. 22, 2003.

170 to save the monument: See Janelle McGrew, "Special Report: Ten Commandments Controversy," *Montgomery Advertiser,* Aug. 29, 2003; and Clarence Page, "Fervor Around 'Roy's Rock' Makes Case for its Foes," *Baltimore Sun,* Aug. 29, 2003.

170 In his brief spell: See Jim Tharpe, "Monument Removed: Ten Commandments Out of Sight," *Atlanta Journal-Constitution,* Aug. 28, 2003.

171 "special concurrence": Roy S. Moore, special concurrence, *Ex Parte HH (in re: D.H. vs. H.H.),* www.findlaw.com, Feb. 15, 2002.

171 "They've bashed the judiciary": Author's interview, Jan. 2005.

172 Focus on the Family: Research by author and Heidi Beirich of the Southern Poverty Law Center, from tax filings by Coral Ridge Ministries, Reclaiming America for Christ, the Center for Christian Statesmanship, and Focus on the Family.

173 "gender hate than to help!": Jerry Falwell, "Ministers and Marches," Mar. 21, 1965; full text in Young, *God's Bullies,* pp. 310–17.

174 "For though we walk in the flesh": 2 Corinthians 10:3.

174 "Be it known to all": Jerry Falwell, "Declaration of War," reprinted in Young, *God's Bullies,* p. 308.

174 "extremely unhappy": Author's interview, Jan. 2005.

175 "civil wrongs rather than civil rights": Quoted in White, *Stranger at the Gate,* p. 103.

175 "While the church leaders are so obsessed": Jerry Falwell, "Ministers and Marches," in Young, *God's Bullies,* p. 315.

175 "Guru of Fundamentalism": Kenneth L. Woodward, "Guru of Fundamentalism," *Newsweek,* Nov. 1, 1983.

175 "Dr. Schaeffer convinced Jerry": Author's interview, Jan. 2005.

176 "The homosexuals are on the march": Falwell quoted in Young, *God's Bullies,* p. 307.

176 Billy James Hargis: For a rousing sample of Hargis's anti-Communist rhetoric, see his 1964 book, Billy James Hargis, *The Far Left* (Tulsa, Okla.: Christian Crusade, 1964).

176 "The rhetoric is highly adaptable": Author's interview, Oct. 2006.

176 "it's the liberals' fault": Author's interview, Apr. 2007.

177 "agents of intolerance": McCain quoted in Elaine S. Povitch and Craig Gordon, "McCain Denounces Leaders of Christian Religious Right," *Newsday,* Feb. 29, 2000.

178 "There is a culture war going on": Pat Buchanan, address to the Republican National Convention, Aug. 17, 1992.

178 evangelical Republicans outnumbered: Barna Research 2006; see also David Paul Kuhn, "The Gospel According to Jim Wallis," *Washington Post,* Nov. 26, 2006.

179 "The pendulum swings": Author's interview, Jan. 2005.

179 The fracturing movement: See "Massachusetts Court Rules Ban on Gay Marriage Unconstitutional," CNN, Nov. 18, 2003, http://www.cnn.com/2003/LAW/11/18/samesex.marriage.ruling/.

179 "The Final Frontier": Paul Weyrich, *Washington Dispatch,* May 11, 2003.

179 "so-called homosexual agenda": *Lawrence et. al. v. Texas* was decided June 26, 2003.

179 Bush . . . support for a Federal Marriage Amendment: "President Calls for Constitutional Amendment Protecting Marriage," Press Release, White House, Feb. 24, 2004, http://www.whitehouse.gov/news/releases/2004/02/20040224-2.html.

180 "It's now or never": Dobson quoted in "Thousands of Christians Rally for Traditional Marriage," Religious News Service, Oct. 19, 2004.

180 "It's a forest fire": Burress quoted in James Dao, "After Victory, Crusader Against Same-Sex Marriage Thinks Big," *New York Times,* Nov. 26, 2004.

180 "I heard evangelicals asking": Author's interview, Oct. 2006.

181–87 Ralph Reed was ready: Material from Ralph Reed's speech to Georgia College Republican Convention is taken from author's notes and transcripts. Quotes from Frederick Clarkson, Clyde Wilcox, and John Green are drawn from author's interviews, notes, and transcripts, Jan. 2005.

181 "The Right Hand of God": Jeffrey H. Birnbaum, "The Gospel According to Ralph," *Time,* May 15, 1995. The cover can be seen online at http://www.time.com/time/covers/0,16641,19950515,00.html.

182 his first notable act of mass deception: Easton, *Gang of Five,* pp. 116–17.

183 reduced to offering twenty dollars: Jim Galloway, "Reed Drums Up Crowd for Evangelical Event," *Atlanta Journal-Constitution,* Jan. 21, 2006.

183 "I resent Christianity being used": Bob Irvin, "Reed an Albatross for GOP," *Atlanta Journal-Constitution,* June 15, 2005.

184 Abramoff's Indian casino clients paid: "Gimme Five: Investigation of Tribal Lobbying Matters," Report of the Senate Committee on Indian Affairs, 109th cong., 2nd sess., Jun. 22, 2006, http://indian.senate.gov/public/_files/Report.pdf.

185 "That's sometimes called laundering": Dorgan quoted in Jim Galloway, "Emails: Reed Knew Tribal Money Funded Anti-gambling Campaigns," *Atlanta Journal-Constitution,* June 23, 2005.

185 "tapped into his vast network": Alan Judd, "Reed as Consultant a Master of Stealth," *Atlanta Journal-Constitution,* Oct. 23, 2005.

185 "an embarrassing silence": Ken Connor, "An Embarrassing Silence," *Baptist Press News,* Jan. 25, 2006.

186 "It's like guerrilla warfare": Reed quoted in Barry M. Horstman, "Crusade for Public Office in 2nd Stage," *Los Angeles Times,* Mar. 22, 1992.

187 "What will happen on Election Day": Joseph Farah, "Judgment Day for Republicans," *World Net Daily,* Jan. 5, 2006, http://www.worldnetdaily.com/index.php?fa=PAGE.view&pageId=34204.

187–92 "You can feel the surge!": Material from Springfield, Missouri, is taken from author's notes and transcripts. Quotes from Steve Helms, Mike Bacheleder, Dee Wampler, and Tom Rollings are drawn from author's interviews, Nov. 2006.

188 "It would be a sin not to": Dobson quoted in Mike Allen, "Take About Five People with You and Vote. It Would Be a Sin Not To," *Time,* Oct. 22, 2006.

188 the faithful had knocked on: According to the Jim Talent for Senate campaign.

188 "It is time for Christians to confront": Austin quoted in David Kirkpatrick, "What Next for Ralph Reed?" *New York Times,* July 22, 2006.

189 admired by 72 percent: "Moore Ahead of Riley in Polls," Associated Press, Jan. 20, 2005.

190 "cells in a petri dish are equivalent": John Danforth, "In the Name of Politics," *New York Times,* Mar. 30, 2005.

190 "God hates you": Keyes quoted in Linda Leicht, "Stem Cell Rally Stirs Christians," *Springfield News-Leader,* Sept. 22, 2006.

191 evangelical voters came out in Missouri: Edison/Misofsky and CNN exit polls, 2006.

191 "Republicans' inability": Marvin Olasky, "Voting Out the Mean-spirited Party," *World,* Nov. 9, 2006.

192–96 On the January Sunday before the 2008 Florida: Material from First Baptist Church is borrowed from *Orlando Sentinel* religion reporter Mark Pinsky, who reported on the service with Governor Mike Huckabee. Material from Northland Church and the Reclaiming the Vote visit to Seminole County is taken from author's notes and transcripts. Quotes from Pinsky and Joel Hunter are drawn from author's interviews, Jan. 2008.

196 "Only people of faith can take on": Author's interview, Jan. 2005.

197 "replaced by Jesus": Wallis quoted in Exley, "What Lessons Can Progressives Learn from Evangelicals?" *In These Times,* Mar. 21, 2007.

197 "Never in history": Boyd quoted in ibid.

197 "[R]eligious people killed Jesus": Rob Bell, interview in *Relevant* magazine, Jan./Feb. 2008, p. 67.

198 "expand the agenda": Author's interview; see also Alan Cooperman, "Second New Leader Resigns from the Christian Coalition," *Washington Post,* Nov. 29, 2006.

198 it set off a major fuss: Laurie Goodstein, "Evangelicals' Focus on Climate Draws Fire of Christian Right," *New York Times,* Mar. 3, 2007.

199 the to-do raised: See David Van Biema, "The Real Losers in the Obama-Warren Controversy," *Time,* Dec. 1, 2006.

199 While they remain overwhelmingly anti-abortion: George Barna, "A New Generation Expresses its Skepticism and Frustration with Christianity," The Barna Group, Ltd., Sept. 24, 2007, http://www.barna.org/FlexPage .aspx?Page=BarnaUpdate&BarnaUpdateID=280; see also "The American Values Survey," People for the American Way Foundation, Aug. 2006, http://media.pfaw.org/pdf/cav/AVSReport.pdf.

199–200 "I'm a Christian, but": Author's interview, Jan. 2008.

200–204 For students at Birmingham's Samford University: Material about Redeem the Vote is drawn from author's notes and transcripts. Quotes from Dr. Randy Brinson, Caroline Bell, and Rob Howell are drawn from author's interviews, Jan. 2008.

201 "thinly veiled GOP vote machine": Jeff Sharlet, "Bolt, Jesus, Bolt!" *The Revealer,* May 3, 2006.

202 When the most popular magazine for young evangelicals: Reader poll, *Relevant,* Jan./Feb. 2008, p. 75.

203 Pew polls found evangelicals' perceptions: Pew Research Center polls, 2003–2006.

203   the Redeemers had made successful stops: Registration estimates from Collier Craft, communications director, Redeem the Vote.

8. Cornbread and Roses

205   "I never intend to accommodate": King quoted in Tyson, *Blood Done Sign My Name*, p. 107.

205–11   "I thought we'd ride right down": Material and quotes from Dick Sloop are drawn from author's interviews, notes, and transcripts, Apr. 2007.

205   per capita income in Dixie lags: "A Profile of the Southern Economy: Living Standards, Economic Structure, and Lower Income Workers," Report by Division of Research, Moore School of Business, University of South Carolina, Oct. 2003.

205   considering where the South had started: Alfred E. Eckes, "The South and Economic Globalization, 1950 to the Future," in *Globalization and the American South,* edited by James C. Cobb and William Stueck (Athens, Ga.: University of Georgia Press, 2005), p. 40.

212   "Get through the culture": Saunders and Jarding, *Foxes in the Henhouse,* p. 81.

212   Chilhowie had lost: Warren Veith, "A Town Traded Away," *Los Angeles Times,* Apr. 19, 2002.

213   Between 1993 and 2000, the South lost: U.S. Census Bureau 2000 and 2005.

214   idea-driven information economy are Southern: Bureau of Economic Analysis, 1999 and 2002 data.

214   79 percent urban by 2006: U.S. Census Bureau statistics.

215–25   Shawn Dixon had to blink back: Material from John Edwards rally, Columbus, Kentucky, Oct. 4, 2007, is drawn from video of the event on YouTube, postings on Eventful.com, and author's interviews with Shawn Dixon, Oct. and Nov. 2007.

217   Hickman County's votes in 2004: General election results 2004, Kentucky State Board of Elections.

220   "In our effort to be reelected": Author's interview, Oct. 2005.

222–23   "a liberal fallacy": Letter to author from William Greider.

222   Bush won them by more than 20 percent: Edison/Mitofsky exit polls, 2004.

223   "What does it mean today": John Kerry, address to Democratic National Convention, July 29, 2004.

225–29   Growing up poor in Neshoba County: Material and quotes from Donna Ladd and Jamie Franks are drawn from author's interviews, notes, and transcripts, Mar. 2007.

230   "No one wants to deal with it": Bob Herbert, "The Blight That Is Still with Us," *New York Times,* Jan. 22, 2008.

230   "what Obama was doing back there": Johnson quoted in Philip Elliott, "BET Bigwig Battles Barack," Chicago *Sun-Times,* Jan. 14, 2008.

230   "roll of the dice": Bill Clinton, *Charlie Rose Show,* Dec. 15, 2007.

231   under-thirty turnout nearly triple the level of 2004: CNN exit polls and www.newvotersproject.org, Jan. 27, 2007.

231   In Georgia, 58 percent of young voters: CNN exit polls.

232   "looking for a job": Huckabee quoted in David Kirkpatrick, "Young Evangelicals Embrace Huckabee as Old Guard Balks." *New York Times,* Jan. 13, 2008.

232 "who are living from one paycheck": Huckabee quoted in Thomas B. Edsall, "McCain Scores Narrow But Crucial Victory in South Carolina," *Huffington Post,* Jan. 19, 2008, http://www.huffingtonpost.com/2008/01/19/mccain-scores-narrow-but-_n_82317.html.

232 "pro-life liberal": Fred Thompson, *This Week with George Stephanopoulos,* ABC News, Nov. 18, 2007.

232 "convince evangelicals to vote Democratic": Brett Grainger, "Will Huckabee's Campaign Encourage Evangelicals to Vote for a Democrat?" *Christian Science Monitor,* Feb. 4, 2008.

232–33 "be conservationists and good stewards": Huckabee quoted in Dick Mayer, "Greens and God," CBS News commentary, Nov. 1, 2007, http://www.cbsnews.com/stories/2007/10/31/opinion/meyer/main3438409.shtml.

233 "If I really know what it means to follow Jesus": Huckabee quoted in Michael Scherer, "Can Mike Huckabee Out-charm the GOP Big Three?" *Salon,* Mar. 5, 2007, http://www.salon.com/news/feature/2007/03/05/huckabee.

233 In South Carolina . . . 220,000 more votes were cast: Edison/Mitofsky exit polls.

234 "You are kept apart": Watson quoted in Woodward, *Tom Watson,* p. 220; Thomas E. Watson, "The Negro Question in the South," *Arena,* vol. VI, 1892.

235 "The spectacle of white farmers": Ibid., pp. 239–40.

235 "Negro plantation hands and laborers": Ibid., p. 241.

SELECTED BIBLIOGRAPHY

Books and Chapters

Applebome, Peter. *Dixie Rising: How the South is Shaping American Values, Politics, and Culture.* New York: Times Books, 1996.

Ayers, Brandt, and Thomas H. Naylor, eds. *You Can't Eat Magnolias.* New York: McGraw-Hill, 1972.

Ayers, Edward L. *The Promise of the New South: Life After Reconstruction.* New York: Oxford, 1992.

Balmer, Randall. *Thy Kingdom Come: How the Religious Right Distorts the Faith and Threatens America.* New York: Basic Books, 2006.

Bass, Jack, and Walter DeVries. *The Transformation of Southern Politics: Social Change and Political Consequences Since 1945.* New York: Basic Books, 1976.

Black, Earl, and Merle Black. *Divided America: The Ferocious Power Struggle in American Politics.* New York: Simon & Schuster, 2007.

———. *The Rise of Southern Republicans.* Cambridge, Mass.: Harvard University Press, 2002.

Boston, Rob. *Close Encounters with the Religious Right: Journeys into the Twilight Zone of Religion and Politics.* New York: Prometheus, 2000.

Boyd, Gregory. *The Myth of a Christian Nation: How the Quest for Political Power Is Detroying the Church.* Grand Rapids, Mich.: Zondervan, 2005.

Bullock, Charles S. III, and Mark J. Rozell, eds. *The New Politics of the Old South.* Lanham, Md.: Rowman & Littlefield, 1998.

Carter, Dan T. *The Politics of Rage: George Wallace, The Origins of the New Conservatism, and the Transformation of American Politics.* New York: Simon & Schuster, 1995.

Cash, W. J. *The Mind of the South.* New York: Knopf, 1941.

Clarkson, Frederick. *Eternal Hostility: The Struggle Between Theocracy and Democracy.* Monroe, Maine: Common Courage Press, 1997.

Cobb, James C. *Away Down South: A History of Southern Identity.* New York: Oxford, 2005.

Cobb, James C. and William Stueck, eds. *Globalization and the American South.* Athens: University of Georgia Press, 2005.

Degler, Carl N. *The Other South: Southern Dissenters in the Nineteenth Century.* Boston: Northeastern University Press, 1982.

Dennett, John Richard. *The South As It Is: 1865–1866.* New York: Viking, 1965.

Drescher, John. *Triumph of Good Will: How Terry Sanford Beat a Champion of Segregation and Reshaped the South.* Jackson: University of Mississippi Press, 2000.

Du Bois, W. E. B. *The Souls of Black Folk.* Chicago: A. C. McClurg & Co., 1903.

Dunbar, Anthony, ed. *Where We Stand: Voices of Southern Dissent.* Montgomery, Ala.: New South Books, 2004.

Duncombe, Stephen. *Dream: Re-Imagining Progressive Politics in An Age of Fantasy.* New York: New Press, 2007.

Easton, Nina. *Gang of Five: Leaders at the Center of the Conservative Ascendancy.* New York: Simon & Schuster, 2002.

Edsall, Thomas. *Building Red America: The New Conservative Coalition and the Drive for Permanent Power.* New York: Basic Books, 2006.

Edsall, Thomas, with Mary Edsall. *Chain Reaction: The Impact of Race, Rights, and Taxes on American Politics.* New York: Norton, 1992.

Egerton, John. *The Americanization of Dixie; the Southernization of America.* New York: Harper's Magazine Press, 1974.

———. "The Southernization of American Politics." In Anthony Dunbar, ed. *Where We Stand: Voices of Southern Dissent.* Montgomery, Ala.: NewSouth Books, 2004, pp. 197–223.

———. *Speak Now Against the Day: The Generation Before the Civil Rights Movement in the South.* Chapel Hill: University of North Carolina Press, 1994.

Frady, Marshall. *Jesse: The Life and Pilgrimage of Jesse Jackson.* New York: Random House, 1996.

———. *Southerners: A Journalist's Odyssey.* New York: New American Library, 1980.

———. *Wallace.* New York and Cleveland: World, 1968.

Frank, Thomas. *What's the Matter with Kansas? How Conservatives Won the Heart of America.* New York: Metropolitan, 2004.

Franklin, John Hope. *The Color Line: Legacy for the Twenty-First Century.* Columbia: University of Missouri Press, 1993.

Frederickson, Kari. *The Dixiecrat Revolt and the End of the Solid South, 1932–1968.* Chapel Hill: University of North Carolina Press, 2001.

Gaston, Paul M. *The New South Creed: A Study in Southern Mythmaking.* New York: Knopf, 1970.

Genovese, Eugene. *The Southern Tradition: The Achievement and Limitations of an American Conservatism.* Cambridge, Mass.: Harvard University Press, 1994.

Gitlin, Todd. *The Twilight of Common Dreams: Why America is Wracked by Culture Wars.* New York: Metropolitan Books, 1995.

Goldfield, David R. *Still Fighting the Civil War: The American South and Southern History.* Baton Rouge: Louisiana State University, 2002.

Greider, William. *The Soul of Capitalism: Opening Paths to a Moral Economy.* New York: Simon & Schuster, 2003.

Goodwyn, Lawrence. *Democratic Promise: The Populist Movement in America.* New York: Oxford, 1976.

———. *The Populist Moment: A Short History of the Agrarian Revolt in America.* New York: Oxford, 1978.

Hackney, Sheldon. *Populism to Progressivism in Alabama.* Princeton, N.J.: Princeton University Press, 1969.

———. "Identity Politics, Southern Style." In Anthony Dunbar, ed. *Where We Stand: Voices of Southern Dissent.* Montgomery, Ala.: NewSouth Books, 2004, pp. 181–96.

Helms, Jesse. *When Free Men Shall Stand.* Grand Rapids, Mich.: Zondervan Publishing House, 1976.

Hertzberg, Hendrik. *Politics.* New York: Penguin, 2004.

Hetherington, Mark J. *Why Trust Matters: Declining Political Trust and the Demise of American Liberalism.* Princeton, N.J.: Princeton University Press, 2004.

Horwitz, Tony. *Confederates in the Attic: Dispatches from the Unfinished Civil War.* New York: Pantheon, 1998.

Hunter, Joel C. *A New Kind of Conservative.* Ventura, Calif.: Regal Books, 2008.

Jackson, Maynard. "Glory, Hallelujah, While They're Trying to Sock It to You." In H. Brandt Ayers and Thomas H. Naylor, eds. *You Can't Eat Magnolias.* New York: McGraw-Hill, 1972, pp. 127–35.

Jarding, Steve, and Dave "Mudcat" Saunders. *Foxes in the Henhouse: How the Republicans Stole Rural America and What the Democrats Must Do to Run 'em Out.* New York: Simon & Schuster, 2006.

Judis, John B., and Ruy Teixeira. *The Emerging Democratic Majority.* New York: Scribner, 2002.

Kazin, Michael. *A Godly Hero: The Life of William Jennings Bryan.* New York: Knopf, 2006.

Key, V. O. *Southern Politics in State and Nation.* New York: Knopf, 1949.

King, Martin Luther, Jr. *Stride Toward Freedom: The Montgomery Story.* New York: Harper & Row, 1958.

———. *Why We Can't Wait.* New York: Harper & Row, 1964.

Lassiter, Matthew. *The Silent Majority: Suburban Politics in the Sun Belt.* Princeton, N.J.: Princeton University Press, 2006.

Lewis, John. *Walking with the Wind: A Memoir of the Movement.* New York: Simon & Schuster, 1998.

Luebke, Paul. *North Carolina Politics 2000.* Chapel Hill: University of North Carolina Press, 1998.

McGill, Ralph. *The South and the Southerner.* Boston: Atlantic-Little, Brown, 1959.

Mencken, H. L. *A Religious Orgy in Tennessee: A Reporter's Account of the Scopes Monkey Trial.* Baltimore, Md.: Melville House, 2006.

Miller, Zell. *A National Party No More: The Conscience of a Conservative Democrat.* Macon, Ga.: Stroud & Hall, 2003.

Moore, Roy. *So Help Me God: The Ten Commandments, Judicial Tyranny, and the Battle for Religious Freedom.* Nashville, Tenn.: Broadman & Holman, 2005.

Nichol, Gene, "Ignoring Inequality." In Anthony Dunbar, ed. *Where We Stand: Voices of Southern Dissent.* Montgomery, Ala.: NewSouth Books, 2004, pp. 61–69.

Novak, Robert D. *The Agony of the G.O.P. 1964.* New York: Macmillan, 1965.

Perlstein, Rick. *Before the Storm: Barry Goldwater and the Unmaking of the American Consensus.* New York: Hill and Wang, 2001.

Phillips, Kevin. *American Theocracy: The Peril and Politics of Radical Religion, Oil, and Borrowed Money in the 21st Century.* New York: Viking, 2006.

———. *The Emerging Republican Majority.* New Rochelle, N.Y.: Arlington House, 1969.

Pinsky, Mark I. *A Jew Among the Evangelicals: A Guide for the Perplexed*. Louisville, Ky.: Westminster John Knox Press, 2006.

Raines, Howell, ed. *My Soul Is Rested: Movement Days in the Deep South Remembered*. New York: Penguin, 1983.

Reed, John Shelton. *The Enduring South*. Lexington, Mass.: Lexington Books, 1972.

Sager, Ryan. *The Elephant in the Room: Evangelicals, Libertarians, and the Battle to Control the Republican Party*. Hoboken, N.J.: Wiley, 2006.

Scammon, Richard, and Ben J. Wattenberg. *The Real Majority*. New York: Coward-McCann, 1970.

Schaller, Thomas F. *Whistling Past Dixie: How Democrats Can Win Without the South*. New York: Simon & Schuster, 2006.

Smith, Lillian. *Killers of the Dream*. New York: Norton, 1949.

Sokol, Jason. *There Goes My Everything: White Southerners in the Age of Civil Rights, 1945–1975*. New York: Knopf, 2006.

Sullivan, Patricia. *Days of Hope: Race and Democracy in the New Deal Era*. Chapel Hill: University of North Carolina Press, 1996.

Tindall, George. *The Ethnic Southerners*. Baton Rouge: Louisiana State University Press, 1976.

Twelve Southerners. *I'll Take My Stand: The South and the Agrarian Tradition*. New York: Harper's, 1930.

Tyson, Timothy B. *Blood Done Sign My Name: A True Story*. New York: Crown, 2004.

Weaver, Richard M. *The Southern Essays of Richard M. Weaver*. Indianapolis: Liberty Fund, Inc., 1987.

Webb, James. *Born Fighting: How the Scots-Irish Shaped America*. New York: Broadway, 2004.

White, Mel. *Stranger at the Gate: To Be Gay and Christian in America*. New York: Plume Books, 1995.

Wilkie, Curtis. *Dixie: A Personal Odyssey Through Events That Shaped the Modern South*. New York: Simon & Schuster, 2001.

Williams, Harry T. *Huey Long*. New York: Knopf, 1969.

Wilson, Charles Reagan, and William Ferris, eds. *Encyclopedia of Southern Culture*. Chapel Hill: University of North Carolina, 1989.

Wilson, Edmund. *Patriotic Gore: Studies in the Literature of the American Civil War*. New York: Farrar, Straus and Giroux, 1962.

Witcover, Jules. *Party of the People: A History of the Democrats*. New York: Random House, 2003.

Woodward, C. Vann. *The Burden of Southern History*. Baton Rouge: Louisiana State University, 1968.

——. *The Future of the Past*. New York: Oxford, 1989.

——. *Origins of the New South, 1877–1913*. Baton Rouge: Louisiana State University, 1951.

——. *The Strange Career of Jim Crow*. New York: Oxford University Press, 1955.

——. *Tom Watson: Agrarian Rebel*. New York: Macmillan, 1938.

Yoder, Edwin, "Southern Governors and the New State Politics." In H. Brandt Ayers and Thomas H. Naylor, eds. *You Can't Eat Magnolias*. New York: McGraw-Hill, 1972, pp. 160–66.

Young, Perry Deane. *God's Bullies: Power Politics and Religious Tyranny*. New York: Holt, Rinehart and Winston, 1982.

Zinn, Howard. *The Southern Mystique*. New York: Knopf, 1964.

Articles, Reports, and Speeches

Armstrong, Jerome. "Harold Ford & the South, Big Tent & 50 State Stategy." *MyDD.com,* Nov. 14, 2006.

Anderson, Kurt. "The Lou Dobbs Factor." *New York,* Nov. 27, 2006.

Bai, Matt. "Is Howard Dean Willing to Destroy the Democratic Party in Order to Save It?" *New York Times Magazine,* Oct. 1, 2006.

———. "Huntin' for Nascar-Lovin', Moon-Pie-Eatin', Bluegrass-Listenin', Shotgun-Totin' Democrats." *New York Times Magazine,* Sept. 15, 2002.

Bankston, Carl L. "New People in the New South: An Overview of Southern Immigration." *Southern Cultures,* Winter 2007.

Beinart, Peter. "The Burbs." *The New Republic,* Oct. 19, 1998.

Bhargava, Deepak, and Jean Hardisty. "Wrong About the Right." *The Nation,* Nov. 7, 2005.

Browder, Glen. "Entrenching Democratic Minority." *Emerging Democratic Majority,* Jun. 10, 2005.

———. "The Real Southern Problem and My Democratic Party's Future." Special Report for the Program on Southern Studies, University of North Carolina at Chapel Hill, 2005.

Carter, Hodding III. "The Southern Press: Yesterday, Today and Tomorrow." Speech delivered at the University of Mississippi, Nov. 20, 2004.

Cooper, Marc. "Thinking of Jackasses." *Atlantic Monthly,* Apr. 2005.

Crouthamel, James L. "Tocqueville's South." *Journal of the Early Republic,* Winter 1982.

Dionne, E. J. "The Liberal Moment." *Chronicle of Higher Education,* Sept. 7, 2007.

———. "Painting the Suburbs Blue." *Washington Post,* Sept. 14, 2007.

Douthat, Ross. "Blue Period." *Atlantic,* Sept. 2007.

Exley, Zack. "What Lessons Can Progressives Learn from Evangelicals?" *In These Times,* Mar. 21, 2007.

Frank, Thomas. "What's the Matter with Liberals?" *New York Review of Books,* May 12, 2005.

Frey, William. "The Electoral College Moves to the Sun Belt." Brookings Institution Research Brief, May 2005.

Green, Jordan. "From Woolworth's to Wal-Mart." *Facing South* and *Yes! Weekly,* July 30, 2005.

Griffin, Larry J., and Katherine McFarland. "In My Heart, I'm an American: Regional Attitudes and American Identity." *Southern Cultures,* Winter 2007.

Hacker, Jacob. "The Rise of the Office-Park Populist." *New York Times,* Dec. 24, 2006.

Kamarck, Elaine C. "Assessing Howard Dean's Fifty State Strategy and the 2006 Midterm Elections," *The Forum: A Journal of Applied Research in Contemporary Politics,* vol. 4, 2006.

Kirkpatrick, David. "The Evangelical Crackup." *New York Times,* Oct. 28, 2007.

King, Martin Luther Jr. "Letter from Birmingham Jail," *Christian Century,* June 12, 1963.

Levenson, Jacob. "Divining Dixie." *Columbia Journalism Review,* Mar./Apr. 2004.

Luo, Michael, and Laurie Goldstein. "Emphasis Shifts for New Breed of Evengelicals." *New York Times,* May 21, 2007.

Meyerson, Harold. "Wal-Mart Comes North." *The American Prospect,* Mar. 18, 2007.

Moser, Bob. "A New-Model Ford," *The Nation,* Oct. 26, 2006.

———. "The Battle of Georgiafornia." *Intelligence Report,* Winter 2004.

———. "Cornbread and Roses." *The Nation,* Nov. 28, 2005.

———. "The Crusaders." *Rolling Stone,* Apr. 7, 2005.

———. "The Democrats' Depressing Debate." *The Nation online,* Apr. 27, 2007.

———. "The Devil Inside." *The Nation,* Apr. 17, 2006.

———. "Endangered Species of the American South." *The Nation,* Oct. 20, 2003.

———. "Holy War." *Intelligence Report,* Winter 2005.

———. "Lincoln Reconstructed." *The Intelligence Report,* Summer 2003.

———. "Purple America." *The Nation,* Aug. 13/20, 2007.

———. "South Carolina: Inside the 'Black Primary.'" *The Nation,* Jan. 7, 2008.

———. "Virginia's Rumbling Rebels." *The Nation,* Oct. 23, 2006.

———. "The Way Down South." *The Nation,* Jan. 25, 2007.

———. "White Heat." *The Nation,* Aug. 28/Sept. 4, 2006.

———. "Who Would Jesus Vote For?" *The Nation,* Mar. 24, 2008.

———. "Yesterday's Gone." *The Independent Weekly,* Aug. 23, 2000.

Noah, Timothy. "Forget the South, Democrats." *Slate,* Jan. 27, 2004.

Perlstein, Rick. "How Can the Democrats Win?" *Boston Review,* Summer 2004.

Pinsky, Mark. "Vox Populi, Vox Dei?" *Harvard Divinity School Bulletin,* Winter 2007.

Reed, Adolph. "A Lost Cause." *Boston Review,* Summer 2004.

Schaller, Thomas. "A Route for 2004 That Doesn't Go Through Dixie." *Washington Post,* Nov. 16, 2003.

———. "The Demographic Case for Whistling Past Dixie." thedemocraticstrategist .org, Oct. 26, 2006.

———. "Do Democrats Need the South?" *Salon,* Nov. 14, 2006.

Sirota, David. "The Democrats' Da Vinci Code." *The American Prospect,* Dec. 8, 2004.

Sokol, Jason. "Epiphanies of a Massachusetts Liberal." History News Network, Nov. 15, 2004.

Sullivan, Amy. "Finding Their Faith." *Time,* Feb. 14, 2008.

———. "When Would Jesus Bolt?" *Washington Monthly,* Apr. 2006.

Teixeira, Ruy. "The Battle for the Exurbs." *New York Times,* Nov. 14, 2005.

Tomasky, Michael. "How Democrats Should Talk." *New York Review of Books,* May 31, 2007.

Walker, Jesse. "We Are All Populists Now." *Reason,* Aug. 21, 2007.

Watterson, Henry. "The 'Solid' South." *North American Review,* no. 266, January 1879.

Zinn, Howard. "Against Discouragement." Spelman College Commencement Address, May 15, 2005.

ACKNOWLEDGMENTS

I can never adequately thank the Southerners who let me into their homes, offices, heads, and hearts while I reported this book. *Why* you let me, I'll never know, but I will always be in your debt for it. Even if I couldn't quote you here, I learned from you—about a whole lot more than Southern politics, too. Along with many others, thanks to Brett Bursey, Dan Carter, Hodding Carter III, Jim Carter, Rick Casares, Collier Craft, Shawn Dixon, Jean and George Edwards, Elena Dubester and Gary Phillips, Kevin Alexander Gray, Susan Glisson, Theresa Harmon, Fred Hobson, Lisa and Richard Howorth, Mark Hufford, Senator Ellie Kinnaird, Chris Kromm, Audrey and Tom Lowe, Representative Paul Luebke, Jerry Meek, Jay Parmley, former Congresswoman Liz Patterson, Jim Pence, John Shelton Reed, Dick Sloop, Diane Tilson, Carol and Harold Trainer, Senator Jim Webb, and Curtis Wilkie.

My enduring gratitude to the editors (and publisher) who believed in me when I needed it most, and who taught me what little

I know about journalism: Gillian Floren, Katherine Fulton, Mark Potok, Karen Rothmyer, and Steve Schewel.

Special holler-outs to:

Deirdre Mullane of Mullane Literary Associates, world's greatest agent and neighbor.

Robin Dennis of Times Books, for her earth-clearing edits.

Rob Fischer, for his fabulous research (and dog-sitting).

The editors who encouraged and enabled me to do the reporting and thinking that became this book: Roane Carey, Katrina vanden Heuvel, and Karen Rothmyer of *The Nation*; Mark Potok of *The Intelligence Report*; Eric Bates of *Rolling Stone*; and Darren Stanhouse, formerly of *The Independent Weekly*.

My beloved fellow Knight Writers and families.

Facing South, the Institute for Southern Studies' invaluable Web chronicle of Southern progressivism.

Tom and M. L. Moser, for their generosity and support.

The Willoughbys, for taking me in.

Lana, Carol, and Melinda. Now it's your turn.

INDEX

ABOUT THE AUTHOR

BOB MOSER is an award-winning political correspondent for *The Nation*. He has chronicled Southern politics for nearly two decades for publications ranging from *Rolling Stone* to *The Independent Weekly*. A native and longtime resident of North Carolina, he is temporarily housed in Brooklyn, New York.